KT-473-962

# Voluntary but not Amateur

A guide to the law for voluntary organisations and community groups

by Duncan Forbes, Ruth Hayes and Jacki Reason
Illustrations by Steve Simpson

**London Voluntary Service Council**
356 Holloway Road, London N7 6PA

**October 1994**

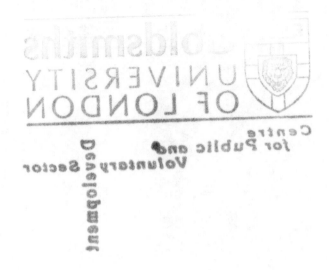

**British Library Cataloguing in Publication Data**

A catalogue record for this book is available from the British Library

ISBN 1 872582 11 7

© 1994 London Voluntary Service Council

Print: Spider Web, 14 Sussex Way, London N7 6RS
Published by LVSC, 356 Holloway Road, London N7 6PA

# Foreword

I am pleased — extremely so — to be writing the foreword for the fourth edition of VBNA.

This is for two reasons. The contents — which are clear, accessible, concise and up to date — speak for themselves and so require little commendation. Also, I can speak from the position of having used VBNA long before joining LVSC, in a variety of roles — as a community worker, trainer and management committee member.

Of course, this is not the only publication a voluntary organisation needs. However, it is essential. The information that VBNA provides enables and assists voluntary and community organisations, of all types and sizes, to carry out their duties lawfully, professionally, efficiently and, most importantly, being adequately informed.

For new and existing organisations which require a structure for delivering effective services and support, need to respond to changing legislation and have increased demands for accountability from both users and funders, VBNA is indispensable.

Many people contributed to this edition. Thanks go to past and present LVSC staff for their comments on particular chapters: David Green, Sue Hutchinson, Martin Rosling and Sandra Vogel; to Stephen Lloyd, for clarifying charity trading; Greyham Dawes from the Charity Commission for helping to unravel charity accounting; Dave Leggett from NCVO for comments on lotteries and raffles; Lorna Dacres from the DSS and Joy Anderton from the Employment Department for checking the maternity pay and leave sections; and Marcia Reid from the Home Office for comments on fundraising. Particular thanks go to Alison Forbes for proof reading and to Sandy Adirondack, for her invaluable comments on the whole publication.

But most importantly we must acknowledge the work of the authors. LVSC is again in gratitude to Duncan Forbes, Ruth Hayes and Jacki Reason for writing this book.

**Janet Hibbert**
Assistant Director, Community Services Division

# Introduction

We delayed publication of the latest edition to enable us to include the recommendations of the Charities and Voluntary Organisations Deregulation Task Force. Throughout the book reference is made to the recommendations and to forthcoming legislation, in particular Part VI of the Charities Act, 1993, and rights of part-time workers. The law as stated is correct as at 1 August 1994.

Booklists are given at the end of each chapter. Addresses of publishers and other organisations referred to within the text appear at the end of the book.

We welcome your feedback. Included you should find an evaluation form: we would be grateful if you could spare a few minutes to complete and return it. If there is no form, let us have your comments anyway. Please send them to Head of Publications, LVSC, 356 Holloway Road, London N7 6PA.

Thank you

# Contents

# Chapter 1: Getting an organisation off the ground

This chapter starts by explaining why a constitution is necessary and then describes the legal structures used by voluntary organisations. The following sections discuss charity status and the advantages and disadvantages of registering as a charity. The next sections look at making the decision about legal structure, setting up the organisation and, in particular, drawing up a constitution. The final section explains how to change from one legal structure to another.

Charity and company law are covered in greater detail in *The voluntary sector legal handbook*.

## Organisational structures

A small group without premises or paid staff may need only a set of basic rules which state its aims and the powers it has to achieve them. However, once an organisation owns or rents property, employs paid workers, raises funds or borrows money, it takes on legal and management responsibilities. It is then essential to adopt a set of rules which define who is responsible for meeting these obligations.

The rules governing an organisation are set out in a **constitution**, the precise form of which depends on the legal structure adopted.

The four types of structure for a voluntary organisation are:

❑ an unincorporated association;

❑ a charitable trust;

❑ a limited company;

❑ an industrial and provident society.

It is no longer possible to register as a new friendly society although those already registered can continue with that structure.

## Why have a constitution?

A constitution is the legal document which sets out the rules for governing an organisation and is necessary for the following reasons:

❑ to ensure an organisation's aims are clear and agreed by its members;

❑ to provide mechanisms for making decisions and resolving disputes;

❑ to gain credibility with bank managers and funders;

❑ to clarify liability and lines of responsibility and in particular reduce the personal financial risk of committee members;

❑ to ensure accountability;

❑ to enable an organisation to take advantage of the benefits of charitable status (a written constitution is needed in order to register as a charity);

❑ to enable trustees to be formally appointed and, if necessary, hold property on trust for an organisation;

❑ to enable an organisation to register as an industrial and provident society or a company limited by guarantee;

❑ to enable an organisation to affiliate to the local council for voluntary service or other coordinating agencies.

The next section examines the legal structures which can be used for setting up a voluntary organisation.

## Legal structures

### Unincorporated associations

A group is not required by law to seek approval of any kind before it sets itself up, nor does it need to register with any regulatory body unless it is going to operate as a charity. Groups with short-term goals and those which do not intend to employ staff or acquire property may need only a set of basic rules under which all members will operate. These should state the organisation's aims, the powers it has to achieve them and its management procedures.

## Advantages

Unincorporated associations are quick and cheap to set up. Unless a group is applying for charitable status other agencies need not be involved. There are no fees to pay, unless the group seeks legal advice on drawing up its constitution. Unincorporated associations are also independent; they do not have to answer to an external authority, for example by submitting accounts (unless the group is a charity, or accounts are required by a funding agency). Because the constitutions of unincorporated associations are flexible, the organisation can be democratic. Finally, an unincorporated association can be wound up relatively easily at a general meeting of its members.

Unincorporated associations can register as charities and if they do, will gain all the advantages of charity status listed later in this chapter.

## Disadvantages

An unincorporated association has no separate legal existence, and remains for most purposes a collection of individuals. As a result in most cases:

❏ it cannot acquire property in its own name; property must be held by individuals acting on behalf of the group;

❏ legal proceedings cannot be taken by the group in its own name, but must be taken by individuals representing the group;

❏ individual members of the management committee (or trustees) can be held personally responsible for the organisation's obligations and debts; this is an important factor to consider when choosing a legal structure and is further discussed below (see 'Liability of committee members').

An unincorporated association may find it difficult to borrow money. Loans can be made only to individual committee members, who become personally responsible for ensuring repayments.

## The constitution

Several organisations have devised model constitutions which can be adopted by local groups. Alternatively, a constitution could be adapted from one being used by a similar group, or be drawn up from scratch. The Charity Commissioners have produced a *Model constitution for a charitable unincorporated association (GD3)*. Points to consider

when using this constitution are set out in 'Setting up the organisation', later in the chapter.

## Charitable trusts

A group wishing to own property and receive grants could consider the structure of a trust. However, only those groups with charitable aims may use this structure and registration with the Charity Commissioners is essential.

Trusts are set up to manage money or property for a clearly defined purpose. They establish a formal relationship between three parties:

❏ the donors of money or property (the people who started off the trust by making the first donation, which may be only a few pounds);

❏ the trustees (the Charity Commissioners usually require three) who become the nominal owners of the trust property;

❏ the beneficiaries (the people who will benefit from the trust).

The trustees must ensure that the property or money is used for the purposes set out in the trust deed; it is generally illegal for them to benefit personally from trust property.

## Advantages

Trusts can be set up quickly and cheaply although legal advice may be needed. Apart from asking the Charity Commissioners to approve the constitution — known as the **trust deed** — and paying 50p stamp duty at the local Inland Revenue Stamp Office (listed in the phone book), other regulatory bodies need not be involved. Small trusts are also cheap to administer. If there is provision for changes in the trust deed, amendments can be made fairly easily; the Charity Commissioners must, however, approve any alterations to the section on aims and objectives.

Trustees can acquire and manage property on behalf of the trust and the trust deed can give the trustees powers to raise and borrow money to fulfil the aims of the organisation.

## Disadvantages

Trusts must register as charities and therefore have all the disadvantages of registered charities set out later in this chapter.

Trusts are essentially non-democratic organisations. Decision making lies with the trustees, who are the only people with legal powers to make decisions relating to the trust. Unlike other legal structures, trusts do not have a membership structure. However, it is possible to have trustees appointed by other bodies, for example other voluntary organisations or local authorities. The trustees usually have an unlimited term of office although this need not be the case. They can only be removed if the trust deed allows for this; the model trust deed recommended by the Charity Commissioners does not have this provision. Trustees generally cannot benefit personally from their role as trustees so that employees working for a trust cannot have a formal role in decision making.

Trustees can be personally liable for contracts entered into on behalf of the trust and for any loss resulting from their actions which are in breach of trust. This is discussed further under 'Choosing the legal structure', later in the chapter.

Since property is vested in the trustees as individuals, transferring it to new trustees may be complicated and expensive. It is important that the original trust deed allows for a change in trustees.

## The trust deed

The *Model declaration of trust (GD2)*, available from the Charity Commissioners, should be used as the basis for a deed of trust for a charity. Always make sure trustees are aware of their legal obligations and potential liabilities.

# Limited companies

There are two types of limited company. In a **company limited by shares** members (shareholders) invest money in the hope of gaining a profit; this type of company is generally found in the commercial sector.

The second kind of company is a **company limited by guarantee.** This is appropriate for organisations which aim to pursue some social or political cause. There are no shareholders and any profits are reinvested in the company. All members must guarantee to pay a nominal sum (usually £1, and almost always less than £5) if the organisation runs into debt.

A limited company may register as a charity, provided it meets the requirements of the Charity Commissioners.

## Advantages

A company limited by guarantee is an **incorporated organisation**. This means that it has a separate legal identity as distinct from that of its members and therefore:

❑ can buy and sell property in its own name;

❑ may take or defend legal proceedings in its own name;

❑ can protect individual members of the organisation and, in almost all circumstances, members of the management committee from personal liability.

The liability of individual members (people who have a right to vote at an annual general meeting) and of committee members (also known as board members or directors) is different. The extent of members' personal liability is limited to the amount they agree to guarantee. Individual members are therefore almost totally protected against personal liability by setting up an incorporated organisation.

Under company law the board of directors is responsible for running the company, although in a voluntary organisation they may be called a committee or management committee.

The directors or committee members have no personal liability unless they:

❑ act fraudulently;

❑ act in breach of trust; or

❑ continue running the company when they know or ought to know it has no reasonable chance of avoiding insolvent liquidation.

What happens when a company is in insolvent liquidation is dealt with in chapter 10. The liability of committee members is dealt with further under 'Choosing the legal structure', later in the chapter.

Companies are democratic. They are required to have a membership which usually has the power to elect, and always has the power to remove, officers and committee members. The structure works equally well for any size of group.

Because a company limited by guarantee is incorporated and therefore has a separate legal identity, owning and transferring property is relatively simple. Even when the committee or membership changes, ownership of the property remains in the name of the company, so there is no need for any documents transferring ownership.

Most companies have to use the word 'Limited' as part of their name, but the majority of voluntary organisations are exempt from this requirement.

It is relatively easy for a company to borrow money because the lender knows that the organisation, rather than a changing group of individuals, is responsible for repayment. However, banks may still ask for personal guarantees that will make individual committee members personally liable to repay the loan if the company defaults.

Once the constitution is agreed within the organisation, company registration (with the Registrar of Companies) takes only about two to three weeks provided there are no complications.

## Disadvantages

Companies are usually subject to more controls and bureaucracy than other legal structures; their activities are regulated by the Companies Acts.

Although the registration fee is only £50, the legal fees for setting up a charitable company limited by guarantee may be considerable if an organisation wants to change the Charity Commissioners' model constitution. A company has to pay a fee when submitting annual returns to the Registrar of Companies (as at April 94, £32).

Companies limited by guarantee have to notify the Registrar of Companies whenever a committee member leaves or a new one is appointed. Companies also have to notify the Registrar of Companies if they enter into any legal charge (for example if they borrow money from a bank and the bank has a mortgage over the company's property).

## The constitution

The constitution of a limited company consists of two parts:

❏ the **memorandum of association**, which contains the aims of the organisation, the powers it has to pursue them, and the extent of members' liability;

❏ the **articles of association**, which describe the company's rules, including its procedures for electing the management committee and keeping accounts.

The Charity Commissioners have produced a *Model memorandum and articles of association for a charitable company limited by guarantee (GD1)* and, subject to the comments made under 'Setting up the organisation', below, this is a useful model.

## Industrial and provident societies

To qualify for registration under the **Industrial and Provident Societies Act, 1965** a society should carry on an industry, business or trade and be either a bona fide cooperative society or acting for the benefit of the community.

The guidelines issued by the Registry of Friendly Societies say a bona fide cooperative society must meet the following criteria:

❏ it must not contain in its constitution artificial restrictions on membership, designed to increase other members' interests and rights;

❏ business must be conducted for the mutual benefit of the society's members;

❏ membership must be open to everyone who works in the organisation;

❏ all members must have an equal say in running the society;

❏ the interest paid to members who have invested money in the society must be restricted;

❏ the society must have at least seven members;

❏ profits must be distributed to members in relation to the extent to which they have participated in the business of the society.

The guidelines say that an organisation for the benefit of the community must usually:

❏ be non-profit making;

❏ have rules forbidding the distribution of its assets among members;

❏ allow all members an equal say in controlling its affairs;

❏ restrict the interest rate paid on its share or loan capital;

❏ be able to show it will benefit non-members.

## Advantages

Industrial and provident societies are incorporated organisations, which means that they can hold property in their own name and take legal action in their own name. Most importantly, committee members are protected from personal liability under contracts and can be personally liable only if they act fraudulently or in breach of trust, or continue to run the organisation when they ought to know that it has no reasonable chance of avoiding insolvent liquidation (see chapter 10).

Industrial and provident societies do not have to submit as much information to the Registrar of Friendly Societies as companies limited by guarantee have to submit to the Registrar of Companies. For example they do not have to notify the Registrar of Friendly Societies about any changes to the committee or about legal charges.

Industrial and provident societies use a set of rules to register with the Registrar of Friendly Societies. A number of umbrella organisations, for example the National Federation of Housing Associations, have had sets of model rules approved by the Registrar. Groups which qualify to join one of these umbrella organisations will probably be able to use their model rules. If there is no such umbrella organisation appropriate for your group, you will have to draw your own rules from scratch. This will be expensive in legal and registration fees.

## Disadvantages

If model rules are not used, registration can be a lengthy, expensive process (as at April 94, £535). If model rules are used, the fee is reduced (as at April 94 to £200) but the umbrella organisation which produced the model rules and which will help with registration may charge an additional fee. Even registration using model rules can take several months.

As with companies limited by guarantee, registration involves loss of privacy. Annual returns and accounts must be submitted to the Registrar, and these are open to the public. Registers of members and officers must be kept and be available for inspection (see chapter 2). It is expensive to amend the constitution (as at April 94, £170 even for a small amendment).

Although the Government has recently removed the audit requirements for small companies limited by guarantee (see chapter 8), no equivalent announcement has been made in respect of small industrial and provident societies. The audit requirements for industrial and provident societies are, therefore, now more stringent than those in force for companies limited by guarantee.

Probably the greatest disadvantage of an industrial and provident society is that it can no longer register with the Charity Commissioners, even if it is a charitable organisation, and therefore will not receive a registered charity number. Many funders, for example charitable trusts, are unwilling to give funds other than to registered charities.

It is still important for the constitution to be approved by the Inland Revenue as charitable, otherwise corporation tax may be payable.

Industrial and provident societies have a shorter period than companies to file their accounts. Those whose year-end is between the end of August and the end of January have to file accounts by the end of March. In other cases accounts have to be filed within three months of the end of the society's financial year. This allows very little time to organise an audit, set up a committee meeting to approve the accounts and hold an annual general meeting. There are financial penalties if the accounts are submitted late.

**NB:** At time of writing (August 94) the Government was intending to lengthen the period for societies to file their accounts to bring it into line with that for companies.

# Local authority influenced companies

The **Local Government and Housing Act, 1989** gave the Government power to introduce controls on local authorities' interests in companies. The aim is to prevent local authorities using local companies to carry out activities which they are prohibited from doing themselves.

The restrictions apply to companies and industrial and provident societies but can be extended to trusts. The legislation has not yet been brought into force (as at August 94), and voluntary organisations will be affected by it only if they fall into one of the categories detailed below.

## Local authority controlled organisations

This is where the organisation is controlled by the local authority, for example the local authority controls the majority of votes at a general meeting or has the power to appoint or remove a majority of the committee or board of directors. This is unlikely to apply to most voluntary organisations.

## Local authority influenced organisations

An organisation is considered to be 'local authority influenced' if it has a 'business relationship' with the local authority (see below) and:

❑ at least 20% of its committee or board of directors are people associated with the local authority; or

❑ at least 20% of the voting rights at a board or committee meeting are people associated with the local authority; or

❑ at least 20% of the voting rights of all members entitled to vote at a general meeting are people who are associated with the local authority.

The Government has the power to define people who are 'associated with the local authority'. This can include former as well as current councillors and officers and their spouses, or indeed anyone who holds or has held an office in a political party which nominated someone for election to the local authority.

An organisation has a 'business relationship' with the local authority where there are financial transactions between the two, and includes organisations:

❑ which, within a period of 12 months, have more than half of their turnover associated with the local authority; or

❑ where more than half of their assets originated from the local authority; or

❑ which occupy land provided by the local authority on terms lower than the commercial rate.

Although many voluntary organisations will have business relationships with the local authority because of grant aid, contracts or subsidised premises, most will not fulfil the minimum membership or committee membership requirements.

## Controls

The Government has power to introduce different controls for local authority controlled organisations and local authority influenced organisations. The details are not clear as the regulations have not been introduced. However, they are likely to require the organisation to obtain permission from the local authority before borrowing any capital and provide information to the local authority about the organisation's activities and finances

# Charitable status

This section describes which groups are eligible for charitable status and examines the advantages and disadvantages of being a charity.

In the strict legal sense, a charity is an organisation established for charitable purposes, and will generally be registered under the **Charities Act, 1993.**

A charitable unincorporated association, a charitable trust or a company limited by guarantee with charitable purposes must register as a charity unless the organisation does not own or use land, has no permanent endowment and its annual income is less than £1,000.

## Charitable purposes

To register as a charity, all the group's aims and objectives as stated in its constitution must be charitable. The four recognised categories of charitable activity (known as the **four heads of charity**) are:

❑ the relief of poverty;

❑ the advancement of religion;

❑ the advancement of education;

❑ other purposes beneficial to the community.

## Relief of poverty

The Charity Commission uses a broad definition of poverty which includes people who are sick, have a disability or are mentally ill.

Relief of poverty can be provided directly, for example through financial help, food, clothing or housing, or indirectly by helping people become more self sufficient, for example through the provision of welfare advice. Unlike the other charitable purposes described below, poverty charities can work with a quite narrowly defined group of people.

## Advancement of education

There is no precise definition of education. The category would include:

❑ promotion of commercial education;

❑ promotion of aesthetic education, for example through concerts and drama;

❑ research activities for public benefit;

❑ education about political principles in the academic sense (the Charity Commission would not accept for registration a group promoting a particular political view).

The advancement of education must be for general public benefit.

## Advancement of religion

This is not confined to the Christian faith. In order to qualify under this head a group must be able to demonstrate that its activities will benefit the general public.

## Other purposes beneficial to the community

As long as a group can demonstrate that its activities are beneficial to the community (or a substantial part of it) there is scope for extending the traditional charitable frontiers. The following activities could fall into this category:

❑ protection of lives or property of the community;

❑ resettlement and rehabilitation of ex-offenders and drug abusers;

❑ promotion of industry, commerce or art;

❏ promotion of moral welfare;

❏ provision of public recreation and leisure facilities;

❏ conservation of the national heritage.

The work of many groups will fit within these categories, although sometimes indirectly. For example a group involved in employment creation and the promotion of economic activity would not be charitable under the above definitions. However, if stated goals were the relief of poverty among unemployed people, the provision of education and training for the relief of unemployment, or the promotion of industry or commerce in general, the group could be eligible for charitable status.

A self-help organisation which exists exclusively for its members would not be eligible, as it does not operate for the general public benefit. However, if the objects clause in its constitution is carefully worded to allow for an unrestricted membership, a self-help group might be able to obtain charitable status.

## Advantages

### Tax relief

The main advantages of charitable status lie in the field of taxation. Charities have the following tax advantages:

❏ **income and corporation tax**: charities do not pay income or corporation tax on their income. Profits earned from trading activities can be exempt from tax (but only if they are used solely for the purposes of the charity and the trade is part of the main function of the charity or the work is mainly carried out by the beneficiaries);

❏ **stamp duty**: charities are exempt from stamp duty

when property is transferred to them, but an exemption stamp must still be obtained;

❏ **capital gains tax**: charities do not pay capital gains tax as long as any gain is used for charitable purposes;

❏ **inheritance tax**: many gifts to charities are exempt from inheritance tax;

❏ **Value Added Tax (VAT)**: sales in charity shops of donated goods are exempt from VAT. So too are fundraising events by charities. Most other trading is, however, taxed in the normal way. Organisations considering contracting with public authorities should check with their accountants and with Customs & Excise to see whether or not VAT should be charged;

❏ **payroll giving**: employees can receive tax relief on regular deductions from their wages if the money goes to charities (the maximum annual limit as at April 94 was £900);

❏ **individual large donations**: individual donations to charities are eligible for tax relief (as at April 94 the minimum donation was £250);

❏ **covenants**: charities can recover income tax under covenants. This means that if a tax-paying person is willing to contribute a regular annual sum for three years or more under a Deed of Covenant, the charity receives back from the Inland Revenue the income tax paid by the donor (contact the Inland Revenue for further details).

### Rate relief

A charity pays only 20% of the non-domestic rate on any building it uses wholly or mainly for charitable purposes (**mandatory relief**). The local authority has the discretion to waive the 20% so that the organisation pays no rates at all (**discretionary relief**). There is no statutory requirement to submit applications for mandatory rate relief but it is advisable to inform the rating authority (see chapter 6 for further details).

## Fundraising

Many funders, particularly trusts, have a policy of grant-aiding only registered charities. Having charitable status and in particular having a registered charity number also gives a group credibility when raising money from the general public through events such as appeals, street collections and raffles.

## Advice

The Charity Commissioners can offer free advice to committee members on all aspects of charity law.

# Disadvantages

## Political activity

Charities must not have directly political aims, and are therefore restricted in the nature of their campaigning work. The law does, however, allow some political activity by charities as long as it is directly relevant to their work and does not involve party politics.

The Charity Commissioners have produced revised guidelines on political activities and campaigning by charities in leaflet CC9.

The general principles are that a charity can engage in political activity if it:

❏ would effectively further the stated purposes of the charity and so benefit its beneficiaries;

❏ is within the powers of the committee under the terms of the charity's constitution; and

❏ is appropriate to a non-political organisation.

In addition, the views must be based on a well-founded and reasoned case and be expressed in a responsible way.

The Charity Commissioners advise that the following activities are acceptable:

❏ seeking to influence government or public opinion through well-founded, reasoned argument based on research or direct experience on matters either relating directly to the achievement of the charity's own stated purposes or relevant to the well-being of the charitable sector;

❏ publishing a response to the Government or a public body considering or proposing changes in the law or to a green or white paper;

❏ in response to a parliamentary bill, supplying MPs with information and reasoned arguments for use in debate which the charity reasonably believes would assist the achievement of its charitable purposes;

❏ advocating a change in the law or public policy which it reasonably believes would help to achieve its charitable purposes, and opposing a change in the law or public policy which the charity reasonably believes would hinder its ability to do so. In either case it can present Government with reasoned arguments in support of its position and may publish its views and seek to influence public opinion in favour of its position by well-founded reasoned argument;

❏ supporting the passage of a bill which the charity reasonably believes would help it to achieve its charitable purposes and oppose the passage of a bill which it reasonably believes would hinder its ability to do so;

❏ spending funds on the promotion of legislation provided the charity has power to do so and believes it will further its charitable purposes;

❏ commenting publicly on social, economic and political issues if these relate to the charity's purposes or the way in which it is able to carry out its work;

❏ advocating a particular solution if the charity reasonably believes that this will further its purposes. A charity may advocate the same solution as a political party, but the charity must make it plain that its views are independent of the political party concerned;

❏ providing factual information to the charity's members and those interested in its work in seeking to inform their MPs and others on matters relating to the purposes of the charity;

❏ employing a parliamentary liaison officer to inform MPs on matters relevant to the charity's purposes;

❏ responding to forthcoming elections by analysing and commenting on the proposals of political parties which relate to the charity's purposes or the way in which it is able to carry out its work, provided that it comments in a way which is appropriate to a non-political organisation and complies with all the relevant provisions of electoral law;

❏ providing prospective candidates in elections with information about issues relating to the charity's purposes or the way in which it is able to carry out its work, and raising public awareness about the issues generally, provided that the promotional material is educational, informative, reasoned and well-founded;

❏ seeking the support of MPs in connection with a Government grant to the charity.

A charity must ensure that any published research work is properly analysed and objective. Proposals advocating political action must arise from a thorough analysis of the research findings and should make clear whether the solutions are those of the author or the charity. The charity must support only those recommendations which, if adopted, have a reasonable expectation of furthering its purposes.

The Charity Commissioners consider the following activities to be unacceptable:

❏ seeking to influence public opinion or put pressure on the Government whether directly or indirectly, through supporters or members of the public, to legislate or adopt a particular policy on the basis of slanted or inaccurate data;

❏ participating in party political demonstrations;

❏ conducting publicity campaigns indicating how individual MPs or parties have voted on particular issues as a means of applying public pressure on those MPs or the Government;

❏ conducting a referendum on a political issue as opposed to a properly constituted study or survey;

❏ providing its supporters or members of the public with pro forma letters or other pro forma material to send to MPs or the Government;

❏ in the case of a charity for the advancement of education, overstepping the boundary between education and propaganda in promoting its educational purpose (the distinction is between providing balanced information designed to enable people to make up their own minds and one-sided information designed to promote a particular point of view);

❏ supporting a political party;

❏ pursuing indirectly a political purpose by financing it through a third party either by making a grant or by affiliation;

❏ providing supporters or members of the public with material specifically designed to underpin a

political campaign, or with material for or against a government or particular MPs;

❏ issuing biased publicity material;

❏ seeking to persuade members of the public to vote for or against a candidate or a political party;

❏ manipulating information in published research to present a partial view or to support a preconceived position or objective;

❏ undertaking research for another body where it is clear that the body intends to use the research for political or propagandist purposes.

To avoid problems with the Charity Commissioners charities should refrain from using words such as 'campaign', 'pressure' or 'action' in their published material unless the activities clearly fall within the Commissioners' guidelines.

Charities that overstep the mark on political activity may receive a demand for income or corporation tax on at least part of their income. Committee members may, in rare cases, be liable for breach of trust. If non-charitable activities continue, the Charity Commission is likely to remove the organisation from the Register of Charities.

Some charities have set up a parallel non-charitable organisation to carry out their political activity. For example Liberty is not a charity, and so is free to campaign. The linked but separate Civil Liberties Trust is registered as a charity. Groups that adopt this strategy should ensure that the charitable and non-charitable bodies have completely separate accounts.

## Trading

A charity has limited powers to trade. It may:

❏ sell goods produced by its beneficiaries, for example items made in a sheltered workshop;

❏ sell donated goods;

❏ sell items that are part of its charitable work;

❏ sell its services as part of its charitable work, for example by providing community care services;

❏ organise occasional modest fundraising events, such as stalls at bazaars.

However, if a charity intends to trade specifically to generate an income and not fulfil its charitable purposes, it could be breaking the law. It can solve this problem by setting up a separate non-charitable trading subsidiary.

## Trading using a subsidiary

A charitable company can set up a subsidiary profit making company. An unincorporated association or charitable trust can set up a trading company with individual committee members appointed as the shareholders.

In both cases the following requirements must be met:

❑ the charity must have the power to purchase shares in a private company as part of its constitution — many charities only have investment powers set out in the **Trustee Investments Act, 1961**, which does not give power to buy shares in a private company;

❑ the trading venture must not be too speculative;

❑ there must be some clear benefits to the charity in having the trading subsidiary — a reasonable expectation of profits and income based on proper assessments of risk and income;

❑ the two organisations must have separate accounts and, if the same staff are employed by both organisations, it should be possible to distinguish the work staff are doing for each organisation;

❑ there must be no subsidy of the trading company by the charity; costs should be properly apportioned between them;

❑ the charity can lend money to the trading subsidiary only if the loan is considered to be a reasonable investment, market interest rates are charged and steps are taken to obtain security for the loan. In addition the charity's constitution must allow for such a loan.

For further details see *Charities, trading and the law.*

## Payments to committee members and employees' involvement

One condition of charitable status is that committee members generally may not gain any personal benefit, in particular financial benefit, from the charity. The normal rule is therefore that employees cannot become committee members and that committee members cannot be paid for any work carried out for the charity. This effectively excludes any worker-controlled organisation from registering as a charity.

There are, however, some exceptions to the above.

### Payments to committee members

Committee members **can** receive financial benefit from the charity provided:

❑ the constitution allows such a payment;

❑ the payment is necessary to ensure that the charity is properly administered; and

❑ the amount paid properly reflects the services provided to the charity and takes account of the charity's financial resources.

For further details see *Decisions of the Charity Commissioners, volume 2.*

For a charity which existed before the above guidance was published (April 94), the Commissioners will take the following into account when considering whether to allow an amendment to the constitution:

❑ the charity's size and administrative complexity;

❑ its activities, in particular whether committee members need to have continual involvement in the day to day management of the organisation;

❑ the specialist nature of the skills required of the committee members;

❑ the cost of obtaining the necessary skills from employees rather than paying committee members.

Where staff are employed, this will generally imply that committee members should not receive any payment, although the Charity Commissioners recognise that in some cases at least one of the committee members, for example the chair, may be so heavily involved that remuneration would be justified.

Charities can apply to the Commissioners for permission to make a one-off payment to a committee member if they can show that:

❑ the work is exceptional and not part of the committee member's duties;

❑ the work is necessary;

❑ the payment is genuine, for example the committee member is not being employed at a greater cost that would be charged elsewhere; and

❑ payment is appropriate for the work done.

### Employees on the committee

A new charity can include a provision within its constitution allowing an employee to be appointed as a committee member provided that he or she is excluded from meetings where terms of employment are discussed. However, it will generally not be possible for the committee to include any significant number of employees. The Charity Commissioners will not permit existing charities to amend their constitutions to allow employees to act as committee members unless the committee can provide strong arguments for it.

Even though restrictions mean that most employees cannot play any formal role in making the most important management decisions, this does not prevent them from being involved through consultation.

## Liability for breach of trust

A charity's committee members can be personally liable if any losses result where they have acted in breach of trust. This is discussed further under 'Choosing the legal structure', below.

## Publicity and administrative requirements

Registered charities lack privacy. They have to submit annual returns to the Charity Commissioners and will have to make their annual accounts publicly available (for further details see chapter 8).

The **Charities Act, 1993** includes requirements relating to disposal of property, for example by mortgage, lease or sale (for further details see chapter 6).

# Choosing the legal structure

This section describes the factors to take into account when deciding which legal structure would be most appropriate.

It is possible to move from one form of legal structure to another as a group develops and its needs change. For example, it may start as a steering group with no constitution, merely a set of agreed objectives, move on to become an unincorporated association with a constitution and then decide to register as a charity. In time it may want to enter into a contract for services with a local authority and may need to become a company limited by guarantee.

## Minimising the risk of personal liability

All voluntary organisations will want to ensure that members and committee members do not end up being personally liable in any way. In many voluntary organisations there is minimal risk. In others, there are risks and these organisations need to choose a legal structure designed to prevent personal liability as far as possible.

## Liability of committee members

Almost all voluntary organisations will be run by a committee. If this is not the case the organisation's members will count as the committee for the purposes of these rules on liability.

A management committee can be known by a number of different titles; some alternatives are listed below.

❑ **unincorporated associations**: committee, executive committee or management committee;

❑ **trusts**: committee or board of trustees;

❑ **companies limited by guarantee**: board of directors;

❑ **charities** (whether incorporated or unincorporated): trustees.

Whatever their title, they have the responsibilities and liabilities set out below, and for the rest of this chapter they will be referred to as 'committee members ' or 'the committee'.

It is important to understand the following three ways in which committee members can become personally liable:

❑ for breach of trust if the organisation is a charity;

❑ for negligence or breach of statutory duties in carrying out the organisation's activities;

❑ under contracts entered into by the organisation.

### Breach of trust

Committee members of a charity who have acted in breach of trust may be personally required to repay the charity for any losses that have been incurred, whatever the legal structure. This can include where:

❑ a committee member has acted fraudulently (for example stealing money from the charity);

❑ someone has gained personal benefit from being a committee member (for example receiving payment not allowed under the terms of the constitution);

❑ committee members have allowed the charity to carry out an activity not permitted under the terms of the constitution (for example engaging in a political campaign or trading which was not within its objects). However, even if the committee has acted in breach of trust in allowing this activity, the members would be required to repay the charity only if financial losses were incurred. For example, if the charity engaged in political campaigning which was not allowed, committee members might have to repay to the charity the cost of any publicity material produced;

❏ the committee has been seriously negligent and this has resulted in losses to the charity (for example by allowing it to engage in some risky venture without taking proper steps to protect its position).

Provided trustees act sensibly and seek advice when necessary from, for example valuers, solicitors or accountants, there should be no reason for them to act in breach of trust. Organisations which operate on the fringe of acceptable charity activity (for example campaigning), in particular will need to get advice if they have any doubt as to whether the activities are permitted under charity law.

Even if a committee member has acted in breach of trust, the court has power to relieve him or her of personal liability if it is satisfied that the individual acted reasonably and honestly.

It may also be possible for the charity to obtain indemnity insurance for the committee against liability for breach of trust (see chapter 7).

### Negligence or breach of statutory duty

In a company limited by guarantee or an industrial and provident society the organisation itself would usually be liable for negligence if a loss, damage or injury arose as a result of an action, or inaction (for example failing to repair a building) by the organisation. The committee members would be protected from individual liability. In unincorporated associations and charitable trusts, the committee would be liable for negligence. In practice, personal liability can be avoided by taking out adequate insurance and the committee should take responsibility for arranging this (see chapter 7).

### Contracts

Voluntary organisations can enter into a number of contracts including:

❏ employment contracts;

❏ office equipment leases;

❏ leases on premises;

❏ contracts to provide services, for example community care.

Many contracts, especially those relating to leasing premises, contain clauses requiring payment over a number of years. Unless there is provision to terminate the contract, an organisation will continue to be liable to make the payments until the lease has ended.

Taking on contracts and leases increases the risk of personal liability. In an incorporated organisation (industrial and provident society or company limited by guarantee) the organisation itself will be liable to make the payments even if the funding has ceased.

An unincorporated organisation (unincorporated association or trust) cannot itself enter into a lease or contract of any kind. It must do so through named individuals, holding trustees (see chapter 2) or the whole committee, who will be responsible for making payments under the terms of any contract or lease. Even if the organisation loses its funding, the individuals will continue to be personally liable until the debt has been discharged.

Personal liability can be limited to some extent by:

❏ ensuring the contract can be terminated at least on reasonable notice if funding runs out;

❏ stating in the contract that it is being entered into by a person in the capacity of a trustee on behalf of the organisation and that the trustee is not to be personally liable for any breach of contract; or

❏ confirming that anyone entering into the contract has a right of indemnity (repayment) from the whole committee. This will enable them at least to spread the loss if the organisation runs out of funds.

## The ability to raise funds

For most voluntary organisations, the ability to fundraise is essential.

An organisation considering setting up as an industrial and provident society should consider the possible disadvantages of not being able to gain a charity registration number. Such organisations should check whether local authorities and other potential funders are restricted to funding registered charities or whether they can also fund charitable industrial and provident societies.

## Status of the organisation

Incorporated organisations may be taken more seriously than unincorporated organisations. This may be particularly important, for example, where groups are competing for grants or contracts.

## The ability to campaign

The restrictions on campaigning by charities are set out on pages 8 and 9. If they are too restrictive it may be better not to set up as a charitable organisation or to consider setting up two organisations, one of which is a charity and one of which is not.

## The ability to trade

Charities face some restrictions on their trading (see 'Trading', above). If trading is essential for raising revenue and would not be allowed within the charitable restrictions, the options are setting up as a non-charitable organisation or setting up a trading subsidiary.

## Size of the organisation

Unincorporated associations and companies limited by guarantee face no restrictions on their size. In practice, charitable trusts usually have a limited number of trustees and no membership so that in effect they are controlled by a small number of people. Industrial and provident societies require a minimum membership of seven but there is no maximum.

## Privacy

Most voluntary organisations are happy to be accountable to the public so that need for privacy is not important. Industrial and provident societies and companies limited by guarantee must record committee members' and members' names in a register which is open for public inspection (see chapter 2). These requirements are not particularly burdensome. However, if privacy is important, consider setting up a non-charitable unincorporated association, where there are no publicity obligations unless required by funders.

## Setting up costs

If adopting a model constitution, the only cost involved in setting up will be the fees payable to registration authorities; these are higher for industrial and provident societies than for companies. Legal advice may be needed when drawing up a new constitution or adapting an off-the-shelf one — this would be an additional cost.

Companies limited by guarantee have to pay when filing their annual returns. No fees are payable for filing returns for other forms of legal structure, although the Charity Commissioners have powers to charge in the future.

## Democracy

Apart from charitable trusts, all forms of legal structure allow for as much participation as desired. However it should be noted that there are limits on the extent to which staff can participate in formal management of registered charities (see 'Employees on the committee', above).

## Administrative requirements

Registered charities, industrial and provident societies and companies limited by guarantee all have to file annual returns with the relevant authority.

Companies limited by guarantee must notify the Registrar of Companies whenever there is a change to the committee membership.

# Choosing the legal structure — summary

In practice there are usually four main factors to take into account when deciding on the type of legal structure: risk, setting up costs, the need to have a charity registration number and the need to be democratic.

## Risk

An organisation which will be entering into contracts (including leasing premises) should generally incorporate either as an industrial and provident society or a company limited by guarantee.

## Setting up costs

It is cheaper to set up a company limited by guarantee than an industrial and provident society.

## Need for a charity registration number

If this is important an organisation will have to register as a charity. This is because industrial and provident societies cannot register.

## Democracy

If this is important, in practice the decision about legal structure will often come down to:

❏ becoming an unincorporated association or a company limited by guarantee; and

❏ whether to register as a charity (this is possible with either of the above structures).

# Setting up the organisation

Setting up a **charitable trust** is straightforward through using the *Model declaration of trust (GD2)* available from the Charity Commissioners, who will also provide advice. **Industrial and provident societies (IPS)** planning to use a set of model rules can obtain advice from the sponsoring organisation. Legal advice will be needed to draw up a tailor-made constitution. The Registrar of Friendly Societies can help with setting up an IPS.

The following section sets out the steps that need to be taken to set up as a **charitable unincorporated association** or a **charitable company limited by guarantee**.

# Decide on the name

Companies limited by guarantee and charities cannot use a name that is the same or similar to that of another company or charity. It is possible to check whether a proposed name is already being used by telephoning Companies House or the Charity Commissioners. Both authorities have the power to restrict the use of certain names.

The general rule is that companies limited by guarantee must have the word 'limited' as part of the company name (or the Welsh equivalent in Wales). However, all charities are exempt and most other voluntary organisations are exempt from this requirement if:

❑ the objects of the company are the promotion of commerce, art, science, education, religion, or any profession or anything incidental or conducive to those objects; and

❑ the company's memorandum and articles:

- require its profits or other income to be used to promote its objects;

- prohibit the payment of dividends to members; and

- on winding up, require the assets to be transferred to some other similar body rather than to the membership.

A company limited by guarantee that wants to be exempt from the use of the word limited must complete form G30(5)(a) — a statutory declaration that the company complies with the requirements set out above — when registering the company.

# Draft and agree the constitution

To register as a charity an organisation must have charitable objects. It is possible to amend objects used by similar organisations. Remember that the **Sex Discrimination Act, 1975** and the **Race Relations Act, 1976** forbid discrimination in the provision of services on grounds of sex and race. The exception is where objects *specifically* state that an organisation is providing services to women or men only or to one racial group (which cannot be defined by reference to colour). If intending to use these provisions, check with the *Equal Opportunities Commission* or the *Commission for Racial Equality.*

The Charity Commissioners have published model constitutions. They are very general in their terms and may need adapting to meet an organisation's specific needs. The following sections examine their clauses and raise points to consider before using them.

# Model constitution for a charitable unincorporated association (GD3)

Throughout the following, the term 'committee' is used, whereas the model constitution uses 'executive committee'.

## Objects and powers

### Equal opportunities
No specific mention is made of equal opportunities, in particular the need to ensure that all applications for membership are treated equally.

## Membership and general meetings

### Membership structure
Although the model constitution allows for both individuals and organisations to join the charity (clause F), there is no provision for different membership structures, for example branches or regional structures. Some organisations may want to specify different categories of membership with rights to elect different parts of the committee.

### Honorary members
The model constitution has no provision for honorary members, who are generally people who have no vote and therefore from a legal point of view are not members. However, organisations may want a category of honorary membership to encourage particular contributions that people can make.

### Expelling members
The model constitution allows for a member to be expelled only if the committee makes a unanimous decision (clause F5). In practice, this could make it impossible to expel a member of the committee or an officer since they would, presumably, vote against their own expulsion. Any procedures for terminating membership need to strike a balance between the rights of the individual and the need of an organisation to be able to remove someone who is behaving inappropriately.

### Annual general meetings (AGMs)
The model constitution specifies that the AGM should take place in a specified month or as soon as possible afterwards (clause Q1). You may want to be more flexible.

### Nominations for election to the committee
The model constitution requires that all nominations for committee places are made 14 days before the AGM (clause Q5). However, some people are prepared to volunteer themselves or nominate others only when they get to the meeting. You may therefore wish to remove this clause.

### Election procedures

Other than the requirement for nominations (see above), the model constitution gives no details about the way in which elections are to be held. You may wish to adapt it to give the committee more flexibility by introducing standing orders relating to elections (which can be changed quite easily). Alternatively, if elections are likely to be contentious, an organisation may want to include election procedures in the constitution, making them far more difficult to change.

### Members' rights

The model constitution does not give members the right to put resolutions on the agenda. If you want to give members this right it should be stated in the constitution. Other rights that could be introduced are a right to:

❑ inspect the register of members;

❑ have copies of non-confidential committee meeting minutes;

❑ receive copies of the accounts on request;

❑ be given a copy of the constitution.

### Holding a general meeting at short notice

There is no such provision in the model constitution; you may want to allow for this with the consent of a certain proportion, for example 90%, of the membership.

### Notice of general meetings

The model constitution only requires members to be informed within a certain period that a general meeting is going to be held (clauses Q2 and R). It does not state what should be included within the notice of a general meeting. Given the importance of a general meeting, you may wish to be more specific, for example by requiring that any resolutions to be discussed at the general meeting are included in the agenda.

### Forgetting to tell a member about a general meeting

If you use the model constitution and omit to tell one member about a general meeting, for example through forgetting to give them a notice, the whole meeting is invalidated. Most organisations would include a clause in their constitution stating that accidental omission to give a member a notice of a meeting should not invalidate the meeting.

### Tied votes

The constitution does not state what happens if there is a tied vote at the general meeting (ie the same number of votes are cast for and against a resolution). Possibilities are to state that a resolution would be lost on a tied vote, or to allow the chair a casting vote.

### Inquorate meetings

The model constitution states a quorum (ie the minimum number of people to enable an inquorate meeting to make decisions) is one tenth of the membership or ten members — whichever is the greater (clause S2). Many constitutions include a provision allowing a meeting to be held the same time the following week, which would be deemed to be quorate however many members attended. This ensures that at least a decision can be made.

### Secret ballots

The model constitution does not describe voting procedures at general meetings. This could result in the chair insisting that votes are taken by a show of hands. You may want to make provision for votes to be taken by secret ballot if requested by a specified number of members.

### Appointing proxies

A proxy is someone who is authorised to vote on behalf of a member. There is no provision in the model constitution for proxies and you may want to introduce this.

### Dispensing with the general meeting

Many constitutions include a provision for a resolution to be passed if it has been signed by all members (thereby dispensing with the need for a general meeting). This is a useful way of enabling decisions to be made quickly while avoiding the administrative requirements of calling a meeting.

## The committee, officers and committee meetings

### Election of officers

The model constitution allows the AGM to elect officers (clause Q3) but many organisations prefer the committee itself to elect them from amongst the committee members.

### Cooptions

The model constitution states that cooptions to the committee can only take place at a special committee meeting (clause H2) and that 21 days' notice has to be given of such a meeting (clause K1). You may wish to allow cooptions to be made at an ordinary committee meeting held on ordinary notice.

### Committee retirements

The model constitution provides for all the committee to retire at every AGM (clause K3) although they can be re-elected or reappointed. Some organisations prefer to have a third of the committee retiring each year.

### Filling committee vacancies

The model constitution does not state how vacancies on the committee should be filled. Most organisations will want the committee to have the power to fill vacancies by cooption until the next AGM. If other organisations can nominate members to the committee, the constitution should state whether they can renominate someone else if their first representative retires or resigns.

## Changing groups that nominate committee members

The model constitution contains a space for details of how nominated committee members, if any, are appointed (clause H1c). You need to decide whether you wish to specify eligible groups in the constitution or have a more flexible mechanism which allows the groups entitled to nominate members to be changed from time to time. This will enable new groups to be included as they become involved in your organisation.

## Expelling committee members and officers

The model constitution has no provision for expelling committee members or officers, even if they are expelled as members. Any procedure for expelling committee members or officers has to balance the rights of the individual concerned against the needs of the organisation. One option is to allow for suspension by the committee with a decision on expulsion being made by the general meeting. Alternatively, the committee could be given the right to expel, with a right of appeal to the general meeting. You could also introduce an external appeal system using someone not involved in the dispute. There should also be a provision stating that if a nominating organisation withdraws its nominee that person automatically ceases to be a committee member.

## Powers to suspend

You may also wish to give powers in the constitution for the committee to suspend officers or committee members or, at the very least, require them to leave the committee meeting.

## Paying reasonable expenses

There is no provision within the model constitution for paying committee members' expenses unless they are solicitors or accountants, in which case they can charge professional fees. You will almost certainly want to amend this clause.

## Paying committee members, and employee involvement

In general, committee members cannot be paid and employees cannot serve on the committee. In order to be able to pay committee members for specific pieces of work, or in exceptional circumstances to allow employees to sit on the committee, the model constitution would need to be amended to allow this.

## Notice of committee meetings

The model constitution does not require specific notice to be given of an ordinary committee meeting. It might be useful, however, to include precise requirements to ensure that all committee members receive proper notice.

## Subcommittees

The model constitution states that a subcommittee can only consist of committee members — at least three (clause K7). You will therefore want to consider whether to adapt this requirement.

## Officers' delegated powers

There needs to be specific provision in the constitution if you want to enable powers to be delegated to individual officers at any stage between committee meetings.

## Dispensing with committee meetings

The model constitution has no provision allowing a decision to be made by all committee members signing a resolution instead of holding a meeting. This is particularly important for dealing with emergencies.

## Altering cheque signatories

The model constitution requires that all cheques are signed by at least two committee members (clause L1). It is possible to amend this to allow a member of staff to be one signatory.

## Other matters

The model constitution states that a notice posted to members is deemed to have arrived ten days after posting (clause T). This would mean that notice of the annual general meeting would have to be sent out to members 32 days beforehand. You may wish to shorten the period.

## Code of conduct

The model constitution contains no provision enabling a code of conduct to be adopted to ensure that members and committee members behave appropriately towards other members, committee members, staff and service users. It is good practice to adopt such a code as part of an equal opportunities policy.

## Adopting the constitution

The model constitution is drafted on the basis that it will be signed by the first committee members. An alternative is to have it adopted by all members at a meeting to launch the organisation. If so, the provisions stating that the signatories are committee members (clause W) will have to be changed.

# Model memorandum and articles of association for a charitable company (GD1)

The term 'committee' is used below when the model memorandum and articles (a company's constitution) uses 'trustees'.

## Objects and powers

### Equal opportunities

There is nothing specific in the model memorandum and articles about equal opportunities and in particular about the need to ensure that all applications for membership are treated equally.

## Membership and general meetings

### Membership requirements

The model memorandum and articles allows the committee to decide who can join the organisation, the cost of membership subscriptions, conditions of membership and the way in which members can be expelled (Article 61). You may wish to set out who can become members in the articles of association and add a clause guaranteeing members' rights, including safeguards against improper expulsion.

### Putting resolutions on the agenda

There is no provision for members to submit resolutions to a general meeting. You may wish to adapt the model memorandum and articles to enable members to put items on the agenda.

### Appointing proxies

There is no provision allowing for members to appoint proxies to vote on their behalf. If this is required the model memorandum and articles will need to be adapted.

### Excluding members from voting

The model memorandum and articles states that members who owe money to the charity cannot vote (Article 21). This allows little leeway in the collection of annual subscriptions and you may wish to be more flexible.

### Categories of membership

There are no provisions in the model memorandum and articles setting out separate categories of committee membership, for example individual membership, voluntary organisations and the statutory sector. There could be an article allowing for various categories of committee membership to be established. There should also be an article requiring the committee to take account of equal opportunities when specifying the categories of committee membership.

## Local and regional structures

If organisations want regional or local structures the memorandum and articles will need to be adapted to permit this.

## The committee, officers and committee meetings

### Committee retirements

The model memorandum and articles requires that a third of the committee retires each year (Article 29). Alternatives are for other proportions or for all members to retire each year.

### Appointing new committee members

The model memorandum and articles requires new committee members either to be appointed by the old committee (Article 32.1) or to be nominated well in advance of the annual general meeting by a member of the company (Article 32.2). In practice, in many voluntary organisations it is not always possible to arrange nominations in advance.

### Removing committee members

Although Article 38 relates to removal of committee members, it does not allow the committee to remove or suspend members in cases of misconduct or fraudulent behaviour. Also there is no provision for cases where a nominating organisation withdraws its nomination.

### Appointing a managing director

The model memorandum and articles allows the committee to appoint one of its members as an unpaid managing director (Article 40). As the position would become permanent this may be unsuitable for many organisations.

### Subcommittees, and officers' delegated powers

The model memorandum and articles allows for subcommittees to be set up comprising only committee members (Article 46). Many organisations would like other people to serve on subcommittees, although the Charity Commissioners are likely to require that committee members comprise the majority of decision making subcommittees. In addition some organisations want to provide for regional committee structures and there may also need to be specific provision to delegate decision making powers to individual officers in certain circumstances.

### Altering cheque signatories

The model memorandum and articles requires that all cheques are signed by at least two committee members (Article 49). It is possible to amend this to allow a member of staff to be one signatory.

### Notice of committee meetings

The model memorandum and articles does not impose any requirement for notice of committee meetings to be given in writing. As a safeguard, you may wish to include such a provision.

### The company secretary

The model memorandum and articles states that the company secretary would not normally be a member of the committee (Article 50). You may want to allow for the company secretary to be a committee member.

### Officers

There is provision only for a chair and secretary in the model memorandum and articles (Articles 46 and A50). You may wish to make provision for other officers or to give flexibility for the committee to create other officer posts in the future.

### Election procedures

There is no provision in the model memorandum and articles for the way in which elections should be held. Whilst elections could be subject to rules made by the committee, many organisations would consider it inappropriate and would rather have rules written into the memorandum and articles.

### Cooptions

The model memorandum and articles does not provide for cooptions of non-members. You may wish to change this.

### Committee membership

The model memorandum and articles does not require that committee members are members of the company. You may wish to specify that only members are eligible for election to the committee, unless they are coopted.

### Election of officers

The model memorandum and articles provides for officers (chair and secretary) to be appointed by the committee (Articles 45 and 50). You may want to have officers elected at the annual general meeting.

## Submit draft constitution to the Charity Commissioners

An organisation wishing to register as a charity should send two copies of its draft constitution to the Charity Commissioners, together with the **Commissioners' questionnaire (form RE96A).**

## Agree any required amendments

The Charity Commissioners often suggest a number of amendments to a draft constitution. These will need to be discussed and agreed. Once the Charity Commissioners have approved the constitution they will supply a **charity registration form (RE1).**

## Adopt the constitution

### Unincorporated associations

Once the constitution has been agreed between yourselves (and, if applicable, with the Charity Commissioners) the next step is for those involved formally to adopt the constitution, either by holding a meeting or by signing the document.

### Companies limited by guarantee

Once the constitution has been agreed amongst yourselves (and, if applicable, the Charity Commissioners) the following procedures need to be followed:

❑ at least one person must sign:

  - both the memorandum and the articles of association as the 'subscriber(s)' (ie the founder member(s)) of the company;

  - **form G10** giving details about his or herself and saying he or she has agreed to be the company's first director(s) and secretary. This form will also give details of the company's registered office. If there are more than two subscribers you will need form G10 continuation sheets, each of which allows for a further two names.

❑ at least one director or secretary, or the solicitor handling the registration must sign a **Declaration (form G12)** confirming compliance with company law.

❑ a charitable company using a name which does not include the word 'limited' must complete form G30(5)(a).

All the above must be submitted to the *New Companies Department* at *Companies House,* together with two bound and signed copies of the memorandum and articles of association and a cheque or postal order for £50, payable to 'The Registrar of Companies'.

All forms mentioned above can be purchased from law stationers (listed in the Yellow Pages under 'stationers'), or are available free of charge from Companies House.

Provided the correct documentation is submitted and the name is acceptable, the Registrar of Companies will register the company, give it a registered number and send a Certificate of Incorporation to its registered office. This process will take two to three weeks.

## Register as a charity

Once the constitution has been formally adopted or the company has been formally incorporated the charity registration application form should be completed and returned to the Charity Commissioners with one copy of the constitution or memorandum and articles of association.

The charity is then entered on the Charity Register and will be notified of:

❑ the registration number;

❑ the details of the charity recorded in the index to the Register;

❑ the requirements after registration.

## Hold the first committee meeting

As soon as the organisation has been formally set up, the first committee meeting should be held. The matters to be discussed at this meeting are considered in chapter 2.

# Changing an organisation's legal structure

Many voluntary organisations start off as unincorporated associations or charitable trusts but as their activities develop and they employ staff they may consider setting up as a company limited by guarantee. This is perfectly possible. A new organisation (the company) will need to be established and the original organisation wound up. The following section goes through the points which need to be considered when making such a transfer.

## Date of transfer

It is most convenient to choose a date which fits in with the original organisation's financial year — either the last date or half-way through. In this way both organisations will have either a full or a six-month period of accounts.

## Bank accounts

The company must open new bank accounts and the new committee of the company will therefore have to pass resolutions appointing new cheque signatories.

## Officers

The new committee will have to meet and elect officers for the company.

## Contracts of employment

Employees will need to have their employment transferred. The company must inform them of the name and address of their new employer, stating that they have continuity of employment from the original organisation. This notice must be issued on or shortly after the transfer to the company.

## Premises

If the original organisation leases premises, agreement will need to be obtained from the landlord to transfer the lease to the company. If the landlord refuses, legal advice should be sought. The rules on disposal of premises are discussed in more detail in chapter 6.

## Equipment

On the date of transfer, all equipment belonging to the original organisation must be transferred to the company. The best way is for an officer representing the original organisation and a committee member or officer from the company to sign a single sheet of paper confirming the transfer of all equipment. Check any guarantees on the equipment because they may be invalidated by a transfer of ownership. If that is the case, it may be advisable to leave them in the name of the trustees of the original organisation until the guarantee has expired.

## Insurance

The company will need new insurance policies. It may be necessary to have additional types of insurance (for further details see chapter 7).

## Funding

Funding agreements will have to be transferred to the company with the funders' permission.

## Membership

When the company is set up, the only members will be those people who signed the memorandum and articles of association. One of the first tasks of the new committee is therefore to agree to admit as members all the members of the original organisation.

## Cooptions

The company will not have any coopted committee members unless they signed form G10 when the company was set up. The new committee must therefore agree to cooptions.

## Letterheads

The new company will need a new letterhead (see chapter 2). It is illegal to continue to use the original organisation's letterhead without the company registration number.

## Charity number

If registered as a charity the company will have a new registration number, which, in most cases, must be included on all relevant documents (for further details see chapter 2).

## Action on the transfer date

The following transfers will take place:

❏ money in bank or building society accounts;

❏ responsibility for outstanding cheques and liabilities;

❏ employees' contracts;

❏ equipment and premises (unless they are to be left in the names of the original trustees).

The original organisation will continue to exist until the final accounts have been prepared and audited, and submitted to a general meeting.

## The final meeting

After the transfer date a general meeting of the original organisation should be held to discuss the following items:

❏ agreement of the audited accounts for the final period up to the date of transfer;

❏ a resolution to wind up the organisation.

Where applicable, once the original organisation has been wound up, the Charity Commissioners should be informed.

# Booklist

A model declaration of trust (GD2), Charity Commission (1993), free

Charitable status: a practical handbook, *Andrew Phillips*, Directory of Social Change (1994), £7.95

The charities manual, Tolley's Publishing, £80 plus updates

Charities, trading and the law, *Stephen Lloyd*, Directory of Social Change (1994), price not fixed

Company secretaries' duties and responsibilities (leaflet CHN16), Companies House, free

Croner's management of voluntary organisations, *Croner Publications*, £113.60 plus update service £69.05

Decisions of the Charity Commissioners, volume 2, Charity Commission (1994), free

Duty free? payments for charity trustees, *Tim Gill and Kate Kirkland*, National Council for Voluntary Organisations (1994), £3.00

Explanatory leaflets (CC1) (lists all the Charity Commission's free leaflets, audio and video tapes), Charity Commission (1994), free

Legal issues for voluntary organisations: a reading list, National Council for Voluntary Organisations, (1994), price not fixed

Model constitution for a charitable unincorporated association (GD3), Charity Commission (1993), free

Model declaration of trust (GD2), Charity Commission (1993), free

Model memorandum and articles of association for a charitable company limited by guarantee (GD1), Charity Commission (1993), free

New companies: notes for guidance, (leaflet CHN1), Companies House, free

A practical guide to company law for voluntary organisations, Directory of Social Change (1994), £7.95

Specimen constitution for an unincorporated charitable organisation having a membership, National Council for Voluntary Organisations (1990), £2.50

The voluntary sector legal handbook, *Sandy Adirondack and James Sinclair-Taylor*, Directory of Social Change (1995) c £20

Other relevant material is available from Community Matters and Companies House

# Chapter 2: Running an organisation

This chapter examines the law and good practice in running an organisation. It starts by explaining some of the terms used to describe an organisation's membership, committee and meetings. The following sections look first at the procedures a group must introduce when setting up and then at day to day administration, including holding an annual general meeting (AGM). The final section looks at good practice in relation to developing equality of opportunity.

Charity and company law are covered in greater detail in *The voluntary sector legal handbook*.

## The structure of organisations

Unincorporated associations, companies limited by guarantee, friendly societies and, in most cases, industrial and provident societies, have a committee to run the organisation. All have a membership which is given certain powers under the constitution.

### Membership

In general there are two categories of members: those with a right to vote, for example 'full members', 'ordinary members', 'voting members', 'individual members', 'group members' or 'corporate members'; and those linked to the organisation but who have no vote, for example 'honorary members', 'associate members' or 'junior members'.

From a legal point of view, a member of an organisation is a person who has agreed to abide by the terms of the constitution and in return has been given rights under the constitution, for example a right to vote at general meetings.

Members of a company limited by guarantee agree to pay a fixed amount (usually £1 or £5) if the company becomes insolvent. Industrial and provident society members agree to buy a share from the society (usually for £1).

There are no specific requirements for members of unincorporated associations. Some have 'open membership', where the constitution states that anyone fulfilling certain criteria is automatically a member. Arrangements of this kind do not impose any obligations on members.

### Group membership

Many constitutions permit groups as well as individuals to become members. In unincorporated associations the constitution can allow any organisation with a constitution to join. However, incorporated organisations (industrial and provident societies and companies limited by guarantee) can allow only other incorporated organisations to join as voting members. A constitution can, however, allow unincorporated groups to nominate an individual to represent them. That individual then becomes a member, whose name should appear in the membership register (see 'Setting up registers', below).

### Members' meetings

Members' meetings are usually called 'general meetings', but may also be described as 'open meetings' or 'council meetings'. The constitution will almost certainly include a requirement to hold an annual general meeting (AGM) which all members are entitled to attend and at which members with voting rights can vote.

Some constitutions state a certain number of general meetings should be held, for example three times a year, or at regular intervals. Other constitutions require only that an AGM is held but allow a group of members to write to the secretary requesting a general meeting. A general meeting arranged in this way may be called a 'special general meeting' or an 'extraordinary general meeting'.

Industrial and provident societies, friendly societies and companies limited by guarantee must hold their first AGM within 18 months of setting up and then once in each calendar year, with no more than 15 months between AGMs.

### The committee

The group of people who run the organisation can have different titles, for example 'council', 'executive committee', 'management committee', 'trustees' or 'the board'. In industrial and provident societies they are usually called the **'committee'**, in companies limited by a guarantee the **'board of directors'** and in charities the **'trustees'**.

People can become committee members in a number of ways.

### Election

Constitutions or **standing orders** (a set of procedural rules made under the constitution covering areas such as elections and conduct of meetings) often describe how elections must be carried out. The constitution will also say how long someone remains in office once elected. The most usual way of becoming a committee member is through election by the membership at an AGM.

## Cooption

Some constitutions allow the committee to coopt additional committee members, usually to:

❑ fill a 'casual vacancy': the committee is given the power to coopt new committee members, at least until the next AGM, to replace anyone who has resigned or retired; or

❑ enable an organisation to introduce additional skills onto the committee, for example financial expertise.

## Nomination or appointment

Committee members can also be nominated, by, for example an organisation's main funder or by groups that use its services.

## Restrictions

There may be restrictions on people who can serve on the committee. In charities the following people cannot be committee members:

❑ anyone aged under 18;

❑ those who have been convicted of any offence involving deception or dishonesty, unless the conviction is spent under the **Rehabilitation of Offenders Act, 1974;**

❑ undischarged bankrupts and people who have made formal agreements with creditors under the **Insolvency Act, 1986;**

❑ anyone who has previously been removed from trusteeship of a charity by the court or the Charity Commissioners;

❑ anyone disqualified from being a company director.

It is an offence to act as a charity trustee whilst disqualified unless the Charity Commissioners have given a waiver under **Section 72(4) of the Charities Act, 1993.**

If it is discovered that an existing committee member falls into one of the above categories he or she cannot attend further committee meetings or vote. Check your constitution to see whether the person concerned automatically ceases to be a committee member. If there is a provision stating that anyone disqualified or incapable of acting is automatically removed, then this will take effect and there will be a vacancy on the committee. If there is no such provision, anyone disqualified will remain as a committee member but cannot act on behalf of the organisation, for example they cannot attend committee meetings or carry out officers' duties. They remain in this position, effectively suspended, until removed under the terms of the constitution, for example by the members under a resolution at a general meeting, when their period of office ends, or if a waiver is obtained from the Charity Commissioners. If a waiver is obtained, they can then continue to serve on the committee as before.

## Holding trustees

Constitutions of many unincorporated associations allow the appointment of 'holding trustees' to make it easier to own or lease property. Since an unincorporated association has no separate legal existence, a lease will usually be granted to named individuals. As it would be impracticable to have the whole committee named as the trustees of the lease, the organisation has the power to appoint a few people to represent it. Holding trustees can (but do not have to) be individual members of the committee. The holding trustees continue their responsibilities until the lease expires.

## The secretary

Companies must appoint a **company secretary** and industrial and provident societies must have a **secretary** to meet statutory as well as constitutional responsibilities. Unless required by the constitution, the secretary need not be a member of the committee, and could be a member of staff who is paid to carry out the work. However, if the organisation is also a charity, a paid employee cannot usually be both the secretary and a member of the committee. Charities cannot pay an honorarium (a fee) to a secretary who is a member of the committee unless this is allowed for in the constitution. Any honorarium must be taxed under PAYE (see chapter 4).

## Other officers

There is no requirement for any organisation to have any officers apart from those set out in the constitution. However, most appoint a chair, secretary and treasurer. Many also have other officers, including a vice chair and membership secretary.

Different constitutions have different procedures for electing officers. Some are elected directly by the membership at the AGM before the rest of the committee is elected and automatically sit on the committee. In other organisations the committee members elect the officers from amongst themselves at their first meeting.

Officers do not have any automatic delegated authority unless it is written into a constitution. A committee meeting generally has to make a decision to delegate powers to officers. Many larger organisations adopt standing orders setting out officers' and subcommittees' delegated powers.

# Terminology used in this chapter

For the rest of this chapter the body which runs the organisation will be called 'the committee', the members of the committee 'committee members', and the company secretary of a company limited by guarantee, the secretary of an industrial and provident society and the secretary of any other organisation 'the secretary'.

# Getting off the ground

## Members, the committee and officers

### Unincorporated associations

An unincorporated association can be set up either by holding a meeting to agree the draft constitution or by getting the first members to sign the constitution. Initially only those who attended the meeting or signed the constitution will be the members. The procedure for admitting new members will have to be used before anyone else can join and have a right to vote (see 'Changes in membership', below).

If a meeting was used to set up the group and agree its constitution, those attending may also have elected the first committee members and officers. If the group was set up by signing a constitution it will need to follow the procedures for electing a committee and officers, probably by holding a general meeting.

### Companies limited by guarantee and industrial and provident societies

The initial members are those who signed the memorandum and articles of association (companies) or rules (industrial and provident societies). A company must name the first committee members and the secretary in its application for incorporation. It may need to increase the committee membership by cooptions or elections and follow the procedures in the articles of association for appointing other officers. An industrial and provident society will have a secretary named in its application for registration and will have to hold a general meeting to elect a committee.

## The first committee meeting

Procedures to be followed before, during and after the first committee meeting are outlined in the checklist at the end of the chapter.

The agenda of the first committee meeting should include the following items.

### Election of officers

The usual options for electing officers are: by members at an annual general meeting (AGM); by the committee at its first meeting; or by the committee pending an AGM. If the constitution does not allow the committee to appoint officers you will have to wait until the first AGM.

### Address for administrative purposes

All charities must notify the Charity Commissioners of their contact address and of any changes to that address. Companies limited by guarantee must notify the Registrar of Companies, and industrial and provident societies must notify the Registrar of Friendly Societies of their first **registered office**, and again of any changes to that address. Industrial and provident societies will be charged (as at April 94, £33) to register a change. The registered address must be printed on all correspondence and many other documents.

Companies and industrial and provident societies must have a nameplate clearly identifying the premises as their registered office.

### Bank accounts

The constitution should describe the requirements for cheque signatories. Before the meeting, obtain the necessary bank forms **(bank mandates)**; most banks have different forms for different legal structures. The bank will require the committee to pass and minute a standard resolution which includes the decision to appoint cheque signatories, who will then need to sign the necessary paperwork. Registered charities should inform the bank of their charitable status because (in most cases) this must be clearly stated on their cheques.

### Insurance

Chapter 7 describes the different forms of insurance that organisations may need. The first committee meeting should delegate responsibility to committee members or officers to liaise with insurance companies and fill in proposal forms.

### Premises

Organisations planning to take on premises should

consider the requirements set out in chapter 6 relating to leasing or owning premises.

## Equal opportunities policy

It is good practice to develop an equal opportunities policy as soon as possible. This should form the basis of any decisions about services, membership, staff and volunteer recruitment, and committee membership. Equal opportunities policy and practice are discussed at the end of this chapter and in chapter 3.

## Cooptions to the committee

Check whether the constitution gives powers to coopt others onto the committee and decide whether to exercise these powers. If an election at a general meeting is the only method of expanding committee membership, it may be necessary to hold such a meeting fairly quickly.

## Membership

Organisations may want to expand their membership as soon as possible. The constitution should describe the necessary procedures. In some cases only the committee can agree new members, but other constitutions allow the responsibility to be delegated to a subcommittee, individual officers or staff.

## The financial year

The constitution may stipulate a financial year; if this is not the case then the committee has discretion. Companies limited by guarantee have to complete a form giving details of their financial year as soon as they receive their certificate of incorporation.

## Auditors

Many voluntary groups have a statutory requirement to have their accounts audited (see chapter 8). Some funders may also require audited accounts. Before the first committee meeting clarify the requirements and in particular check whether the auditor needs to be a qualified accountant.

An auditor should be appointed as soon as possible and certainly before the end of the first financial year.

## Letterheads

The letterheads of companies limited by guarantee and industrial and provident societies must contain reference to their legal status ('*Company limited by guarantee no ... registered in England*' or '*Registered as an industrial and provident society no ...*') and must give the address of the registered office. Registered charities whose income exceeded £5,000[1] in the previous financial year must give this status on their letterhead ('*Registered charity*'). It is useful to include the registration number ('*Registered charity number ...*').

Companies are not legally obliged to have directors' names on their stationery. However, if they do so they must include the names of **all** directors.

## Other publicity material

Registered charities whose income exceeded £5,000 (see footnote) in the previous financial year must have this status printed on all publicity material and stationery such as order forms and invoices. A company must also have its company registration number and the address of its registered office printed on these documents.

## Delegating powers

Check the constitution to see whether decision making can be delegated. It may be appropriate for larger organisations to establish standing orders which delegate powers to a number of sub-committees. In smaller organisations it may be sufficient to delegate responsibility to officers.

## Annual general meetings (AGMs)

The first committee meeting should consider when to hold the first AGM. This could take place before the end of a financial year because there is no need to present accounts and so could be combined with a launch of the organisation and the first democratic election of a committee. AGMs are discussed in greater detail later in the chapter.

## Taking over from a previous organisation

If one organisation has been set up to take over the activities of another, additional decisions need to be made. The new organisation will formally need to agree to take responsibility for the employees, equipment and property as well as all liabilities of the old organisation so that it can be wound up (for further details see chapter 1).

## Appointment of staff

Organisations appointing staff should deal with the following :

❑ an equal opportunities policy covering recruitment;

❑ job particulars and contracts of employment; and

---

[1] The Government has accepted the Charities and Voluntary Organisations Deregulation Task Force recommendation that this figure should be increased to £10,000. This had not been implemented at time of writing (August 94).

❏ interview procedures.

(all of the above can be delegated if the constitution allows)

Staff recruitment is covered in chapter 3.

## Setting up registers

Companies limited by guarantee, industrial and provident societies and friendly societies are all legally required to keep certain registers, some of which must be open to public inspection. Failure to keep registers up to date can lead to an imposition of a fine. Registers can be contained in a simple bound book, which can be purchased from any stationers. There should be separate pages for the different kinds of register, for example membership, committee membership and secretaries. Although there are no obligations on unincorporated associations to keep such registers, it is good practice to do so.

### Register of members

Companies limited by guarantee, industrial and provident societies and friendly societies must have a register of members. It must include:

❏ names and addresses of all members;

❏ date of joining;

❏ date when people ceased to be members.

The register must be updated whenever a member is admitted or someone resigns or is removed. The register, or a duplicate, is usually held at the registered office. If the register of members of a company limited by guarantee is not at the registered office, Companies House has to be notified on form 353 where it is kept. The register of members of companies limited by guarantee must also be available for public inspection, and kept in a form which prevents it being falsified.

If there are more than 50 members of a company limited by guarantee, the register must have an index unless the membership list itself is in alphabetical order.

The register of members for an industrial and provident society must state the number of shares owned by each member.

### Registers of officers and committee members

Industrial and provident societies must keep a separate register of officers' names and addresses, showing when they were appointed and when they ceased to hold office.

Companies limited by guarantee must have a register of directors (committee members) and a separate register of company secretaries. A company secretary who is also a member of the committee has to be entered in both registers.

The register of company directors must contain the following:

❏ date of appointment;

❏ full name;

❏ any previous name (apart from any change of a woman's name on marriage);

❏ home address, including post code;

❏ date of birth;

❏ nationality;

❏ business occupation;

❏ a list of every company of which the person concerned is a director or has been a director at any time in the previous five years, including companies limited by guarantee. If there are no such companies, the register should say so.

The register of company secretaries need only include their name and home address.

### Register of charges

This is necessary if a company, industrial and provident society or friendly society enters into any charges, ie securing a loan given by a bank or building society.

## Day to day administration

### Holding meetings

The constitution should set out the notice required for general meetings, usually either 14 or 21 days. Some also specify notice for committee meetings, and the method of giving notice. If the constitution does not specify notice for meetings the committee should adopt standing orders setting out its requirements.

Some constitutions also describe the content of agendas and meetings (for example a requirement that the date, time and place of the meeting, and the nature of the business to be covered is given).

Other issues which need to be clear before any meeting are:

❏ whether the chair has a casting vote in case of a tie;

❑ the quorum;

❑ who is taking minutes;

❑ whether a subcommittee has delegated powers to make required decisions;

❑ in the case of a company limited by guarantee, that the auditor is given notice of all general meetings and is clear that he or she is entitled to speak on matters concerning the audit and accounts.

# Changes in membership

## New members

The constitution should describe the procedures for admitting new members; both individual and, where relevant, organisational. In some cases the committee must make a decision; if so, new membership should be an item on every agenda. Some groups may want to delegate the decision to a subcommittee, officers or staff. If this is the case, the committee should pass a resolution to this effect, which should be recorded in the minute book.

Companies limited by guarantee and industrial and provident societies can accept only other incorporated organisations as organisational members. An unincorporated association wishing to join must name an individual to act as its representative, whose name must be entered into the register of members.

In industrial and provident societies, members usually pay £1 for their share and receive a share certificate. Other organisations may charge a membership subscription, if this is allowed in the constitution.

Companies limited by guarantee and industrial and provident societies must enter details of new members in the register of members.

All organisations should have a method of recording acceptance of membership, for example an application form that includes the statement *'I wish to become a member of ... and agree to abide by its constitution'*, together with the member's signature. All new members should be given any appropriate written material, for example a copy of the constitution.

An equal opportunities policy should ensure that any decision to refuse membership is justified and that reasons are recorded.

## Terminating membership

A constitution should describe the circumstances in which membership will end. For example, it may state that anyone who fails to pay their membership subscription will cease to be a member. It may also allow the committee or a general meeting to expel a member. It is good practice, even if not set out in the constitution, to ensure that anyone whose expulsion is proposed is notified of the reason and given an opportunity to state their case. The reasons for expulsion should be recorded. When a person or organisation ceases to be a member for any reason the register of members should be updated (within 14 days for a company limited by guarantee). Members of industrial and provident societies should have their £1 refunded in exchange for their share certificate.

# Changes in committee membership

## Ending membership

The constitution should describe ways in which people can cease to be committee members, for example when their term of office expires, through non-attendance, or on grounds of misconduct. The members of a company can remove a committee member by passing a resolution on a simple majority at a general meeting. Special notice needs to given of any such resolution.

If a committee member can be dismissed through non-attendance ensure:

❑ regular checks are kept on attendance;

❑ any member nearing the limit is warned;

❑ the committee is informed if someone's limit is reached.

If it is proposed to remove a committee member on grounds of misconduct ensure:

❑ any proposed resolution conforms with the constitution and that proper notice has been given;

❑ the committee member is informed of the meeting at which the removal is to be considered and is given written details of any allegations;

❑ sufficient time is allocated at the meeting for the matter to be properly considered and for the committee member to have an opportunity to speak;

❑ the vote on any resolution is counted and recorded in the minutes;

❑ any provisions of the equal opportunities policy are complied with and in particular that reasons for removal are recorded.

## Filling vacancies

The constitution should also describe the procedures for filling vacancies on the committee, for example by election, cooption or appointment (nomination). The way in which a member is replaced will be determined partly by their category of membership. For example, a person nominated by a local authority will usually have to be replaced by a further nomination from that authority; a person elected by the AGM can probably be replaced until the next AGM by someone coopted by the committee.

## Recording changes

All changes in committee membership must be recorded in the register of committee members.

Companies need to notify Companies House if a committee member leaves for any reason and the secretary must update the register of committee members. Details of any changes of committee membership must be sent to Companies House on form 288 within 14 days.

## Information for new committee members

All new committee members should be given information required to carry out their responsibilities, for example a copy of the constitution, induction pack, annual report and equal opportunities policy.

## Changes in officers

The constitutions of industrial and provident societies and companies limited by guarantee usually require that secretaries are appointed by the committee, who can remove them at any time. The register of secretaries must be updated if the secretary is replaced.

In the case of other officers, the same rules apply as for committee members. In companies limited by guarantee and industrial and provident societies the register of officers or committee members must be updated where there is a change in the officers. No such requirements will be needed in the case of an unincorporated association or charitable trust but you may wish to do this as a matter of good practice.

Always ensure that the appointment of officers is minuted for the meeting at which the appointment took place (general meeting or committee meeting).

Companies must inform Companies House within 14 days of any changes in secretary and of new officers who are also new committee members, using form 288.

Where officers' names appear on an organisation's stationery, ensure it is amended as necessary.

## Changing the administrative office

An organisation changing its administrative office should carry out the following procedure:

❏ check whether the constitution has specific rules about changes to the registered office;

❏ ensure that the decision is made by a meeting and recorded in the minutes;

❏ companies limited by guarantee and industrial and provident societies must include the new registered office address on stationery and some other documents. Other organisations have discretion about which address to use for which purposes but in most cases will want to use the new address;

❏ ensure other organisations have the new address including, in particular, the bank and the Charity Commissioners if relevant;

❏ companies must submit form 287 to Companies House;

❏ industrial and provident societies must inform the Registrar of Friendly Societies and pay a fee (as at April 94, £33);

❏ companies limited by guarantee and industrial and provident societies must move their nameplate to the new registered office.

## Annual accounts, annual returns and annual reports

### Accounts

Chapter 8 explains the law and good practice concerning bookkeeping and producing accounts. This section looks at the role of the committee in managing the annual audit and producing annual reports.

If an audit is required, the audited accounts of a company limited by guarantee or an industrial and provident society must be approved by the committee before being presented to the membership at an AGM. The approved accounts must be sent out at least 21 days before the AGM.

The following procedure will therefore need to be carried out:

❏ the audit is completed and the auditor satisfied that he or she can give the necessary certificate;

❏ the auditor presents a draft set of accounts to the committee;

❏ the committee approves the draft and authorises the necessary signatures to the accounts as required by the auditor;

❏ those authorised sign a copy of the accounts;

❏ signed copies of the accounts are sent to members with a copy of the auditor's certificate.

The timescale of organising the audit means that a committee meeting to approve the accounts will need to take place at least two months before an AGM.

The first auditor of any organisation will have been appointed by the committee. After that, in the case of a company limited by guarantee or an industrial and provident society (IPS), the AGM should appoint the auditor and either decide how much the auditor should be paid or pass a resolution delegating this responsibility to the committee, since the audit is carried out on behalf of the membership. In other charities which have to have an audit (see chapter 8), the committee should appoint the auditor.

## Annual returns and reports

Registered charities, IPS and companies limited by guarantee have to submit annual returns to the relevant bodies. Charitable companies have to submit separate annual returns to the Registrar of Companies and the Charity Commissioners.

*The Government has accepted the Charities and Voluntary Organisations Deregulation Task Force recommendation that charities with an annual income of less than £10,000 should only have to confirm each year that information held by the Charity Commissioners is correct, rather than provide a full annual return. This had not been implemented at time of writing (August 94).*

In each case the relevant body will send the annual return for completion. It is then simply a case of following the necessary instructions on the form and submitting it within the deadline. Companies limited by guarantee must pay a fee (as at April 94, £32).

A charity whose sole aim is the relief of poverty and which operates wholly or mainly for the benefit of an area of England and Wales which is:

❏ within one county; or

❏ not more than five adjoining parishes; or

❏ Greater London;

must send a copy of its accounts to the local authority. The local authority will make the accounts available for public inspection. They must have been signed by the committee and, if audited, must contain a copy of the auditor's certificate.

Under **Part VI** of the **Charities Act, 1993** (due to be implemented during the 1995/96 financial year) all charities will have to produce a trustees' annual report, and those with an annual income of more than £10,000 will have to send the report to the Charity Commissioners (for further details see chapter 8).

## Charity investments

There are some restrictions on the kinds of investments that charities can use over and above bank and building society accounts. Where relevant, charities should seek advice from a specialist in charity investment, or the Charity Commissioners.

## Annual general meetings (AGMs)

There are two important legal functions of an AGM: to consider the accounts and elect committee members.

Some constitutions will specify the agenda for the AGM. If not it should include the following:

❏ to receive the audited or examined accounts (if appropriate) and balance sheet approved by the committee;

❏ to receive the auditor's or examiner's report on the accounts (if appropriate) and balance sheet;

❏ to receive a report from the committee on the activities of the organisation;

❏ to elect committee members and, if appropriate, officers;

❏ to appoint auditors (if necessary) and either to fix their fees or authorise the committee to do so;

❏ to consider any resolutions put forward.

### Elections

Some constitutions detail the election procedures. If there are no requirements, the committee should agree the format for the election, including: whether it should take place by secret ballot or open show of hands; methods of making sure that only those entitled to vote do so; and procedures for taking nominations.

Some constitutions allow different sections of the membership to elect a proportion of committee members. For example, there may be places on the committee reserved for member organisations, local authorities and individual members. Different categories of elected committee membership will need different elections taking place at the AGM. It is important to devise a system for ensuring that only those entitled to vote in each election receive ballot papers or voting cards for that election.

# Changes to the constitution

Most constitutions describe procedures for amending clauses. This will often involve a specific meeting, with a certain amount of notice to be given of any resolution, and for a particular majority voting in favour of any amendment.

Under **company law**, the constitution can be changed at a meeting for which 21 days' notice of the full resolution has been given and on a resolution passed by 75% of those attending and voting. This includes any change of name. A copy of the revised memorandum and articles (constitution) must be submitted to the Registrar of Companies, together with a copy of the special resolution which made the change, signed by the secretary, showing the date on which it was passed.

An **industrial and provident society** must submit a copy of the amended rules to the Registrar of Friendly Societies together with the registration fee (as at April 94, £170 for minor amendments; £370 for major amendments).

A **registered charity** must receive the Charity Commissioners' consent before any amendment to the constitution's objects or any provision relating to the use of its income or property is considered. As soon as any amendment has been passed, a copy of the revised constitution should be sent to the Charity Commissioners, together with a copy of the resolution making the change.

Most banks need to be informed of any amendment to the constitution; check the original bank mandate for details.

If an organisation changes its name, it should ensure the new name is printed on all stationery, cheques and other necessary financial documents and publications. Companies limited by guarantee and industrial and provident societies must also change their nameplate on their registered office.

# Dealing with crises

## Emergency decisions

Constitutions may include provisions for making decisions in between the normal committee meeting cycle. Some allow a committee meeting to be held at short notice at the chair's discretion. Others may allow a decision to be made by circulating a copy of a proposed resolution to each committee member and asking for their signature.

A third option in some constitutions is to delegate decision making to a subcommittee or officers.

## No quorum

Without a quorum (which should be specified in the constitution), a meeting cannot make a decision. The constitution may describe procedures to follow if insufficient members attend a meeting. In many cases, the committee has the power to coopt if it does not have enough members to form a quorum, and could hold a committee meeting solely to agree cooptions.

Some constitutions give procedures for dealing with inquorate general meetings, for example adjourning the meeting to a later date and deeming the reconvened meeting as quorate however many people turn up, thus enabling decisions to be made.

## Misconduct by officers or committee members

A company limited by guarantee can expel a committee member by passing a resolution with an ordinary majority at a general meeting called on 21 days' notice. In other organisations there must be specific provision in the constitution to expel a member or officer. If not, a general meeting must be called to amend the constitution to give the committee or the general meeting power to remove the person concerned.

In all cases, if a committee member or officer is guilty of misusing funds, the committee has authority to remove that person's ability to sign cheques. The committee also has power to require the person concerned to return immediately any property belonging to the organisation, and can take legal action to recover this property if required.

## Winding up

This is dealt with in chapter 10.

# Equal opportunities

Many people are discriminated against because of prejudice in our society. For example some people are discriminated against because of their racial origin, skin colour, religious or cultural beliefs; women because of their gender; gay men and lesbians for their sexual preference; people who are HIV positive or have AIDS because of ignorance; young people, elderly people and people with disabilities by lack of understanding about their capabilities and experiences. Such discrimination often denies access to employment, financial and other services and opportunities.

Discrimination also means that certain groups are excluded from the decision making processes on matters that affect their lives. People are portrayed in a negative and stereotypical manner and denied social interaction that others enjoy or take for granted. Discrimination manifests itself in various ways, both directly and indirectly.

Voluntary organisations have a responsibility to oppose discrimination and have a role to play in highlighting injustice and promoting good practice. They must ensure that their services, employment opportunities and decision making processes are accessible to everyone. As part of this obligation, every group should develop, and keep under review, an equal opportunities policy, the aim of which should be to help both the staff and management committee eliminate direct and indirect discrimination in decision making, employment practices and service provision.

Organisations should avoid simply adopting an existing equal opportunities policy. The process of developing a policy involves increasing awareness of the different forms of discrimination and how these are manifested, both at an individual and organisational level. This awareness enables the individual and organisation to develop appropriate ways of addressing discrimination and bring about change. Furthermore, an essential part of developing equality of opportunity is the actual process of examining current practices and ensuring that access to services is not denied by discriminatory practices or behaviour. Finally, in developing an equal opportunities policy and strategies it is important to involve people living within the catchment area, especially those who have traditionally been underrepresented in the organisation and in its decision making processes. It is vital to involve the staff, trade union and management committee in drawing up the policy and in monitoring its implementation and effectiveness, as this ensures that everyone's skills and experiences are drawn upon and the policy and strategies are owned by the organisation.

The following sections describe the points to consider when developing an equal opportunities policy.

## The policy

The first step is to identify how you wish to challenge discrimination. Some groups may choose to tackle all forms of inequality at once; others may decide to address one form of discrimination at a time. For example a group may feel that racial inequality is the major problem within its organisation and the area it serves. It would therefore develop a programme

aimed at ensuring that Black and ethnic minority people are treated fairly. Once this programme is in motion, the organisation may then begin to focus on other forms of discrimination, having learned from the experiences of developing and implementing a policy to redress one form of inequality. It is also important to remember that some people suffer discrimination because of a combination of prejudicial views.

An equal opportunities policy should have four components:

❑ a declaration of intent to combat discrimination;

❑ the organisation's objectives concerning equal opportunities;

❑ measures to implement the policy;

❑ monitoring and review processes.

## Declaration of intent

This is a public statement that an organisation recognises that certain groups of people suffer discrimination, is opposed to this situation, and will take steps to challenge it.

The statement should be issued to and supported by all staff and management committee members. Many organisations include the statement in their publications and publicity material, and incorporate it into their job advertisements. Some also have their statement clearly visible in their public areas.

## Objectives

Possible objectives include:

❑ to increase the number of member organisations representing people who face disadvantage;

❑ to ensure that the composition of the management committee reflects that of the local population;

❑ to make adaptations to premises and equipment

and ensure that they are accessible to staff and users;

❑ to increase the number of staff from minority groups, especially in senior positions and in posts with access to the decision making process;

❑ to establish better links with groups of people facing disadvantage;

❑ to increase awareness within the organisation of minority groups' needs in order to provide more relevant services;

❑ to review and adapt the organisation's services to meet the needs of people facing disadvantage;

❑ to introduce an equal opportunities dimension in all areas of work and proposed ventures;

❑ to consider establishing special projects to combat discrimination;

❑ to advocate equal opportunities policies throughout the voluntary sector;

❑ to ensure that no member of staff, management committee member or service user suffers discrimination;

❑ to ensure that staff and management committee members understand the reasons for, and the effects of the different forms of discrimination that exist. For example, Black people have different experiences of discrimination; the racism that Black women suffer is often compounded by sexism.

## Implementation

Points to consider when implementing a policy include:

❑ monitoring the organisation's work in order to identify where discrimination exists and what form it takes;

❑ examining the structure and composition of the management committee and other decision making groups;

❑ monitoring and reviewing services;

❑ developing a code of conduct so that staff, members, committee members, officers and users all know of the procedures for dealing with discrimination and the standards of conduct expected from them during their work or at organisation or committee meetings; the code should be made publicly available;

❑ developing procedures for dealing with breaches

of the code of conduct, not just by staff in the form of a disciplinary policy, but also by the organisation's members, committee members, officers and users. This could include a commitment to take steps to remove a committee member guilty of misconduct. It is important that safeguards are built in to ensure that these actions are taken only in appropriate cases and are not themselves used in a discriminatory way;

❑ staff recruitment;

❑ staff training;

❑ conditions of service;

❑ physical access and working arrangements;

❑ the allocation of responsibility for implementing the equal opportunities policy. Many groups set up a subcommittee of the management committee for this purpose. A member of staff should be given the task of reporting to the subcommittee.

## Monitoring and review

Equal opportunities strategies need to be continually monitored, reviewed and, where necessary, revised. It is important to state the process and who is responsible for this exercise.

Chapters 3 and 4 discuss the law and good practice concerning equal opportunity employment; chapter 9 examines how to make services more relevant to groups facing disadvantage.

The next section describes how management and decision making processes may need to be examined to ensure that they are not discriminatory.

## Management of the organisation

The management committee of a voluntary organisation is often made up of representatives of the consumers of its services and people with a specialist knowledge of its work.

An equal opportunities policy should require a regular analysis of the composition of the organisation's membership, management committee, subcommittees and working parties to ensure they reflect the diversity of people who suffer discrimination.

As well as examining who is involved in formal decision making, organisations should also review their informal decision making processes. Quite often key decisions are made in discussions that take place before and after meetings. It is therefore important to check that this practice does not lead to discrimination.

## Membership

An equal opportunities policy should require a regular analysis of an organisation's membership to identify which communities are underrepresented. It may be necessary to amend the constitution and in particular the membership clause, to enable greater participation. Remember, registered charities must have any amendments to their constitution's objects or any provision relating to the use of the charity's income or property approved by the Charity Commission. Companies and industrial and provident societies must also submit copies of revised constitutions to the relevant registrars.

It is more likely, however, that the actual membership recruitment practices of the organisation will need to be altered, so the policy should outline measures for attracting organisations into membership. These could include:

❑ consulting groups on how to make your organisation more relevant to groups facing disadvantage;

❑ translating written material into other languages, into braille and onto tapes;

❑ preparing publicity material specifically aimed at certain types of organisations;

❑ organising open days and conferences to describe the work of your organisation (make sure that interpreters and signers are present).

Existing members and new applicants for membership should be encouraged to develop equal opportunities policies. Some voluntary organisations have introduced criteria that state only those groups with equal opportunities policies can be accepted into membership.

Also look at how your organisation could help other groups develop equal opportunities strategies.

### Management committees

#### Composition
A regular analysis of the composition of the management committee, subcommittees and other working parties and advisory groups is important to monitor the effectiveness of the equal opportunities policy.

The policy should also describe measures to ensure that minority groups can be represented. One way is to pass a resolution at the AGM stating that a certain number of places on the committee will be reserved for people who can make a special contribution.

A temporary measure is to increase representation through cooptions. Make sure that your constitution allows for this (if necessary make amendments) and ensure that cooptees have full voting rights.

Make sure that all members of the management committee are involved in all discussions. For example do not expect Black representatives to debate race issues alone.

Also check the constitution to ensure that the procedures for appointing committee members encourage new members. For example, constitutions that require nominations to be submitted 21 days in advance of an AGM may discourage people from standing. Even worse is a provision in the constitution that states that a former committee member is reappointed automatically unless the committee is given advance warning of any new nomination.

## Access to committee meetings

Think about where and when committee meetings take place. Some members, especially women and elderly people, may dislike travelling at night. Childcare facilities should be offered. Make sure that all parts of the buildings used are accessible to people with disabilities. Signers, and equipment such as induction loops, may need to be used to enable people with hearing difficulties to participate. Produce committee papers in braille or on tape for blind or partially sighted committee members. Also consider whether committee members need drivers to take them to and from meetings.

## Training committee members

The equal opportunities policy should consider the training needs of management committee members. These would include:

❑ management for the first time;

❑ equal opportunities legislation. All members should know of their obligations under the **Disabled Persons (Employment) Acts, 1944 and 1958**; the **Equal Pay Act, 1970**; the **Equal Pay (Amendment) Regulations, 1983** the **Sex Discrimination Acts, 1975 and 1986**; and the **Race Relations Act, 1976**;

❑ working as a team. Existing members must learn how to involve newcomers and how to challenge discriminatory actions whether made intentionally or otherwise;

❑ equal opportunities interviewing techniques.

## Implementing the policy

The management committee should delegate the responsibility for ensuring that the equal opportunities policy is implemented and developed to a senior member of staff with the necessary authority.

This would involve:

❏ ensuring all employees and management committee members know how the policy works and the process for its review and development;

❏ identifying staff members' equal opportunities training needs;

❏ involving the union on the content and implementation of the policy;

❏ examining the composition of the workforce, management committee, subcommittees and advisory groups;

❏ reviewing the recruitment procedures;

❏ establishing systems to monitor the delivery of services;

❏ reporting to the management committee and membership on the progress of implementing the policy.

Make sure the worker is given time to perform these duties effectively and is given certain rights. These include:

❏ the ability to report directly to the management committee;

❏ powers to investigate discrimination;

❏ powers to examine all written material in the organisation;

❏ management of a budget.

## Booklist

**Charity trustees: 'the crucial guide'** (video), Charity Commission, free

**The effective trustee: part one — roles and responsibilities**, Directory of Social Change (1994), £7.95

**The effective trustee: part two — aims and resources**, Directory of Social Change (1994), £7.95

**The effective trustee: part three — getting the work done**, Directory of Social Change (1994), £7.95

**Equal opportunities: a practical handbook**, *Gill Taylor*, The Industrial Society (1994), £19.95

**Equal opportunities in voluntary organisations — reading list no 2**, National Council for Voluntary Organisations (1993), £2.50

**Equality in action: introducing equal opportunities in voluntary organisations**, *Mee-Yan Cheung-Judge and Alix Henley*, National Council for Voluntary Organisations (1994), £12.95

**The good trustee guide: a resource organiser for members of governing bodies of charitable companies**, *Kate Kirkland (editor)*, National Council for Voluntary Organisations (1994), £14.95

**Just About Managing?**, *Sandy Adirondack*, London Voluntary Service Council (1992), £12.45

**The trustee organiser: for the organised trustee**, Directory of Social Change (1993), £12.50

**The voluntary sector legal handbook**, *Sandy Adirondack and James Sinclair-Taylor*, Directory of Social Change (1995), c £20

**Volunteers on management committee: a good practice guide**, *Rodney Hedley and Colin Rochester*, Volunteer Centre UK (1994), £5.50

# CHECKLIST:

## FIRST COMMITTEE MEETING

### Before the meeting

❑ set up the necessary registers;

❑ set up a system for keeping minutes of committee meetings and general meetings. Companies must keep minutes in a form which prevents tampering or forgery (for example a book or numbered loose leaf pages initialled by the chair);

❑ organise safe storage for:

- the original of the constitution;

- copies of documents submitted to the Registrar of Friendly Societies, the Registrar of Companies or the Charity Commissioners;

- registers of members, committee members and officers;

- minute books;

- audited accounts, agendas and other documents such as leases, contracts of employment and insurance policies;

❑ check the constitution for procedures to elect officers;

❑ obtain bank mandate forms and clarify the documentation required by the bank;

❑ check the constitution for rules on cheque signatories;

❑ obtain quotes and proposal forms from insurance companies;

❑ obtain information necessary for the committee to make decisions about entering into licences or leases of premises;

❑ draft an equal opportunities policy;

❑ where relevant invite organisations entitled to appoint (nominate) committee members to put forward appointees;

❑ check the constitution for:

- the committee's powers to coopt additional committee members;

- rules on admitting new members to the organisation and whether the committee can delegate this responsibility;

- the financial year end;

❑ check funders' requirements regarding year end;

❑ check the rules on audits of accounts and in particular whether a qualified accountant is required;

❑ obtain quotes from potential auditors;

❑ organise draft stationery ensuring that it complies with legal requirements;

❑ check the constitution for any rules about delegation to subcommittees, officers or staff;

❑ make a note of important deadlines that have to be met for the AGM;

❑ if relevant, note decisions that need to be made to take over responsibilities from another organisation;

❑ if staff are to be recruited draft an employment contract, job descriptions and job adverts.

## At the meeting

In particular ensure that:

❑ decisions are made about:

- cheque signatories;
- insurance policies;
- delegating authority for completing and signing insurance proposal forms;
- staff recruitment.

❑ resolutions are passed relating to:

- cheque signatories;
- taking on premises;
- delegating responsibility to subcommittees, officers or staff (where relevant);
- taking over from a previous group.

## After the meeting

❑ update the necessary registers;

❑ order stationery, ensuring it complies with legal requirements;

❑ notify, as appropriate, Companies House, the Registrar of Friendly Societies or the Charity

Commissioners of any change to the registered office;

❑ obtain necessary signatures on the bank mandate if not already done at the meeting;

❑ enter into the minute book the requirements for the bank resolutions, and sign the bank mandate to confirm that this has been done;

❑ return forms to the bank and set up account(s) and, where relevant, ensure that cheques include the words 'registered charity';

❑ obtain the necessary insurance policies and file them for safe-keeping, ensuring copies of proposal forms are kept;

❑ ensure everyone involved with the organisation is made aware of their responsibilities under the equal opportunities policy;

❑ if a company limited by guarantee:

- inform Companies House on form 288 of any new committee members or other changes;

- return the notice of accounting reference date to Companies House on form 224 supplied on registration;

- notify Companies House on form 353 if the register of members is to be kept somewhere other than the registered office;

❑ if a company, ensure the organisation's name and a statement that it is a company appears on all cheques, bills, receipts and publications;

❑ if a charity, ensure the organisation's name and a statement that it is a charity (if required) appears on all cheques, bills, receipts and publications;

❑ keep a record of all decisions to delegate authority to subcommittees, officers or staff.

For further details on running meetings see chapter 5 of *Just About Managing?*.

# CHECKLIST:

## ANNUAL GENERAL MEETING

### Before the meeting:

❑ check the period within which the AGM must be held;

❑ where relevant, ensure the accounts are submitted to the auditor in time for the audit to be completed and for approved accounts to be sent to members;

❑ ensure that audited accounts and the balance sheet approved by the committee and signed by two committee members and the auditor, are ready for distribution to members with the AGM agenda;

❑ check the constitution for any agenda requirements;

❑ check the rules on elections;

❑ ensure correct notice is given of the AGM and that notices are sent in accordance with the constitution;

❑ ensure that the auditor is informed of the meeting (this is a legal requirement for companies and industrial and provident societies);

❑ companies must ensure they have a sufficient supply of forms 288 to be completed at the AGM by new committee members;

❑ prepare the necessary material to hold elections.

### At the meeting

Ensure that:

❑ resolutions are passed receiving the accounts and the committee's report;

❑ elections are held;

❑ new committee members provide the information required for company or industrial and provident society registers;

❑ a company's new committee members sign form 288;

❑ minutes are kept.

## After the meeting

- ❑ submit accounts (audited if required), balance sheet and the committee's report to Companies House, the Registrar of Friendly Societies and/or the Charity Commissioners as appropriate.;

- ❑ ensure that a copy of the audited accounts, annual report, annual return and balance sheets are available for inspection by all members in line with the constitution and, in the case of a company limited by guarantee or an industrial and provident society, at the registered office;

- ❑ for a company limited by guarantee, inform Companies House on form 288 of any changes in committee members and officers;

- ❑ update the appropriate registers;

- ❑ ensure that the minutes are written up;

- ❑ carry out induction procedures for new committee members.

# CHECKLIST:

# ELECTIONS

## Before the meeting

Check:

- ❑ categories of elected committee members;

- ❑ who can vote for which categories;

- ❑ nomination procedures, including timescales.

Circulate (as appropriate):

- ❑ requests for nominations with instructions;

- ❑ information about nominees with the AGM papers.

Prepare (as appropriate):

- ❑ ballot papers;

- ❑ a list of those entitled to vote for each category of member;

- ❑ the agenda in such a way that vote counting can take place without interrupting the flow of the meeting.

## At the meeting

Ensure (as appropriate):

- ❑ ballot papers are given to those entitled to vote, with an explanation of the voting procedure (including who can vote for particular categories of members);

- ❑ people not involved in the elections are available to count votes;

- ❑ results are announced, and recorded in the minutes;

- ❑ the necessary information relating to new members is completed for the register of committee members, and that companies complete form 288 and return it to Companies House.

# Chapter 3: Your responsibilities in recruitment

Taking people on brings new responsibilities, and before doing so employers must be aware of their legal responsibilities and employees' rights. Organisations should have an equal opportunities policy which covers all forms of paid and unpaid employment to ensure that everyone is treated fairly.

This chapter starts by summarising employees' rights (which are discussed in further detail in chapter 4), and looks at the rights of trainees, volunteers and consultants. It then describes the law and good practice concerning equal opportunities in both paid and unpaid employment. The last two sections examine the process of appointing employees and consultants. The insurance requirements relating to employees are discussed in chapter 7.

## Employees' rights

Employees' rights fall into two categories: individual entitlements and rights acquired through trade union membership.

Some rights apply to all employees; others depend upon their length of service and on the number of hours worked each week. Although the law does not define 'part-time', at the time of writing (August 94) there is generally a distinction between people who work for 16 hours or more each week and those who work less than 16 hours. However, in February 1994 the House of Lords decided that the United Kingdom's laws which distinguish between part-time and full-time employees are incompatible with European Union (EU) law and all employees should have the same rights. The Government announced that it would respect the judgment and introduce changes in the law. Details have not been announced but it is likely that there will be major changes to employees' rights.

Until the Government has changed the law in the light of the House of Lords' decision, people working 16 or more hours a week gain statutory rights which depend on a period of continuous service. Those working between eight and 16 hours generally gain these rights only after five years' continuous service. Those working less than eight hours do not benefit from any rights attached to continuous service.

## Part-time and casual workers

The definition of 'employees' also covers part-time staff, including job sharers, casual workers, temporary workers and people with fixed-term contracts. Whether or not they have any statutory rights will usually depend upon their period of continuous employment.

The rights of part-time, temporary and casual workers can be increased by ensuring that they work 16 or more hours a week, or by writing better terms than the legal minimum into their contracts of employment.

## Agency and seconded staff

Agency staff are placed to work for an organisation for a limited period. There is usually a contract between the agency and the organisation as well as one between the agency and the staff member; these contracts should make clear who is the employer.

Seconded staff are employed by another organisation, for example a local authority or company, and are placed with an organisation for a limited period. There should be a written agreement between the seconding employer, the voluntary organisation and the member of staff concerned clarifying who is to be the employer during the secondment.

## Rights of all employees

All employees, regardless of their length of service, have the right:

❑ to equal pay for work of equal value: **Equal Pay Act, 1970**;

❑ not to be discriminated against on grounds of race (except where race is a genuine occupational qualification for the job): **Race Relations Act, 1976**;

❑ not to be discriminated against on grounds of sex or marital status (except where sex is a genuine occupational qualification for the job): **Sex Discrimination Act, 1975**;

❑ not to disclose spent convictions or be penalised for the failure to disclose a spent conviction (except in certain jobs, for example where children are involved): **Rehabilitation of Offenders Act, 1974**;

❑ to work in a healthy, safe environment: **Health and Safety at Work Act, 1974**;

❑ to union membership (in almost all cases) and to take part in union activities;

❑ not to belong to a trade union;

# Rights acquired through continuous service

*Note that the qualifying periods set out below are subject to any changes the Government may make during 1994/95 to implement the House of Lords' decision regarding the difference between part-time and full-time workers' rights*

| Right | Qualifying period | |
| --- | --- | --- |
| | Employees working 8-15 hours each week | Employees working 16 or more hours each week |
| Statement of employment particulars | Within two months | Within two months |
| Itemised pay statement | Five years if fewer than 20 employees; no qualifying period where there are 20 or more employees | None |
| Pay during medical suspension | Five years | One calendar month |
| Statutory maternity pay[1] | 26 weeks as at the 15th week before the expected date of childbirth | 26 weeks as at the 15th week before the expected date of childbirth |
| Longer maternity leave (some of it paid) and the right to return to work at the end of this leave | Five years | Two years |
| Reasonable time off (with pay) to carry out duties as an official of a recognised trade union | Five years | None |
| Reasonable time off (which need not be paid) for other union members for activities of a recognised trade union | Five years | None |
| Time off work (with pay) to perform functions as a safety representative (in organisations with five or more staff) | Two years | Two years |
| Reasonable time off (which need not be paid) for public activities | Five years | None |
| Minimum period of notice | Five years | One month |
| Not to be unfairly dismissed [2] | Five years | Two years |
| Written statement of reasons for dismissal within 14 days of dismissal | Five years [3] | Two years [3] |
| Redundancy payment and reasonable time off to look for work or for training if under notice of redundancy | Five years | Two years |

[1] If average weekly earnings are at least the Lower Earnings Limit during the eight weeks prior to the 15 weeks before the baby is due.

[2] All pregnant employees have the right not be unfairly dismissed for any reason connected with their pregnancy.

[3] Any female employee is entitled to written reasons for dismissal if she is dismissed at any time while she is pregnant or after childbirth where her 14 week maternity leave period ends because she is dismissed. The written reasons have to be given automatically whether or not they are requested.

❏ not to have trade union dues deducted from wages without written consent;

❏ not to be victimised or unfairly dismissed on grounds of trade union membership or activities;

❏ not to be victimised or unfairly dismissed on grounds of activities as a safety representative, for making a complaint about a health and safety matter or for taking steps to protect themselves or leaving a place where they reasonably believe they are in danger: **Trade Union and Labour Relations Act, 1993;**

❏ not to be victimised or unfairly dismissed because they have asserted a statutory right (ie the employee has required the employer to comply with statutory obligations): **Trade Union and Labour Relations Act, 1993;**

❏ to statutory sick pay (if earnings exceed a specific amount each week); however, there are some exceptions to this right (see chapter 4);

❏ to compensation if they become ill or injured during the course of employment.

All female employees are entitled to:

❏ paid time off for ante natal care;

❏ 14 weeks' maternity leave; and

❏ the right not to be unfairly dismissed for any reason connected with their pregnancy (see chapter 4 for further details).

The table opposite describes workers' rights acquired through continuous service. These are explained in greater detail in chapter 4.

## Trainees' rights

Whether trainees have employees' rights depends on the circumstances. Those placed by colleges and who are not paid by the organisation will not usually be employees and therefore will have no rights associated with employment. Those placed for longer periods and who are paid may acquire employment rights. An organisation should clarify whether or not trainees are to be treated as employees and wherever possible they should be given some employment rights. In all cases the organisation has responsibilities to trainees under the **Health and Safety at Work Act, 1974** (see chapter 5). Trainees who are not employees will not be covered by employers' liability insurance if there is an accident. It is therefore essential to ensure that public liability insurance covers trainees whilst they are working for the organisation (see chapter 7).

An organisation's equal opportunities policy should cover the recruitment and management of trainees and include procedures for dealing with complaints of discrimination or harassment.

## Volunteers' rights

Volunteers are not employees and have no rights associated with employment, but they will be owed responsibilities under the **Health and Safety at Work Act, 1974** (see chapter 5). As with trainees, organisations should ensure that their public liability insurance policy covers volunteers. The equal opportunities policy should include the recruitment and management of volunteers and include procedures for dealing with any complaints of discrimination or harassment.

## Consultants

Consultants, sometimes called freelance workers, work on short-term contracts to carry out a specific piece of work. If self-employed, they pay their own tax and national insurance and are responsible for their own public liability insurance. The organisation will still owe a responsibility to them under the **Health and Safety at Work Act, 1974** (see chapter 5).

It may be tempting to contract people on a freelance basis to avoid employment responsibilities, in particular employer's national insurance payments. However, to qualify for self-employed status, people have to meet a number of criteria relating to their working practices (see below). If an organisation treats staff as self-employed when they should be employees, the Inland Revenue and Contributions Agency can demand payment of tax and national insurance even though these have not been deducted from the fees paid to the individual for their work. There may also be penalties and interest due for late payment.

### Self-employment

When deciding if someone can be treated as self-employed consider the following:

❏ whether the person is told how and when to do their work and the degree of responsibility they have for making their own decisions in this respect;

❏ whether they can be suspended and dismissed during the contract;

❏ the degree of risk they take — if they underestimate the time required, do they bear the burden of the extra cost?;

❏ whether they use their own equipment and premises;

❑ whether they can employ sub-contractors to do some of their work, for example if they are ill;

❑ whether they work for other organisations;

❑ whether they have an opportunity to make a profit, for example if they do the work more quickly than they anticipated;

❑ whether they receive holiday or sick pay (because these are generally incompatible with being freelance).

Anyone who is genuinely self-employed has no employment rights in relation to the organisation which is using their services. Their rights will be decided by the contract that exists between them and the organisation. Suggestions for what this contract should contain are given in the final section of this chapter.

# Discrimination

Employers should be aware of their statutory duty not to discriminate on the grounds of race, sex, marital status, trade union activity or lapsed criminal conviction.

## Sex and race discrimination

The **Sex Discrimination Acts, 1975 and 1986** and the **Race Relations Act, 1976** state that it is illegal to discriminate against people because of their sex or (for employment purposes) marital status, or because of their race, colour, ethnic origin, nationality (including citizenship) or national origin.

In particular, discrimination is forbidden in the following areas:

❑ arrangements for recruiting;

❑ shortlisting and appointments;

❑ terms of appointment;

❑ promotion and training;

❑ fringe benefits;

❑ redundancy;

❑ retirement ages.

The Acts govern both direct discrimination (treating someone less favourably than others in similar circumstances because of their race, sex or marital status) and indirect discrimination (applying a condition which puts a racial group, one sex or married people at a disadvantage). Victimisation

(treating people less favourably as a result of their complaints under the Acts) is also unlawful.

There are some circumstances in which the Acts allow positive action for women and people from black and ethnic minorities, for example in training. Before using any of these exceptions seek legal advice, or consult the *Equal Opportunities Commission* or the *Commission for Racial Equality.*

The main exceptions are:

❑ if sex or race is a genuine occupational qualification. For example a job involving personal welfare services for a specific black and ethnic minorities' or women's group might best be done by a member of that group (see **Section 5** of the **Race Relations Act, 1976** and **Section 7** of the **Sex Discrimination Act, 1975**);

❑ training schemes set up for existing workers of a particular racial group to enable those employees to do specific work. The employer must show that at some time in the past 12 months there were no employees or a very small number of the specified racial group employed in the specified work (see **Section 38** of the **Race Relations Act, 1976**);

❑ schemes established specifically to train people of one sex or designed to encourage people of one sex to take up specified types of work. The employer must show either that in the past 12 months there were no employees or a very small number of that sex employed in that type of work in the local area, or that the training is needed because the potential trainees have not been in full-time employment due to domestic or family responsibilities (see **Section 47** of the **Sex Discrimination Act, 1975** as amended by **Section 4** of the **Sex Discrimination Act, 1986**);

❑ schemes providing access to facilities, or services to meet the particular needs of a racial group, in education, training or welfare, for example providing special language training to help people who do not speak English as a first language to apply for promotion. Schemes solely to establish jobs for a particular racial group are not allowed under this provision (see **Section 35** of the **Race Relations Act**).

Discrimination on grounds of language is potentially indirect discrimination. However, it may be possible, for example, to advertise for a Bengali speaker, provided that the language requirement can be shown to be a genuine occupational qualification, because the worker will be providing personal services to the Bengali-speaking community.

You can encourage members of one sex or racial group to apply for a job by, for example stating in an advertisement that applications from women and ethnic minorities would be particularly welcome. However, other people must not be discouraged and all applications should be judged on their merit.

The **Equal Pay Act, 1970** and the **Equal Pay (Amendment) Regulations, 1983** entitle men and women to be paid the same if they do work which is the same or of a broadly similar nature, or is rated as equivalent or of equal value (in relation to, for example demands made on the employee in terms of effort, skill and decision making).

## Offenders

The **Rehabilitation of Offenders Act, 1974** gives people the right not to reveal certain convictions after specified lengths of time, which vary according to the sentence and the age of the person when convicted. For example, for people aged 17 or over when convicted, a period of imprisonment of between six and 30 months becomes spent after ten years, but longer sentences are never spent.

Any employment in the social services field (including within the voluntary sector) is likely to fall outside the provisions of the Act. In these circumstances, applicants have to disclose spent convictions provided that they are told that the **Rehabilitation of Offenders Act, 1974** does not apply. Ideally, application forms for posts outside the remit of this Act should ask about criminal convictions and state that the post is exempt. Most social services departments have a specimen wording for such application forms.

Some professions, including teaching, accountancy, law, nursing and social work (including youth work and those working with elderly people), require applicants to reveal all previous convictions. The Home Office can advise whether a particular job is included in the Act.

## People with disabilities

The **Disabled Persons (Employment) Acts, 1944 and 1958** state that if 20 or more people are employed, at least 3% of workers must be registered disabled people.

Prosecutions are seldom brought under this Act, so many employers ignore the quota. Do not, however, use this as an excuse to avoid making jobs available for people with disabilities. See the section below on employing people with disabilities. Also refer to *Employing people with disabilities.*

Send details of jobs to local disability organisations and to the disablement employment adviser at the local job centre or employment office.

# Equal opportunities: good practice

The law concerning equality of opportunity in employment is limited and has no provisions for volunteers, trainees or consultants. Therefore organisations should adopt an equal opportunities policy to ensure that no member of staff, volunteer, trainee or consultant, or any potential applicant for any of these posts, suffers direct or indirect discrimination or victimisation.

The responsibilities of organisations as equal opportunities employers are to ensure that:

❑ posts are advertised to encourage applications from a wide variety of communities;

❑ all job applicants are treated fairly;

❑ all employees are treated equally;

❑ the training needs for specific groups of people are recognised;

❑ the needs of people with disabilities are met through adaptations to premises and the purchase of specific equipment;

❑ the equal opportunities employment policy is regularly monitored.

Organisations have similar responsibilities in respect of volunteers, trainees and consultants; for example they should ensure volunteers are treated equally and their training needs identified and met.

## Monitoring

It is essential to establish systems for monitoring the effectiveness of an equal opportunities policy. Begin by analysing the composition of your workforce to identify posts or departments where people likely to suffer discrimination are over-represented (in poorly paid jobs) or under-represented (in more senior posts). The policy should state how often this analysis should be carried out.

It should also require that there are systems to record the composition of:

❑ those applying for posts;

❑ those being shortlisted;

❑ people being appointed;

❑ employees seeking career training and development;

❑ employees seeking promotion;

❑ employees being promoted;

❑ employees seeking redress under the grievance procedure;

❑ employees against whom the grievance procedure is used;

❑ employees receiving disciplinary action;

❑ employees issuing disciplinary action;

❑ employees being dismissed;

❑ employees being made redundant.

The policy should also require systems to record how people learn about vacant posts, so that the procedures for advertising can be monitored. It is also essential to monitor the composition of volunteers, trainees and consultants.

Monitoring should be based on a system of records covering race, gender and disability. Groups may wish to consider monitoring other characteristics, such as age and sexual preference. Some voluntary organisations adopt a system of self classification by asking 'How would you describe your race or ethnic origin?'. Others have introduced a standard classification system within the organisation to enable them to monitor and compare composition of membership, management committees and users of the services as well as employees. It is important to involve staff and users in the process of introducing a standard ethnic classification system.

There are many different systems for classifying race. The one recommended by the Commission for Racial Equality is:

❑ White
❑ Irish
❑ Black - Caribbean
❑ Black - African
❑ Black - other (please specify)
❑ Indian
❑ Pakistani
❑ Bangladeshi
❑ Chinese
❑ Other (please describe)

Whatever system is used, people should be told why monitoring is necessary and that participation is voluntary. The names of those being monitored must remain confidential, and information should be stored in a statistical form only.

# Flexible working arrangements

Employers should consider introducing flexible working arrangements to increase access to work for paid staff, trainees and volunteers.

The standard work pattern of an eight-hour day, five-day, 40-hour week discriminates against some people including parents, other carers, people with disabilities, people who wish to retrain, and those with other commitments — business, political, religious or social.

## Flexitime

Many organisations operate a system of flexitime which gives workers more freedom to work the hours that suit them so far as this is consistent with the needs of the organisation. The key elements of a flexitime scheme are:

❑ **band width:** the hours over which the system operates, ie the earliest starting and latest finishing times; a limit is often placed on the number of hours which can be worked in one day — often nine hours;

❑ **core times:** the periods when all employees must be present, other than for authorised absence, for example 10.00 am - 12.00 pm and 2.00 pm - 4.00 pm;

❑ **flexible times:** the periods during which starting and finishing times may be varied, subject to the demands of the job. The hours worked during these periods are credited to the employee's total working hours;

❑ **lunchtime:** in general a break of between half an hour and two hours (ie employees have to take at least half an hour) — usually between the core hours;

❑ **accounting period:** the period in which employees must complete their contractual hours — often four weeks. For example a full-time worker contracted to work a 35-hour week will need to work 4 x 35 (140) hours during a four-week accounting period.

Flexitime allows staff to self-manage their time outside the core hours and has several equal opportunities implications. It is of particular benefit to employees with caring responsibilities, employees with disabilities and those wishing to study or pursue outside interests.

## Job sharing

Another method of increasing access to work is through job sharing: where two people share one full-time job. Each sharer does half the work and receives half the pay, holidays and other benefits. Job sharing is becoming popular with employers because it does not require any organisational restructuring or changes in establishment levels.

## Term-time working

Some employees operate term-time working, whereby staff are given unpaid leave during school holidays but have the same conditions of service as their full-time colleagues.

Introducing flexible working patterns will have implications for management practices, monitoring and supervision of staff. Nevertheless, there are advantages, both in terms of implementing equal opportunities and in relation to recruitment and retention of employees. Employees are more likely to stay in a job providing good benefits, and this reduces recruitment and training costs. This is particularly relevant for the voluntary sector, which is often unable to compete in the labour market in terms of salaries and other benefits.

For further information on flexible working patterns contact *New Ways to Work.*

## HIV and AIDS

Employers have a role to play in providing accurate information on HIV (Human Immunodeficiency Virus) — the virus that can lead to AIDS (Acquired Immune Deficiency Syndrome) — for their employees. By now many workplaces may employ people who are affected by HIV or AIDS. Existing employment, equal opportunities and health and safety policies should be reviewed to ensure that people who are HIV positive or have AIDS are not discriminated against, and to safeguard their right to privacy and medical confidentiality.

By providing accurate information and education about HIV and AIDS, employers can play a major part in countering fear and prejudice. It is particularly important to give information on methods of transmission to dispel myths. For example it should be emphasised that developing AIDS can result from unsafe sexual behaviour, and not because an individual is perceived to be part of an 'at risk group'. Equal opportunities policy statements should include a firm organisational commitment not to discriminate against people who are HIV positive or have AIDS or ARC (AIDS Related Complex), and employment contracts should take into account sick leave, flexible, phased return and time off for carers of people with AIDS.

## People with disabilities

Consider whether the premises and equipment are suitable for people with disabilities. Do not wait until you are about to employ a worker with a disability before making necessary adaptations.

Are there potential hazards for people with restricted sight, for example unmarked pillars, unmarked glass doors, poor lighting, loose mats or holes in carpets? Steps with contrasting edges are easier to see. Check the parking facilities and whether there are kerb ramps in the vicinity. Is there level access, are gradients on ramps too steep, are there lifts accessible to wheelchair users? Don't assume that a goods lift is adequate; a person who is wheelchair bound should have the same access as anyone who is able to walk. Check the width and weight of doors, make sure there

are handrails on steps and that there are separate male and female WCs with wheelchair access.

Whenever possible seek advice from people with disabilities about the suitability of the premises. Remember that a building suitable for wheelchair users may be unsuitable and even dangerous for a blind person, so make sure you get advice from people with different disabilities.

Reconsider the layout of offices for use by a person with a disability. For example wheelchairs require space to manoeuvre, and visually impaired employees can be seriously injured on sharp edges of desks, or filing cabinets sticking out into the room.

Also review office equipment. For example braille equipment may be required, filing cabinets may have top drawers that are too high for a person in a wheelchair, and chairs may be too low to get into or out of easily.

The Employment Service runs the **Access to Work Scheme** to provide people with disabilities and their employers with practical advice. This includes paying for:

❑ a communicator for people who are deaf or have a hearing impairment;

❑ a part-time reader or assistance at work for someone who is blind;

❑ a support worker for someone who needs practical help either at work or in getting to work;

❑ equipment, or adaptation to existing equipment, to suit individual needs;

❑ adaptations to a car, or taxi fares or other transport costs for those who cannot use public transport to get to work;

❑ alterations to premises to enable an employee with a disability to be employed.

The maximum entitlement per applicant (employer or employee) is £21,000 over five years, after which time entitlement begins again.

For further details contact the local *Placing, Assessment and Counselling Team (PACT)* or job centre. Their numbers are listed in the phone directory under 'Employment Service'.

The *National Council for Voluntary Organisations' Training and Employment Network* administers funds from a charitable trust to make small grants available for the promotion of employment and training opportunities for people with disabilities.

The local authority may be prepared to help with adaptations, particularly to WCs, if the organisation agrees to make them available for use by the public.

Further information is available in the **Buildings Regulations 1985: approved document M.**

## Setting standards and dealing with complaints

The equal opportunities policy should ensure that volunteers, trainees and consultants are aware of the standards of behaviour acceptable when dealing with anyone connected with the organisation. Just as an employee guilty of discriminatory behaviour might face disciplinary action, so too should volunteers and trainees have their services terminated where appropriate. Contracts with consultants should give the organisation the right to terminate their services in the event of inappropriate behaviour.

As with employees, consultants, trainees and volunteers should have access to a grievance procedure if they consider they are being discriminated against, harassed or treated unfairly.

## Harassment

When sexual or racial harassment occurs at work it can seriously affect employees' confidence and consequently their ability to do their work. It could also affect their physical and mental health. It is therefore essential to have clear and sympathetic processes of dealing with complaints, including the following:

❑ specify what behaviour is considered to be inappropriate;

❑ make clear that employees have a duty to comply with the policy and that failure to do so is a disciplinary offence;

❑ describe the complaints procedure and specify to whom a complaint should be made;

❑ allow people to complain to someone of their own sex and race;

❑ allow people to be represented throughout the process by a trade union official or friend;

❑ ensure that the person dealing with the complaint is independent of the situation;

❑ guarantee confidentiality and protection against victimisation or retaliation;

❑ ensure that all employees are told about the policy;

❑ ensure that those who have responsibility for dealing with complaints are properly trained;

❑ make provision for an adviser or counsellor for employees suffering harassment who can try to resolve the situation with them;

❑ allow for regular reviews to monitor the effectiveness of the procedures.

For further information on sexual harassment see *Sexual harassment in the workplace: a guide for employers.*

# Workers from abroad

## European Union (EU — formerly EEC) nationals

All EU citizens can work in this country in any type of job.

## Non-EU nationals

Most people from non-EU countries require a work permit. The following are exceptions:

❑ Commonwealth citizens, one of whose grandparents was born in the UK;

❑ people who have been given the right of settlement in the UK, including those married to British citizens and people who have been in approved employment for four or more years;

❑ Commonwealth citizens aged 17-27, who are

allowed to come to the UK for a working holiday of up to two years;

❑ those in permit-free employment, including journalists and ministers of religion, but entry clearance is still required;

❑ those who are coming to the country to work under the training and work experience schemes (see below);

❑ people who have been granted political asylum.

## Work permits

It is the employer's responsibility to apply for a work permit. Before the Employment Department (ED) will consider an application the employer must have advertised the job for four weeks during the previous six months in a 'quality' newspaper with national circulation or in a trade magazine, to allow a suitable worker to be found from within the United Kingdom or other EU countries.

If a non-EU worker is to be recruited, the employer must be able to show that the person has particular qualifications or skills not held by EU applicants and will have to submit details of the worker's professional qualifications and a copy of the his or her references to the ED.

An application for a work permit should be made on form OW1, available from job centres, and sent with the relevant documents to the *Employment Department's Overseas Labour Section*. Work permits are issued only for named workers and are granted for a maximum of four years. After the permit has expired, an application must be made to the Home Office and Employment Department for it to be extended.

The Overseas Labour Section will send an information pack on the work permit scheme on request.

### Training and work experience schemes

People from non-EU countries can come to the UK to obtain professional qualifications or gain specialist experience. To qualify for the **training scheme** they must be aged 18 or over, be given the same salary as a UK trainee and have a qualification equivalent to either a UK degree or a National Vocational Qualification (NVQ) level 4 or above. They are expected to train for at least 30 hours each week and must sign an agreement to leave the country at the end of their training.

To qualify for the **work experience scheme,** the applicant must be between 18 and 35 and be given a supernumerary post which is not available to a UK national. They can be paid only a 'modest personal allowance', probably something equivalent to a student grant. Their work must be at a level which is equivalent to that carried out by someone with an NVQ at level 4 or above and they must spend at least 30 hours per week on the work experience excluding any studies. Details of these schemes can also be obtained from the *Employment Department's Overseas Labour Section*.

## Overseas students

Overseas students can, with the permission of their colleges and the Employment Department, take part-time jobs during their studies. However, a student requiring a full-time job in the UK must leave the country before an employer can start the process of obtaining a work permit.

For further information on employing people from abroad contact the *Joint Council for the Welfare of Immigrants* or the *Migrant Support Unit*.

# Making an appointment

## Reviewing posts

The following sections give suggestions for recruitment practice; none are legal requirements.

As soon as an employee gives notice review the job description. Its content should be based on the needs of the organisation, not the skills and qualifications of a previous postholder.

Examine each vacant post to see whether it is appropriate to take positive action to assist recruitment of women or black and ethnic minority people, using the exemptions in the Sex Discrimination and Race Relations Acts referred to under 'Sex and race discrimination', above. Consider whether the post is suitable for job sharing or flexitime. Also see whether it is particularly appropriate for a worker with a disability.

## Selection panels

The composition of selection panels depends on the nature of the job and organisation. It could include people who will be working closely with the new worker, and members of the management committee. The equal opportunities policy may state the necessary composition and require that panel members have special training in interviewing techniques and equal opportunities law and good practice. Some groups invite outsiders with specialist knowledge of equal opportunities policies and practices to take part in shortlisting as observers, advisers or participants. No more than six people should sit on a panel, and candidates should never be interviewed by one person alone.

# The recruitment process

Making an appointment is a lengthy process. Time will need to be allowed for the panel to:

❑ finalise the job description (up to half a day);

❑ draw up the selection criteria (up to half a day);

❑ draw up questions and decide who will ask them (up to half a day);

❑ shortlist (allow up to a day);

❑ prepare for the interview (1 hour);

❑ interview the candidates (one day per 5 or 6 candidates).

From advertisement to starting date could take at least ten weeks:

| | |
|---|---|
| week 1 | advertisement appears |
| week 4 | closing date |
| week 4/5 | shortlisting |
| week 7 | interviews |
| | offer of appointment made verbally, and accepted |
| | offer made in writing |
| | candidate hands in notice |
| week 11 | employee starts (if four weeks' notice given) |

The time between shortlisting and interviewing could be cut down if interview dates are included in the information sent to applicants.

# Job descriptions

All employees should have a job description outlining the tasks and responsibilities involved in their work. It should form part of a contract of employment and cannot be changed without the worker's agreement.

It should include:

❑ the job title;

❑ the main purpose of the job;

❑ to whom the worker is responsible;

❑ for whom the worker is responsible;

❑ main working contacts;

❑ the key areas of the job;

❑ the main tasks of each key area;

❑ hours of work.

# Special conditions

### Two workers with the same job description

An organisation may receive funding for an area of work which involves two similar jobs. Rather than employing two people with the same job description and then refining the jobs to take into account the individuals' particular knowledge and experience it is preferable to consider specialising the two jobs in some way.

### Job sharers

It is essential to include information about how responsibilities will be shared in job descriptions for job sharers. If some areas are specific to one post, this must be absolutely clear. List shared work areas under a separate heading.

# Person specifications

A person specification describes the knowledge, abilities, skills and experience needed for the post, and should be based on the tasks outlined in the job description.

All specifications should state the minimum qualifications and experience needed to be eligible, which should have been examined to ensure that they are absolutely necessary. Consider whether academic qualifications or previous experience in similar employment are necessary. Other qualities may be just as important, for example personal knowledge of a community, or personal experience of a disability.

# Application forms

Examine the organisation's application form to ensure that it is clear, well structured, and asks only for information relevant to the post.

Use a standard form rather than ask for a curriculum vitae and letter of application. It is far easier to compare applications without bias if the information is presented in the same way.

Application forms should include:

❑ name (ask for 'forename' rather than 'Christian name' as this may deter members of other religious groups. Some organisations ask just for initials, to remove the possibility of discrimination on the grounds of sex);

❑ address, home and work telephone numbers;

❑ details of current or most recent employment, duties involved, date of joining and leaving, if appropriate, and pay;

❑ details of past employment;

❏ education and qualifications of relevance to the post;

❏ relevant experience (paid and voluntary) — make clear that applicants should address their answers to the person specification; an effective method is to include the headings on the application form;

❏ when the applicant would be able to take up the post;

❏ names and addresses of two referees, one of whom should be the current or most recent employer or college or school (ask whether the current employer may be contacted before interview and whether the applicant wishes to be informed before referees are contacted).

Allow enough space for employment details and a general statement in support of the application. Make it clear that applicants should base their replies on the person specification. Do not ask irrelevant discriminatory questions such as marital status, place of birth, religion or details of dependents.

Many application forms include questions on date of birth and age. This may discourage young and older people from applying. Consider whether such information is really necessary. For example do you operate a compulsory employees' insurance or pension scheme for which age is a criterion? It may be more appropriate to include these questions on a separate monitoring sheet (see below) to see whether your organisation treats young and older people fairly.

## Monitoring

Application forms should include a section for monitoring responses from ethnic minority applicants and people with disabilities, and to record the sex of the applicants. Some organisations also include questions relating to age and sexual orientation. These questions should be on a separate sheet, used only for monitoring purposes. It must be made clear that completion of the form is voluntary and failure to take part will not affect the success of an application.

## Job advertisements

Review the practice of advertising posts to ensure that vacancies are communicated to people from groups likely to suffer from discrimination.

This may involve the use of journals for particular groups, for example *The Voice, Caribbean Times, Asian Times, Everywoman* and the *Pink Paper*; local organisations including places of worship and radio stations; and local publications such as a talking newspaper or the local disability organisation's newsletter. The *Commission for Racial Equality* has a list

of newspapers serving the black community. The Disablement Employment Adviser at the local job centre and careers offices in the area should be informed of all vacancies.

Also remember the voluntary sector networks including the magazines *Voluntary Voice* (published by the London Voluntary Service Council) and *Third Sector*. Many councils for voluntary service produce newsletters and will include an advertisement.

Think carefully about the wording. It is important not only to attract good applicants, but also to deter unsuitable enquirers.

Advertisements should include:

❏ name of the organisation;

❏ job title (and department, if appropriate);

❏ brief description of the job;

❏ skills, knowledge, experience and qualifications needed;

❏ salary and salary scale;

❏ hours, stating whether full or part-time and any flexible working arrangements;

❏ whether the post is open for job sharing;

❏ nature of the job: whether permanent or temporary;

❏ name, address and telephone number of the contact for further information and application forms;

❏ closing date for applications;

❏ a statement of the equal opportunities policy operated;

❏ any further information, for example whether applications are particularly welcome from certain sections of the community and if so, under which section of which Act the post is being advertised and whether the offices are accessible for people with disabilities.

## Information for enquirers

Enquirers should be sent a copy of the job description, person specification, a statement of the equal opportunities policy, together with details of the main conditions of service (see chapter 4) including:

❏ salary and salary scale, including any cut-off point for starting salary;

❏ method and frequency of pay;

hours of work including flexitime arrangements if applicable;

place of work;

overtime: say whether this is paid or time off is given in lieu of extra hours worked;

annual leave in addition to bank holidays;

pension scheme;

the name of any recognised union;

maternity/paternity leave arrangements;

any other points, for example car allowance or removal expenses.

Whenever possible let candidates know shortlisting and interview dates.

Enquirers should also receive details of the organisation, ideally including a copy of the latest annual report (although this may be financially unrealistic if there are a large number of enquirers), and details of funding sources (this is particularly important given the uncertainty of voluntary sector funding). If you have received funds for a particular project you may wish to send shortlisted applicants a copy of the funding application.

## Shortlisting

Before shortlisting, the monitoring forms should be separated from the application forms and analysed. The results should be stored for future reference.

Shortlist soon after the closing date. All members of the selection panel should have copies of the job description and person specification and should shortlist separately before meeting to decide on the final shortlist. The decision to shortlist a candidate must be based on whether that person fulfils the knowledge, skills and experience requirements detailed in the person specification.

The panel should record reasons why each applicant has or has not been shortlisted. An applicant who feels discriminated against on grounds of race or sex has up to three months to complain to an industrial tribunal under the terms of the Race Relations or Sex Discrimination Acts. Shortlisting forms should therefore be kept for a minimum of three months. The tribunal can grant an extension so it is advisable, as well as good practice, to keep them for 12 months.

Invite the shortlisted people to an interview, and let others know they have not been successful. If necessary, ask for the candidates' consent if references are to be taken up before interview, then write to the referees, enclosing a stamped addressed envelope and a copy of the job description and specification. Even if references are taken up at this stage they should not be referred to until after the interviews have taken place and a decision has been made.

Letters to interviewees should state:

the date and time of the interview;

its approximate length;

whether any tests will be included and if so, their nature and length;

where it is to be held and how to get there;

whether travel expenses will be paid;

that referees have been contacted (if appropriate);

who will be on the interview panel.

Ask candidates to confirm the interview time as soon as possible.

Tell candidates when they will be informed of the decision.

# Interviews

It is sometimes useful for applicants to visit the organisation before a formal interview. This should be entirely for their benefit; the visit should not form part of the selection process.

## Planning the interview

It is essential to plan interviews well. If any candidate needs an interpreter or signer arrange this as early as possible; ask the candidate if there is an interpreter or signer he or she would prefer. The whole panel should draw up a list of questions relating to the skills and qualities relating to each key area; each set of questions should be asked by one person. Look at the forms to see if there are specific questions that should be asked. Do not ask questions that are discriminatory, for example about childcare arrangements, unless they are directly relevant to the job, in which case question all the candidates in the same way.

Elect someone to steer the interviews and decide who will answer questions on specific topics. One member of the panel should be able to give information about terms and conditions.

Make sure someone is available to welcome applicants, and that there is a suitable waiting area with access to a toilet. Have material prepared for any skills being tested (for example bookkeeping, writing or typing). Each candidate should have the same material.

Organise arrangements for paying expenses.

## Conduct of the interview

Each candidate should be allocated the same amount of time for an interview, and tests if being used. Always allow time for candidates to question the panel and at least ten minutes between each interview for the panel to make notes. It is good practice to wait until all the interviews have been completed before discussing the candidates. Extra time may be needed for some applicants, for example job sharers may need to be seen separately and then together; more time may be needed to interview a candidate who needs an interpreter or signer to communicate with the panel. Remember to include a proper break for lunch.

Whoever is steering the interviews should welcome the candidate, introduce the panel members, outline the structure and say the panel will be making notes. Allow the candidate to do most of the talking and avoid questions that can produce one word answers. Always allocate time for the candidate to ask questions and do not let the interviews overrun.

# Selection

Every member of the panel should make notes on each candidate after the interview. One method is to have a list of the skills, qualities and type of experience needed and record whether each has been partly, fully or not met. Candidates must always be assessed on the selection criteria, and not against each other. Each member of the panel must be able to justify his or her individual decisions with evidence. Always keep a record of the reasons why people were not selected. This is a useful part of an equal opportunities policy, enabling you to check why certain applicants were rejected. The records are also necessary if a decision is questioned by an unsuccessful candidate. As with shortlisting, a candidate who feels he or she has been discriminated against on grounds of race or sex has up to three months to apply to an industrial tribunal under the terms of the Race Relations or Sex Discrimination Acts. Interview records should therefore be kept for a minimum of three months. The tribunal can grant an extension so it is advisable, as well as good practice, to keep the records for 12 months.

Once all the interviews are over, the panel should discuss the applicants. Sometimes one candidate stands out and everyone will agree that person should be offered the job. At other times considerable discussion will be needed before a decision can be reached. If references have been taken up this is the time to read them.

Contact the successful candidate as soon as possible. A telephone call should be immediately followed by a formal offer in writing — be clear if the offer is subject to references.

If the panel genuinely cannot reach a decision consider whether it would be useful to re-interview any of the candidates in a key area. It is possible that the panel was unable to gather enough evidence about a candidate's ability in a particular area because of the questions asked. It may, however, be necessary to readvertise. If this is the case, look again at the job description, person specification and advertisement. Are they realistic?

The letter of appointment forms part of the contract of employment (see chapter 4) and should contain the following:

❏ starting date;

❏ starting salary;

❏ job title;

❏ any conditions of appointment, for example whether it is subject to a medical or to satisfactory references;

❏ a request for any further information or documentation needed, for example a P45 (see chapter 4);

❏ a request for a reply in writing.

# Taking on consultants

It is important to ensure that the equal opportunities policy includes procedures for recruiting consultants. As small contracts may not justify the expense of advertising and staff time in recruitment it may be necessary to specify the size and type of consultancy contracts that will be openly advertised. However, if more informal processes are used to appoint consultants these should be monitored to safeguard against possible discrimination. In any event, always ask consultants for examples of previous work and for references.

## Contracts

Consultants are not employees and are bound only by the terms of the contract made with the voluntary organisation. The following section looks at the clauses that should be included in such a contract.

A contract with a consultant does not need to be drafted by a lawyer and need not be complicated. Some freelance workers will have their own contracts. It is in everyone's interests to ensure that responsibilities are clear.

## Essential matters

The following should be included in a contract.

### Names of the organisation and of the consultant

### The agreed fee

### VAT and expenses

The contract should state whether the agreed fee is exclusive or inclusive of VAT. It should also state whether any expenses (for example travel, telephone or secretarial support) are payable in addition to the fee. If expenses are payable state how they will be calculated. You may want to give a maximum budget for expenses, state how they will be agreed and ask for proof of how they have been incurred.

### Arrangements for invoicing and payment

Payments can be made monthly or weekly in arrears or at specified stages during a longer contract. Some work is paid partly in advance. Always ensure that you owe the consultant money until the work has been completed to your satisfaction but always make prompt payments.

### Start and completion dates for the work

Agree a completion date for a specific piece of work. For more open-ended tasks the contract may continue until the work is completed.

### Work to be done

It is imperative that the contract is clear about the work required from the consultant. This information may be contained in a separate brief to which you can refer. It needs to be as specific as possible to reduce the possibility of misunderstandings.

### Copyright or patent

Clarify who will have the copyright or patent if written material or a new product is produced. If a consultant is contracted to produce a book which may run to a second edition the parties' rights and responsibilities in relation to that edition must be clear.

### Self-employment, tax and national insurance

Make clear that the agreement does not create a contract of employment and that if self-employed, the consultant is responsible for his or her own tax and national insurance.

### Insurance

Depending on the kind of work, it may be necessary for the consultant to have public liability and/or professional indemnity insurance (see chapter 7). If so the contract should state that a copy of the policy or schedule should be submitted as proof of cover.

### Equal opportunities

The contract must make clear that the consultant is expected at all times to comply with the organisation's policy on equal opportunities and abide by the code of conduct adopted as part of that policy.

### Grievance procedure

The contract should either explain or refer to the procedure to be used if the consultant has a complaint about his or her treatment.

### Termination

Clarify the circumstances in which the agreement with the consultant could be terminated before the end of the contract, for example if the consultant:

- fails to comply with any aspect of the contract;

- cannot complete the work within the agreed timescale or any agreed extension; or

- has brought the organisation into disrepute.

Similarly, the consultant should be able to terminate

the contract if payment is not received or the organisation fails to supply information or anything else necessary for the work (in such cases the consultant must be paid any fees owing).

## Confidentiality

Consultants as a matter of course should always respect confidentiality, but it is useful to include a clause in the contract restricting disclosure of information.

## The agreement

There should be a simple phrase stating that the consultant agrees to carry out the work within the timescale and on the terms and conditions included in the contract in exchange for the fee. It should be signed by or on behalf of both parties.

## Optional matters

The following may be included in a contract.

### Increased time required

It is sometimes difficult to assess accurately the time required for a piece of work. It may therefore be helpful to set out what will happen if the job overruns. You should state whether the consultant is expected to complete the piece of work even if more time is required, or allow the option for renegotiation.

### Other responsibilities on the consultant

For longer pieces of work the contract should require regular progress reports on specified dates with details of the time worked and expenses incurred. If the brief demands a policy decision by your organisation during the course of the work, the contract should require the consultant to follow your directions. It should also state that the organisation will pay for any additional time arising from the policy decision. You may also wish to ensure that you have access to any documents collected by the consultant in connection with the work.

### Obligations on the organisation

Always agree to provide the consultant with any information needed to carry out the work. If you are providing any form of administrative or other support this should be made clear.

### Arbitration

You may wish to put an arbitration clause in the agreement, in the event of a dispute. This should contain a procedure for an arbitrator, agreed by both parties, to be appointed, and allow for an independent third party to appoint an arbitrator if the organisation and consultant cannot agree.

The terms and conditions should be set out in a letter or simple contract to be signed by the consultant and the organisation.

# Booklist

**A guide to the Sex Discrimination Act** (PL858), Employment Department, free

**AIDS and work: a guide for employees** (PL916), Employment Department, free

**Be flexible: a guide to flexible working** (PL927), Employment Department, free

**Changing times — a guide to flexible work patters for human resource managers**, New Ways to Work (1994), £19.50

**Employing people with disabilities: sources of information and advice**, Employment Service, free

**Employment rights: a guide for disabled people,** RADAR (1992), £7.00

**Equal opportunities: ten point plan for employers** (PL922), Employment Department, free

**Guidelines for policies on the employment of disabled people**, RADAR (1991), 75p

**Job advertisements and the Race Relations Act: a guide to section 5 for advertisers and publishers**, Commission for Racial Equality (1994), free

**Job descriptions**, *Gill Taylor*, Federation of Independent Advice Centres (1994), £9.95

**Making employment policies for disabled people work in practice**, Lambeth ACCORD, £5.50

**New ways to work: the video**, New Ways to Work (1994), £25

**Sex discrimination in employment** (PL887), Employment Department, free

**Sexual harassment in the workplace: a guide for employers** (PL923), Employment Department, free

**Job sharing: a practical guide**, *Pam Walton*, New Ways to Work (1990), £7.99

**Thinking of taking someone on? PAYE for employers** (IR57), Inland Revenue (1993), free

**Volunteers first: a guide to employment practice**, *Angela Whitcher and Angie McDonough*, Volunteer Centre, £1.50

# Chapter 4:
# Your responsibilities as an employer — during employment

This chapter starts by describing the components of a contract of employment. Further sections cover the role of a trade union, the processes involved in reorganisation and the implications of changing the way staff work. An example of a contract of employment is given at the end of the chapter.

The health and safety responsibilities of employment are described in chapter 5, employers' responsibilities for insurance are given in chapter 7 and redundancy procedures are covered in chapter 10.

# Contracts of employment

Legally, a contract of employment exists as soon as someone accepts the offer of a job, and it is binding on both sides.

Contracts consist of **express terms** and **implied terms.** Express terms are those which have been specifically agreed in the letter of appointment, job description (see chapter 3), terms and conditions of employment and any trade union agreement. Implied terms are those which are not actually stated. These include the employer's duty to pay wages, provide a safe work environment and treat the employee with respect. The implied terms of an employee's contract are to be ready and willing to work, to obey reasonable instructions and to give an honest and faithful service.

## Deciding terms and conditions

The following sections sets out the **minimum** rights of employees under statute (usually the **Employment Protection (Consolidation) Act, 1978**). Employers may provide more generous terms and conditions, and some suggestions are given under each section

and shown in the model employment contract at the end of the chapter. However, before deciding to offer more generous terms and conditions, the financial implications — particularly in relation to sick pay, maternity pay and redundancy — must be considered. A balance needs to be struck between the needs of the organisation to be able to function effectively with adequate resources and the wish to provide good terms and conditions to employees.

## Statement of employment particulars

Every person working eight or more hours a week is entitled to a statement of employment particulars, within two months of taking up the employment (even if the employment ends within two months of starting work). An employee who is to work outside the UK within two months of starting work must receive the written particulars before leaving the UK. However, it is good practice to give all employees a written contract of employment which contains terms and conditions of service as well as the legal requirements for the statement of employment particulars.

The employer must give the employee written notice of any change to particulars of employment within one month of them taking effect.

The **Employment Protection (Consolidation) Act, 1978** as amended by the **Trade Union Reform and Employment Rights Act, 1993** requires that the statement of employment particulars must contain the following:

❏ name of employer;

❏ name of employee;

❏ job title or brief description of the job;

❏ whether previous service with the same employer, or service with a previous employer counts for the purposes of continuous employment;

❏ the date on which the employee's period of continuous employment began, taking into account any employment with a previous employer which counts towards that period (this will normally be the date when the employee began working for the current employer);

❏ scale or rate of pay, including overtime and bonuses;

❏ pay period;

❏ hours of work (including any terms and conditions relating to normal working hours and overtime);

❑ holiday entitlement (including public holidays), holiday pay and rights to accrued holiday pay if employees leave without taking their full entitlement;

❑ terms and conditions relating to incapacity for work due to sickness or injury, including sick pay arrangements;

❑ pension rights, including whether the employer is contracted out of the State Earnings Related Pension Scheme (SERPS);

❑ amount of notice the employer must give: the legal minimum notice to staff working 16 or more hours each week is one week after four weeks' service, two weeks after two years' service and one additional week for every year of employment, up to a maximum of 12 weeks' notice. The amount of notice to be given by the employer can be increased above the statutory minimum in the contract of employment. If a contract is for a fixed term, the date of expiry should be given here and the statement should make clear that the contract is for a fixed term;

❑ amount of notice employees must give: employees working 16 or more hours a week (and those working between eight and 16 hours a week for at least five years) must give one week's notice after four weeks of employment;

❑ the job title or a brief description of the work; this may make reference to a job description;

❑ the place(s) of work or, where an employee is required or permitted to work at various places, an indication of that fact and the address of the employer;

❑ where an employee is required to work outside the UK for more than one month:

- the period of work outside the UK
- the currency in which salary will be paid
- any additional pay and benefits to be made while the employee is working outside the UK
- terms and conditions relating to the employee's return to the UK;

❑ any collective agreements which directly affect the terms and conditions of employment and, if the employer is not a party to them, the persons by whom they were made;

❑ name or job title of the person to whom the employee should go with a grievance;

❑ grievance procedure or details of where the grievance procedure can be obtained;

❑ for organisations with 20 or more employees, disciplinary procedures or details of how they can be obtained.

Some organisations will have a collective agreement between the union and management regarding most aspects of employment, to which an employee may refer.

If any of the above particulars have no related terms and conditions, the statement should specify those items where there is no entitlement.

Employers are not obliged to include the following in the terms and conditions of employment, but it is good practice to do so:

❑ parental leave arrangements;

❑ arrangements for compassionate leave;

❑ time off for public duties and trade union activities;

❑ redundancy notice and pay;

❑ reimbursement arrangements for travel and subsistence;

❑ religious holidays: the conditions of service should make provision for those workers who wish to take leave at times other than the established Christian festivals;

❑ extended leave to allow workers to visit relatives abroad;

❑ dependants' leave: parents and other carers may need time off to look after relatives or other dependants who are ill. The conditions of service may allow staff to take dependants' leave and if so should state the length of this entitlement;

❑ childcare: a voluntary organisation may not have the funds to run a crèche, however, it could consider contributing towards the costs of its workers' childminding costs;

❑ flexitime arrangements: some employees, for example parents and carers, may need to work outside conventional office hours, and the contract may state if this is allowed.

The terms and conditions should include a clear statement that acceptance of the organisation's equal opportunities policy is a condition of appointment. Employers should also make it clear in a separate equal opportunities code of conduct that harassment or discrimination by any employee towards another member of staff, management committee member or service user is a disciplinary offence, and that no worker who provides information about discrimination will be victimised.

The terms and conditions should either include specific grievance procedures for staff who feel they are being harassed or discriminated against or make reference to another document which they may read.

Funding bodies may lay down conditions concerning terms of employment. For example, some local authorities state that grant aided organisations must offer terms similar to those given to local government employees. A voluntary organisation should be clear about what it is committing itself to before accepting such conditions.

## Fixed-term contracts

A fixed-term contract is one that comes to an end after a specified time. If such a contract is not renewed, employees can claim unfair dismissal or redundancy pay if they have worked long enough to qualify. However, the law allows employers to exclude the unfair dismissal and redundancy provisions and to terminate the contract at the end of the fixed term if the employee agrees in writing. If an organisation requires this agreement, it should be made clear in the recruitment process. The agreement to exclude the unfair dismissal and redundancy provisions should be contained in the initial contract of employment.

Fixed-term contracts are not a good way of dealing with short-term funding. It is better, if possible, to give open contracts and deal with unavoidable dismissals through a good redundancy agreement (see chapter 10).

The next section describes terms and conditions of employment and some of the statutory requirements in greater detail.

## Holidays

There is no legal minimum entitlement to holidays or holiday pay. Good practice would be four or five weeks' paid annual leave in addition to public

holidays. The leave year normally runs from January to December or from April to March; some organisations allow employees to carry over some unspent leave entitlement for three or four months.

## Sickness

Employers operate the **statutory sick pay scheme** (SSP). This entitles most workers who earn more than the Lower Earnings Limit (LEL), set in April each year, to payment for the first 28 weeks of sickness. The exceptions include:

❑ men and women over 65;

❑ employees under 16;

❑ people engaged on a fixed-term contract of three calendar months or less, who have been employed for 13 weeks or less (two contracts separated by no more than eight weeks are counted together to determine whether or not the employment has lasted, or is likely to last, for more than 13 weeks);

❑ pregnant women during the period from 11 weeks before the expected date of birth to six weeks after;

❑ those who have received sickness, invalidity or maternity benefit within the previous 57 days;

❑ new employees who have not worked at all under their contracts, unless they were previously employed by the same employer and the two contracts are separated by no more than eight weeks;

❑ employees who have reached their maximum entitlement to SSP;

❑ employees who have provided a leaver's statement which shows that 28 weeks' SSP has already been due from a former employer and there is a gap of 56 days or less since the last day of SSP shown on the statement;

❑ anyone abroad in a non-EU country;

❑ employees who are detained in legal custody or who are in prison;

❑ people who become ill while on strike.

The employer pays out SSP to the employee. Only 'small employers' — those which pay less than £20,000 gross employer's and employees' national insurance contributions in a tax year, or less than £1,666 national insurance contributions per month (as at April 94) — can reclaim SSP. This is done by deducting SSP from monthly Inland Revenue payments. SSP can only be reclaimed after the first four weeks of sickness.

There are two rates of statutory sick pay, depending on the level of the employee's earnings (the up to date figures can be obtained from the Benefits Agency).

Before operating the scheme, the employer needs to:

❏ agree qualifying days (days for which SSP is paid) with employees. These are usually regular working days but may include weekends;

❏ decide rules for notifying absence through sickness;

❏ tell employees what evidence of incapacity is needed. It is normal practice to phone in on the first day of sickness, or as soon as possible. If the absence lasts for at least three days many employers require the employee to send in a completed DSS self-certification form (SC2). After this time the employer is entitled to ask for a doctor's certificate.

The employer also needs copies of:

❏ **changeover form** (SSP1): issued to employees who have received their full SSP entitlement (ie 28 weeks) and would therefore have to be transferred to social security benefits;

❏ **leaver's statement** (SSP1.L): supplied to those who have received SSP within eight weeks before the end of their employment;

❏ **record sheet** (SSP2): to calculate the sick pay and record the details required by the Benefits Agency;

❏ **employee's statement of sickness (SC2)**: to give details about absences of between four and seven days;

❏ the booklet *Statutory Sick Pay manual for employers (NI 270)*, and supplement.

It is good practice to give each employee a copy of the leaflet *Statutory Sick Pay; check your rights (NI 244)*, available from the Contributions Agency.

If someone is often sick, the management committee will need to know why. Is there a long-term sickness? Is the illness due to work-related stress, or unhealthy working conditions? If so, what can be done to improve matters?

Employers should try to improve on the legal requirements by including additional provisions relating to sick pay in the contract of employment. However, consider the financial position of the organisation before any provisions are incorporated. Small groups can be particularly hard hit by staff illnesses.

# Maternity

Women who become pregnant have certain entitlements.

## Paid time off for ante natal care

All pregnant employees, regardless of length of service, are entitled to reasonable time off without loss of earnings for ante natal care. Except in the case of the first appointment, an employer can ask for an appointment card and a medical certificate confirming the pregnancy.

## Maternity leave and returning to work

The **Trade Union Reform and Employment Rights Act**, 1993 introduced new rights to maternity leave.

### Rights of all pregnant employees

All pregnant women, regardless of hours of work and length of service have a right to 14 weeks' maternity leave (**'basic leave'**).

A pregnant employee may start her maternity leave period any time after the beginning of the eleventh week before the expected week of the childbirth (EWC). She must give her employer 21 days' notice of the date she has chosen.

If that is not reasonably practicable she must give notice as soon as possible, informing the employer that she is pregnant and the EWC or, if the child has been born, the date on which this occurred. A week begins on a Sunday for this purpose. Employers can request a medical certificate stating the EWC. If the baby is born before the date given to the employer, or the woman is absent from work wholly or partly because of the pregnancy at any time after the beginning of the sixth week before the expected week of delivery, the maternity leave period will start automatically.

Under the EC Pregnant Workers Directive women are not allowed to work within two weeks of giving birth. Therefore, if the normal 14 week leave has expired before she is allowed to return to work under the Directive, the maternity leave will continue until two weeks after the child's birth.

Whilst on basic maternity leave a woman is entitled to her normal terms and conditions of employment except that she is not entitled to her normal pay. However, she may be entitled to statutory maternity pay or maternity allowance (see 'Maternity pay', below). Because her contract continues, she has a right to return to work in the same job when the leave ends.

## Summary

Basic leave can begin in one of three ways:

❑ the employee taking leave, having given 21 days' notice; or

❑ childbirth (regardless of notice); or

❑ any absence wholly or partly because of pregnancy or childbirth after the beginning of the sixth week before the expected week of birth (regardless of notice).

## Extended maternity leave

A woman who has worked 16 or more hours a week for at least two years, or between 8 and 16 hours for at least five years at the beginning of the eleventh week before the baby is due, is entitled to return to her old job after taking a longer period of maternity (**'extended leave'**). She must inform the employer in writing 21 days before stopping work that she is taking extended maternity leave and wants to return to work, and must return within 29 weeks of the birth, although this can be extended by four weeks if a medical certificate is produced.

*The above qualifying periods are subject to any changes the Government may make during 1994/95 to implement the House of Lords' decision regarding the difference between part-time and full-time workers' rights (see chapter 1 for further details).*

It is up to the employer whether a woman's terms and conditions continue during the period between the end of her basic leave and the end of her extended leave and this must be stated in the conditions of service.

The employer can write to the woman once she has been absent for at least 11 weeks, to ask whether she intends to return to work. The woman has to reply within 14 days of receipt of the letter, or as soon as is reasonably practicable, in order to keep her right to return to work. This time limit means that almost at the same time as having their babies (even beforehand in some cases), many women may be asked to make a decision (although this need not be binding), as to whether or not they will be returning to work. It is therefore good practice to delay seeking confirmation that a woman intends to return to work for as long as possible.

The woman must again confirm her intention to start work by writing to the employer at least 21 days before she is due to return. The employer can postpone return for four weeks.

If, after all this, the employer fails to give the woman her job back, she can take out a claim for unfair dismissal.

## Maternity pay

A woman who has worked for 26 weeks by the fifteenth week before the baby is due is entitled to **statutory maternity pay** (SMP), if her average earnings in the eight weeks before the fifteenth week were more than the Lower Earnings Limit (as at April 94, £57).

SMP is payable for up to 18 weeks: the first six weeks at 90% of earnings, the remaining 12 weeks at £52.50 (as at October 94).

Women who do not qualify for SMP may be able to claim Maternity Allowance from the DSS.

Employers paying £20,000 or less in gross national insurance contributions will be reimbursed in full; others will be reimbursed 92% of SMP.

## Right not to be dismissed

No woman, regardless of length of service or hours worked can be dismissed because of pregnancy, for any other reason connected with the pregnancy, or for the following:

❑ reasons connected with her having given birth;

❑ taking advantage of the benefits of maternity leave;

❑ being absent for up to four weeks after the maternity leave period if she has provided a medical certificate saying she is incapable of work for that period.

Any woman who is dismissed during her 14 week basic maternity leave period is automatically entitled to receive written reasons for her dismissal.

A woman has the right to be offered a suitable alternative vacancy, where available, if she would otherwise have to be made redundant while pregnant or on maternity leave.

Any dismissal which is in breach of these requirements will automatically be unfair.

## Improving on the statutory requirements

Employers should improve on the legal requirements. The letter writing process could be simplified. In particular, employers should not require women to state at or around the time of the child's birth whether they are going to return to work. In addition, the qualifying period could be reduced, the period of right to return to work extended and the period of receipt of maternity pay increased. Whatever improvements are agreed should be included in the written statement of terms.

## Partner and compassionate leave

Although there is no legal duty to offer partner or compassionate leave it is good practice to do so. Each request for compassionate leave should be considered on its own merit.

## Retirement

The law now requires that men and women have equal retirement ages even though women continue to be eligible for a state retirement pension at 60.

## Pensions

National insurance (NI) contributions provide employees with a basic pension and the additional **State Earnings Related Pension Scheme** (SERPS) when they reach retirement age. However, the state scheme does not give a pension on earnings above the national insurance upper earnings limit, a lump sum on retirement or a benefit other than a pension for a widow. Many people, therefore, choose to make additional provision for their pension.

In April 1988 the Government changed benefits given under SERPS. For anybody who retires after the year 2000 the benefits have been decreased, and for those retiring after 2010 it is better to make alternative arrangements. Under the law as it now stands employees have the choice of joining their employer's scheme (if there is one), which can be either '**contracted out**' or '**not contracted out**' (see below), or of setting up a personal pension, to which an employer can, but is not obliged, to contribute. These are additional to the basic state provision and are '**topping up**' plans.

### Contracted out schemes

If an employer's scheme is contracted out, employers and employees pay NI at a reduced rate which entitles the worker to receive only the basic rate pension. Instead of SERPS the worker will receive benefit from the employer's pension scheme. Any contracted out scheme must meet certain standards laid down by the Occupational Pensions Board. It involves the employer in a good deal of administration and depends on an open ended commitment, which a small, insecurely funded voluntary group may not want to undertake.

### Not contracted out schemes

If an employee is in a pension scheme which is not contracted out, higher rate NI contributions are paid to SERPS. To contract out of SERPS an employee can set up a personal pension scheme into which the DSS will pay the higher rate NI contributions. This scheme would be independent of any other arrangements.

### Topping up

There are two types of topping up plans. In a **final salary scheme** the benefit received relates to an employee's pensionable earnings for a period ending at or before normal pension date or leaving service; it is usually also based on pensionable service. A **money purchase scheme** is directly related to the amount of money paid in. Under either of these schemes it is possible for both employer and employee to contribute. The maximum the employee can contribute and claim tax relief on is 17.5% of earnings; for the employer it is a sum related to salary.

It is difficult to get unbiased advice about pension schemes. Many voluntary organisations belong to the *Pensions Trust*, which runs a number of pension schemes especially designed for voluntary groups. Voluntary sector workers and employers are represented on the Trust's management committee.

Organisations funded by local authorities may be able to become admitted bodies to the *Local Government Superannuation Scheme*. This enables organisations to provide their employees with occupational pensions without having to set up their own scheme. Contact the local authority for details.

## Disciplinary and grievance procedures

### Disciplinary procedures

When drawing up a disciplinary procedure, follow the ACAS code of practice: *Disciplinary practice and procedures in employment*, which says that procedures should:

❑ be speedy;

❑ be in writing;

❑ specify to whom they apply;

❑ make clear the range of disciplinary actions;

❑ state who has authority to discipline;

❑ allow for individuals to be told about complaints and to be given an opportunity to state their case;

❑ allow for individuals to be accompanied by a union representative or colleague when stating their case;

❑ give workers the right to be told of reasons for disciplinary action;

❏ ensure no one is dismissed for a first offence, except in cases of gross misconduct, for example serious racial abuse, serious sexual harassment, assault or theft;

❏ give the right of appeal;

❏ specify the appeals procedure (an appeals panel should be made up of people not involved in the disciplinary action).

An initial disciplinary decision could be taken by a line manager, senior staff member or the chair of the management committee, and the appeal might be to a subcommittee of the management committee.

Failure to comply with a disciplinary procedure may be taken into account by an industrial tribunal, should an employee take out a claim for unfair dismissal.

Always check the facts before embarking on a disciplinary procedure. Disciplinary action should only be started if informal discussions and supervision sessions with clear targets for improvement have proved ineffective, or if there has been misconduct or a breach of rules too serious to be dealt with informally. For further discussion on dealing with problems see chapter 10 of *Just About Managing?*.

If a problem does arise that cannot be resolved informally then follow the agreed stages. These should consist of at least two verbal and one written warning before notice is given. At each stage, a full explanation of the reasons for invoking the procedure must be given and employees should be allowed to state their case. They should also be told of their right of appeal. Any record of a disciplinary procedure, apart from those relating to some serious offences, should be removed from an individual's file after an agreed period, say six months.

An employee who is accused of gross misconduct should be suspended on full pay while an investigation is carried out.

### Grievance procedures

A formal procedure is necessary to enable employees to bring a grievance to the attention of management. This procedure can also be used to enable an employee to appeal against a disciplinary matter.

Grievances should be dealt with rapidly. The stages could be as follows:

❏ the employee raises the matter with his or her manager or, if the grievance is with the line manager, to that person's manager;

❏ if the matter is not resolved within five working days it goes to the head of the organisation;

❏ if not resolved within the next five working days it goes to the honorary officers or staffing committee;

❏ if not resolved within the next five working days it goes to the management committee, who should call a special meeting if necessary within the next ten days;

❏ if no satisfactory conclusion is reached by this stage, the employee is entitled to approach ACAS for advice and assistance.

The organisation should consider having a separate grievance procedure under its equal opportunities policy to deal with complaints about harassment or discrimination. It should take account of the difficulties employees face in making complaints of harassment or discrimination and give them access to someone to whom they can turn for support and advice. This is dealt with in chapter 3.

# Paying people

Employers are responsible for paying staff and providing them with payslips. They must also make the following deductions:

❏ national insurance (NI);

❏ income tax;

❏ pension contributions (where appropriate);

❏ union subscriptions (by agreement).

The employer must pay the workers' income tax and NI contributions, together with the employer's NI contributions, to the Inland Revenue. Employers must complete a **deductions working sheet** (P11), for each employee. These should be kept for at least three years after the end of the tax year to which they apply.

The **Wages Act, 1986** prohibits any deduction from wages unless an employee has consented, the deductions are required by statute (for example, tax and national insurance) or it is a term of the contract of employment that the deduction will be made. There are some exceptions which include:

❏ reimbursing an overpayment made by the employer in the past;

❏ deductions made under agreed arrangements for payment to a third party to which the employee has agreed (for example union dues);

❏ deductions where an employee is on strike or engaging in industrial action;

❏ sums due to the employer under an industrial tribunal settlement or court settlement.

Many large organisations have computerised salary payments. All the necessary calculations and deductions are made using the computer. Some banks and accountants offer a salary-paying service to small businesses — including voluntary organisations — for a modest fee and some local authorities provide a similar service at no cost to organisations which they fund. There are also community accountancy projects which provide payroll services for a small charge; see *Accountancy services for voluntary organisations* or contact the local council for voluntary service for details. An organisation without experience of the paperwork associated with employing staff might want to investigate these possibilities.

## Payslips

All employees working more than 16 hours each week (and in organisations with 20 or more staff, employees working more than eight hours each week) are entitled to a detailed payslip containing the following information:

❏ gross amount earned;

❏ amounts of variable deductions such as tax, NI and pension contributions;

❏ amounts of fixed deductions, such as union dues;

❏ any other deductions;

❏ net amount earned.

Preprinted payslips can be purchased from office stationery suppliers.

As a matter of good practice, payslips should be given to all employees.

## Income tax

The method used for deducting income tax on a regular basis is **Pay As You Earn** (PAYE). It applies to all employees who receive an earned income exceeding the annually fixed minimum rate.

Ask the local Inland Revenue office for the address of your tax office as soon as you know you will be employing staff. The tax office will allocate you a reference number and send all the necessary forms, including the **employer's guide to PAYE** (P7) and the **blue card** (P8).

Each month, the employer has to pay to the Inland Revenue the total amount of tax deducted, minus any tax refunded, plus the employer's and employees' NI contributions, less any statutory sick pay (SSP) (if it

can be reclaimed) or statutory maternity pay (SMP) deductions. These are all entered onto the **employer's payment record** (form P32), which is a record of the amount required to be paid to the Inland Revenue. The amount due, together with a form of **record of payment** P30(Z) must be sent to the Collector of Taxes within 14 days of the end of each tax month. At the end of the year, form P35 must be sent to the Inland Revenue.

Employers who are likely to pay less than £450 tax and national insurance per month (as at April 94) may choose to make contributions on a quarterly basis on 5 July, 5 October, 5 January and 5 April. Contact your local *Inland Revenue Accounts Office* to make the arrangements.

The amount of tax deducted depends on:

❏ the employee's code number;

❏ the amount of gross pay earned since the beginning of the tax year;

❏ the amount of income tax already deducted.

The Inland Revenue provides employers with weekly or monthly tax tables from which tax deductions are calculated. They are divided into two sections:

❏ **table A — the free pay table** — which lists code numbers with the appropriate free pay to date;

❏ **table B — the taxable pay table** — which shows the total tax due on taxable pay.

New employees will normally bring form P45 parts two and three, giving details of their tax code, NI number, amount of pay received and tax paid to date. Part two is kept by the employer and part three is sent to the tax office.

If no P45 is provided and the employee will be working more than a week, complete form P46 and send it to the tax office to obtain the correct tax code. In the meantime, the emergency tax code will have to be used.

A deductions working sheet, P11, should be completed for each new employee.

## Employees leaving

When someone leaves:

❏ fill in the appropriate section on the P45;

❏ send part one to the tax office;

❏ give the employee parts two and three.

## At the end of the tax year

At the end of each financial year (5 April) an employer must give each employee a **certificate of earnings and tax deducted** (P60). This records earnings while in employment, and the tax deducted, less refunds.

Send to the Tax Office:

❏ form **P14** (a summary of the deductions working sheet: DWS) for each employee for whom a DWS has been used at any time in the year; and

❏ a **P35**, listing all employees and their pay, tax, statutory sick pay and statutory maternity pay.

These make up the **End of Year Return.**

If expenses have been reimbursed to staff, these must be declared to the Inland Revenue on form P11D for each member of staff who has earned over £8,500 in the year (as at April 94) unless there has been a dispensation given to the relevant employees by the Tax Office. For further details see the *Employer's guide to PAYE (P7).*

## Temporary and casual staff

If anyone is employed on a temporary or casual basis whose wages are not being paid by an agency keep a record of:

❏ their name and address;

❏ their NI number;

❏ dates of their employment;

❏ the amount they were paid.

A deductions working sheet must be completed in the following circumstances:

❏ the employee gives you a P45; or

❏ the employee earns more than £57 per week; or

❏ the employee works for you for more than one week; or

❏ the employee is taken on for one week or less but will be working for you again.

If casual workers have more than one job, complete a P46 when they start and use the emergency code until you are told the correct amount to deduct.

## National insurance (NI)

The lower earnings limit (LEL) and higher earnings limit (HEL) usually change each April (as at April 94 the limits were £57 and £430). Employees who earn more than the LEL have to pay Class 1 NI contributions on all earnings up to the HEL. The employer has to pay NI contributions on all earnings (including those above the HEL) if the employee earns more than the LEL. The rates are on a sliding scale according to how much the employee earns. Lower rates are payable if the employee is contracted out of SERPS (see 'Pensions', above).

Contribution tables are issued by the Contributions Agency each year and employers should receive them by mid-March. If they do not arrive by then, contact the local Contributions Agency office for tables (CF391) if you have not contracted out of the state scheme, or the Contracted Out Employment Group if you have contracted out.

NI numbers for employees who have not worked before can be obtained from the Contributions Agency.

Some married women pay a reduced rate contribution. People over pensionable age do not pay NI contributions although the employer's contribution is still payable; anyone to whom this applies should provide the employer with a certificate stating the position. If no certificate is available make the normal deductions and arrange a refund when a certificate is produced.

Anyone paying contributions in another job must provide a certificate of non-liability stating that contributions are already being made. In this case the second employer does not pay a contribution.

## Keeping records

Employers have a legal duty to keep records of tax and NI deductions, and statutory sick pay and statutory maternity pay. It is also useful to keep basic information about employees, such as addresses, NI numbers, next of kin, job descriptions, a signed copy of their employment contract containing employment particulars, together with holiday and sickness forms. Keep a file for each person. These should be available for inspection by the employees involved.

Someone who leaves or applies for another job may ask for a reference. An employee has no legal right to see a reference, but it is a good practice to make it available. Keep a copy on file.

# Unions

Almost all employees have the right to belong to a trade union and to take part in union activities outside working hours, and during working hours if this is agreed by the employer. Industrial action does not count as a union activity for this purpose. Employees also have the right not to belong to a union.

## Union/management agreement

If several employees join a trade union, their representatives are likely to request official recognition, which will allow the representatives to negotiate with the employer over terms and conditions.

The agreement can either cover only disciplinary or grievance matters relating to individuals (**an individual agreement**), or it can cover the whole range of conditions affecting employees, including pay (**a procedural agreement**). If a majority of employees belong to a trade union, it is advisable to draw up a procedural agreement.

If employees belong to more than one union, the employer may decide to recognise the union with the greatest number of members in a procedural agreement and recognise the others for discussing individual rights only.

An alternative is to ask the representatives of the various unions to form a joint committee. The employer will then negotiate with the committee's chair and secretary.

Contact *ACAS* for further information about union recognition and agreements.

## The rights of recognised trades unions

Once an employer has given a union official recognition the union acquires the following rights:

❑ to receive information for collective bargaining purposes. ACAS lists the following as possibly relevant for collective bargaining: pay and benefits; conditions of service; staffing; performance; and finance (see *ACAS Code 2: Disclosure of information to trade union officials for collective bargaining purposes*);

❑ to appoint safety representatives;

❑ to be consulted over redundancy (see chapter 10);

❑ to allow union officials (working 16 or more hours

each week, or those working at least eight hours with five years' continuous service) reasonable time off with pay for union duties and relevant training.

## Union representatives

The union should notify management of the names of the elected representatives who will have been given credentials (papers authorising them to act for their union). Representatives have a right to some facilities, and it is good practice to provide others, including:

❑ a desk and a lockable filing cabinet;

❑ use of a phone to make calls in private;

❑ a union notice board;

❑ use of a photocopier and mailing facilities;

❑ use of a typewriter or computer;

❑ meeting space.

An employer can encourage people to join the union by:

❑ negotiating with the union rather than with individuals;

❑ enabling union representatives to talk to all new employees as soon as they start;

❑ arranging for union contributions to be deducted direct from pay (often called **'check off'**) if members agree.

The main unions in the voluntary sector are:

❑ MSF (formerly ASTMS)
❑ ACTSS (the white collar section of the TGWU)
❑ UNISON (an amalgamation of NALGO, NUPE and COHSE)

# Reorganisation

Voluntary organisations, like other employers, sometimes have to reorganise. This may involve changes to contracts of employment, for example a change in workplace, different jobs and, in some cases, different terms and conditions of employment.

Where possible, amendments to a contract of employment should be made only with the agreement of the employee concerned or, where applicable, negotiated with the trade union.

However, in some cases it may be essential to make changes to contracts of employment whether or not employees agree. For example, contracts of employment may state that staff have one place of work but the organisation may need to move offices. In such a case there will be little choice but to insist upon a change to the contract.

If someone does not agree to a change in his or her contract of employment then the only way to achieve the change is to terminate the old contract and re-employ the worker on a new contract containing the new terms and conditions. The worker must be given the required notice to bring the old contract to an end. A worker who objects to the new terms and conditions may seek to claim a redundancy payment or claim unfair dismissal.

Obviously, wherever possible, organisations will want to reach agreement with their staff about changes to their employment. If this is not possible, some organisations may be prepared to make staff redundant, but many will want to avoid the costs of redundancy payments or having to pay compensation for unfair dismissal.

If it is not possible to obtain the agreement of all staff affected by a reorganisation, get legal advice and carry out the consultative procedure set out below before any change is imposed as a last resort.

# Claiming redundancy

By law an employee is dismissed because of redundancy if:

❏ the employer has ceased or intends to cease carrying on the activities for which the employee was employed; or

❏ the employer has ceased or intends to cease carrying on the activities in the place where the employee was employed; or

❏ the need for the employee to carry out particular work has ceased or diminished or is expected to do so; or

❏ the need to carry out particular work in the place where the employee was employed has ceased or diminished or is expected to do so.

## Change of place of work

Whether or not a move of offices or workplace involves redundancy will depend on the contract of employment. If it is specific about where the worker is employed, for example a particular address, then any move to a new address will involve an amendment to the contract. It will probably also mean that the employer has ceased or plans to cease to carry on the activities in the specific place 'where the employee was employed' and so will fall within the definition of a redundancy situation. By contrast, if the contract of employment contains a general description of where staff are employed (for example anywhere within a particular borough or a city) then any move within that borough or city will not involve an amendment to the contract, so there will be no redundancy. It is therefore advisable to allow some flexibility for a change in place of work within the contract of employment.

## Change in the work required

Whether or not a change to an employee's work involves a redundancy situation depends on whether another member of staff is going to be asked to do that work. There will only be a redundancy situation if the work the employee was doing under his or her contract of employment has ceased or diminished.

## Other changes

Other changes to terms and conditions are likely to be caused by a financial crisis. Whether this constitutes a redundancy situation depends on whether the organisation is scaling down its activities.

## Avoiding liability for a redundancy payment

An employee who is offered alternative employment on new terms and conditions, or a new place of work, or with a slightly different job will not receive a redundancy payment if he or she refuses an offer of suitable alternative employment.

# Unfair dismissal

The **Employment Protection (Consolidation) Act, 1978** states that employees are dismissed fairly if they are dismissed 'for some substantial reason which justifies dismissal'. The courts have ruled that a necessary reorganisation by the employer counts as a 'substantial reason'. Provided that there are good reasons for a reorganisation, an employee who has been offered reasonable alternative terms and conditions is unlikely to be able to claim unfair dismissal.

## Offering reasonable alternative terms of employment

Employees who consider they have a valid redundancy or unfair dismissal claim on reorganisation can take the complaint to an industrial tribunal. The tribunal will decide whether the offer of alternative employment was suitable and whether the refusal of the offer was unreasonable. Organisations should therefore take account of the effects on each employee of any revised terms and conditions, pay, job description or place of work.

Changes may need to be adapted to take account of staff members' particular circumstances to ensure that they are reasonable for those individuals.

## Procedure for reorganisation

In order to protect itself from claims for redundancy payments or unfair dismissal an organisation should ensure that:

❑ it has seriously considered the need for reorganisation so that it can be carefully and objectively justified;

❑ all the possible alternatives to reorganisation have been examined;

❑ all employees affected by the potential reorganisation have been consulted and justification for the proposed changes has been explained;

❑ views expressed by those employees or on their behalf have been considered, and suggested alternative strategies examined;

❑ the final decision has not been made until employees' views have been taken into account;

❑ even in the light of employees' views it is decided that there is no reasonable alternative available but to reorganise;

❑ in amending the terms of the contract of employment, it has considered each employee's needs;

❑ as far as resources allow, it has introduced flexibility and protection for employees who will be substantially affected by the changes.

If the reorganisation will involve substantial extra expense or substantial loss of income for an employee, changes could be phased in by, for example paying extra travel expenses to work for a limited period. Such payments will be subject to tax and NI in the usual way.

# Industrial tribunals

Employees who consider their employment rights have been infringed usually have the right to apply to an industrial tribunal. Amongst other matters, industrial tribunals can deal with the following:

❑ claims for unfair dismissal;

❑ claims for redundancy payments where these have been refused by the employer;

❑ complaints of race or sex discrimination in employment, and for equal pay;

❑ an application for employment particulars to be determined if they have not been given by the employer;

❑ an application for pay details to be determined if an itemised pay statement has not been given by the employer;

❑ a complaint that time off has not been given in line with the statutory requirements;

❑ a complaint that ante natal leave has not been provided;

❑ unauthorised deductions from wages.

Most complaints to an industrial tribunal must be made within three months. A tribunal has power to award compensation for unfair dismissal within a statutory limit. There is no longer any financial limit to compensation that can be awarded in cases involving sex or race discrimination.

No legal costs are awarded at an industrial tribunal. Employees may be represented by trades unions or receive financial assistance from the Equal Opportunities Commission or the Commission for Racial Equality. This can place small organisations at a disadvantage because they will have to pay for their own legal representation and cannot recover any of the legal costs even if successful. For this reason it is often less costly to settle a complaint to an industrial tribunal by making a payment to the employee even if the employer considers itself to have been entirely justified.

# MODEL CONTRACT OF EMPLOYMENT

The example employment contract given below includes all the information that must be included in the statement of employment particulars. If it is used it is therefore unnecessary to give employees a separate statement of employment particulars unless and until the details change.

**Terms given in this contract are generous, and increasing the legal minimum can involve extra expenditure. Organisations should therefore think carefully about financial implications, particularly in relation to sick pay, maternity pay and redundancy.**

Some matters are not covered in detail in the following contract, including grievance and disciplinary procedures, equal opportunities and redundancy policies. Details should be given in a separate staffing policy document, issued at the same time as the statement of conditions.

Reference is made in the contract to the need to obtain permission or documentation from someone within the organisation. Where this occurs the symbol (**) will appear. Decide who will provide this information and enter their job title. Clauses making reference to a fixed-term or temporary contract should be deleted if not applicable.

# CONTRACT OF EMPLOYMENT

This is a contract of employment which also sets out particulars of the terms and conditions on which *(name of organisation)* will employ you:

*(name of employee)*

The *(name of organisation)* issues, together with this statement of conditions of service, a staffing policy document as negotiated with *(name of trade union)*.

Your continuous employment (taking into account any service with a previous employer) began on:

This is a fixed-term contract which ends on the ... of ... 19.. (delete if not applicable)

This is a temporary contract expected to run until .:. of ...19.. (delete if not applicable)

1. **JOB TITLE:**

2. **REMUNERATION**
   Your grade runs from point * to point *    on the *(name of local authority)*'s spinal column scale. You will start at point __ £ __ *(plus £__ London Weighting allowance)*, making a total of £ __ per year.

   Salaries are paid monthly in arrears on the last day of each month, normally by bank transfer.

   Your salary grade will be reviewed if and when you receive increased responsibility.

   A salary increment will be paid annually on 1 April in addition to any general adjustment to scales, except if:

   (a) increments are being withheld from all staff because of the *(name of organisation)*'s financial position.

   (b) your salary is at the highest point on the scale, in which case transfer to another scale will automatically be considered and you will be notified of the outcome in writing.

   (c) disciplinary proceedings up to stage 3 (see attached staffing policy document) have been invoked for reasons of unsatisfactory work and/or conduct. If your work and/or conduct are agreed to have improved for three months from the issue of a written warning then the increment will become payable from that date unless clause 2(a) or 2(b) applies.

### 3. YOUR PLACE OF WORK

Your initial place of work is at (*enter address*).

(*name of organisation*) has other offices at (*enter addresses*) and you may be required to work at any of these offices from time to time.

You may also be required to work at any other place within (*enter area*) from time to time: you will be consulted about such requirement before it is put into effect.

### 4. HOURS OF WORK

The ordinary (*name of organisation*) office hours are 9.30 am to 5.30 pm Mondays to Fridays. A 35-hour working week is required from all full-time staff (this does not include time taken off for meals). Staff normally work the 'core' hours of 10.00 am to 4.00 pm, but the remaining are 'flexi' hours and can be varied by agreement with (**).

Time off will be allowed in lieu of extra hours worked, with the prior approval of (**). Such time off must be taken as soon as reasonably possible in consultation with (**).

### 5. ANNUAL HOLIDAYS AND HOLIDAY PAY

The normal annual holiday with pay is 25 working days in each leave year with two extra days being taken between Christmas and the New Year. This is in addition to public holidays. In addition one extra day's leave is given at the Easter, Spring, and Christmas public holidays. The leave year runs from 1 April to 31 March and the annual holiday should normally be taken within that year. In exceptional cases holiday not taken within the year may be taken before 30 September of the following leave year. Employees joining after 1 April will be granted leave pro rata in their first leave year. Five extra days will be added to the basic leave period after ten years' service.

Part-time employees are entitled to (a) the extra holiday given at Easter, Spring and Christmas public holidays provided these holidays fall on a day that the part-time employee normally works, (b) the basic 25 working days up to ten years service and 30 working days thereafter as for full-time staff, pro rata. Part-time employees are required to take a day's leave if their normal working day falls on the extra two days the office closes between Christmas and the New Year.

Employees whose contracts are terminated for any reason will not receive any pay for accrued holiday entitlement which has not been taken during the period of employment.

### 6. SICK PAY AND ABSENCE DUE TO ILLNESS

Notification of absence from work owing to illness or any other cause should be made on the first qualifying day of the spell of sickness (by phone or by letter) direct to (**). If absent for more than seven calendar days, a doctor's statement should be obtained and sent without delay to (**). On your return to work you must see (**) and complete an absence statement form.

In addition to the entitlements under the statutory provisions an employee is, in any 12 consecutive months, permitted:

| | |
|---|---|
| During the first year of service | 4 weeks' full pay and (after completing 4 months' service) eight weeks' half pay (less any statutory sick pay (SSP) or NI benefits) |
| During the second year of service | 8 weeks' full pay and 8 weeks' half pay (less any SSP or NI benefits) |
| During the third year of service | 16 weeks' full pay and 16 weeks' half pay (less any SSP or NI benefits) |
| During the fourth and fifth years of service | 20 weeks' full pay and 20 weeks' half pay (less any SSP or NI benefits) |
| After five years' service | 24 weeks' full pay and 24 weeks' half pay (less any SSP or NI benefits) |

### Qualification for entitlement

(a) Any previous period of sickness absence for which benefit was payable in the 12 months preceding the first pay of a new period of absence will be counted against the above limits for the latest absence.

(b) If, during a period of absence, an employee's service reaches a new qualification period, the duration of the payment will be based on the newly acquired qualification.

### Sickness during holiday

When sickness accruing payments under these provisions occurs during annual holidays, the employee will be credited with the equivalent number of days' holiday to be taken at a later date.

### Phased return

In cases where a doctor advises an employee to work less than normal hours per day for a period on return to work after sickness as a temporary measure, full pay will be given.

### Damages

Where absence results from an occurrence where damages may be recoverable from a Third Party (for example a road accident), employees must sign a form undertaking to repay sick pay up to the amount of any damages for loss of earnings received.

### Discretion

(a) Continuation of sick pay beyond the limits laid down may be made in cases which (**) sees as exceptional or deserving of particular compassionate treatment.

(b) At (**)'s discretion an employee or an intending employee may be examined by a doctor nominated and paid for by the (*name of organisation*).

(c) At (**)'s discretion an employee may be required to produce a medical certificate confirming the reasons for absence even on the first day of any future absence provided he or she has been notified in advance that such a requirement may be made.

## 7. EXTENDED LEAVE

The (*name of organisation*) will give favourable consideration to staff with families abroad to take up to one month's additional unpaid leave. In addition, up to two weeks' holiday entitlement may be carried over from the previous year for the purpose of such visits. Timing of this leave must be agreed as far as possible in advance, but in any case not less than one month in advance so that adequate arrangements for cover can be made.

## 8. MATERNITY LEAVE AND PAY

### a. Basic maternity leave

Provided she informs (**) in writing at least three weeks before her absence, or as soon as reasonably practicable thereafter, any female member of staff shall have the right to maternity leave as follows:

(i) the leave may begin at any time after the beginning of the eleventh week before the expected week of childbirth;

(ii) the staff member may choose when the leave is to begin, but if not already started, it will begin automatically on the day the child is born or on any day the staff member is absent wholly or partly because of pregnancy after the beginning of the sixth week before the expected week of childbirth, whichever occurs first;

(iii) the leave will be for 14 weeks or until the child is born, whichever is the later;

(iv) if the staff member is prohibited from returning to work under legislation, the leave will last until the prohibition ends;

(v) the contract of employment continues during the basic maternity leave period; there is no right to contractual pay, but the staff member will receive any pay due under statute (for example statutory maternity pay) to which she is entitled;

(vi)    the staff member has the right to return to her previous post at the end of her maternity leave.

**b. Maternity pay: qualification**
A member of staff who is absent from work because of pregnancy or confinement is entitled to maternity pay (as set out below) if:

(i)    she continues to be employed by the (*name of organisation*) (whether or not she is at work) until 11 weeks before the expected week of confinement;

(ii)    she has at least 26 weeks' continuous service by the fifteenth week before the baby is due;

(iii)    she informs (\*\*) in writing, three weeks beforehand, or as soon as reasonably practicable thereafter, that she wants her SMP to start; and

(iv)    she produces a maternity certificate MAT B1 stating the expected week of confinement.

**c. Maternity pay will be payable as follows**
(i)    six weeks on full pay including any statutory maternity pay (SMP) or maternity allowance (MA). Providing the maternity allowance is claimed and paid to the (*name of organisation*), then the amount involved will be reimbursed as a tax free payment, thus restoring the salary to the full rate. The Benefits Agency Giro cheque received should be sent to (\*\*) at the end of the first six week period or any convenient time during this period.

(ii)    a further six weeks on half pay, including any statutory maternity pay (SMP) or maternity allowance (MA).

(iii)    a final six weeks on half pay including any statutory maternity pay, less the amount of any maternity allowance. The (*name of organisation*) expects that the pregnant member of staff who has no intention of returning after confinement will claim only her statutory entitlement during this final six weeks.

**d. Extended maternity leave**
Provided she complies with conditions b(i)-(iv) above, and provided she informs (\*\*) in writing at least 21 days before her absence, or as soon as reasonably practicable thereafter, that she intends to return to her previous post, a member of staff will have the right to a total of 52 weeks' leave and to return to her previous post at any time within 52 weeks of the date of childbirth. A request to return on a part-time basis will be viewed sympathetically subject to the requirements of the post. At least 21 days before she proposes to return to work she must inform the (*name of organisation*) of her intention. The (*name of organisation*) may delay her return for up to four weeks on giving specified reasons, and she may delay it for the same period. Failure by the employee to comply with the requirements will lose her the right of return to work.

**e.** A member of staff will be allowed reasonable time off with full pay for attendance at ante and post natal clinics and this will not count against sick leave entitlement.

**f.** If a post is declared redundant whilst the occupant of the post is absent on maternity leave she will be entitled to receive redundancy pay. This will be payable on the date she would have returned to work.

## 9. PARENTAL/ADOPTION LEAVE
Subject to a qualifying period of nine months' service, a member of staff who is the parent or prospective parent of a newly born or newly adopted child is entitled to up to ten days' paid childcare leave, providing that she or he resumes work and continues to be employed by the (*name of organisation*) following the period of childcare leave, and providing that the childcare leave is taken within three months either side of the date of birth or adoption of the child.

## 10. CHILDCARE LEAVE
Parents and adoptive parents are entitled to up to ten days' paid leave per year to care for children if they are sick.

## 11. DEPENDANTS LEAVE

Staff are entitled to up to five days' per year to care for a sick dependant other than a child.

## 12. COMPASSIONATE LEAVE

The (name of organisation) will give sympathetic consideration to any hardship or difficulty which might arise and necessitate a request for absence from work on compassionate grounds.

Such difficulties might include bereavement, religious holidays or illness of a close or dependent relative. Each request for compassionate leave will be considered on its merits without recourse to any precedent, and leave may be granted with or without pay, or on reduced pay. Requests for compassionate leave should be made to (**).

## 13. PENSIONS AND RETIREMENT

Employees shall be entitled to join the (name of organisation)'s pension scheme with (enter name of scheme) when they have completed six months' service unless they give express notice in writing before the expiry of six months that they do not wish to do so. The (name of organisation) and employees are each required to contribute to the (enter name of scheme).

A contracting out certificate under the Social Security Act, 1975 is/is not in force in respect of this employment.

Existing contracts of employment will normally end on employees reaching the age of 65. The (name of organisation) may, in exceptional circumstances, by agreement with the employees concerned, extend service beyond the relevant age for one year or any less period, and for such further periods of not more than one year at a time as the (name of organisation) may deem expedient.

## 14. TERMINATION OF EMPLOYMENT

(a) The (name of organisation) will give at least four weeks' notice in writing to all members of staff and at least eight weeks' notice in writing to those who have served for more than two years and less than nine years.

Thereafter, the (name of organisation) will give notice in writing as follows:
    9 weeks' notice after 9 years' service
    10 weeks' notice after 10 years' service
    11 weeks' notice after 11 years' service
    12 weeks' notice after 12 years' service

The maximum period of notice given will be 12 weeks.

(b) An employee is required to give at least four weeks' notice in writing. For some senior appointments a longer period may be specified in the letter of appointment.

## 15. TRADE UNION

The (name of organisation) has recognised (enter name of union) as the sole representative body for staff for the purposes set out in the Procedural Agreement, a copy of which may be obtained from (**). You are recommended to join (enter name of union). As a result of negotiations with (enter name of union), you may be asked from time to time to accept changes in your conditions of service.

## 16. TIME OFF FOR PUBLIC DUTIES

The (name of organisation) will allow reasonable time off for employees to carry out:

(a) Trade union duties

  (i)    to officers of such a union in order to carry out industrial relations duties. Time off is also allowed for training for these duties, provided such training is approved by the Trades Union Congress or by the independent trade union of which the member of staff is an officer. The (name of organisation) will pay for time spent on these activities.

(ii)   to any member of staff who is a member of such a union in order to take part in its union activities, excluding industrial action. The *(name of organisation)* will not pay for time off spent on these activities except as more fully set out in the Procedural Agreement.

(b) Public duties

The *(name of organisation)* will permit such time off work to be taken for public duties as is set out under the Employment Protection (Consolidation) Act, 1978 and in addition as is reasonable. Payment will be in accordance with the Act and in addition at the discretion of *(name of organisation)*. Part-time employees will also be eligible at the discretion of the *(name of organisation)*.

This will apply to a member of staff who is:

(i)    a justice of the peace, a member of a local authority or member of a statutory tribunal;

(ii)   a member of a regional health authority, district health authority or community health council;

(iii)  a member of the managing or governing body of an educational establishment maintained by a local education authority;

(iv)   a member of a water authority;

(v)    a member of any other body at the discretion of (**);

(vi)   a member of an interpreters service, or any other service at the discretion of (**).

Employees are required to claim attendance allowances/loss of earnings/expenses and to remit them to *(name of organisation)*, excluding travelling and subsistence costs, to set against salary costs.

(c) Safety representatives

People appointed as safety representatives to carry out their functions as such, including obtaining the necessary training to carry out such functions effectively.

## 17. SUBSISTENCE AND TRAVELLING EXPENSES

These are paid when employees are away from their normal place of work on duty. The current scale of allowances can be obtained from (**). The allowances may be altered at the discretion of *(name of organisation)* annually and may be either increased or decreased.

## 18. REMOVAL

Removal expenses on taking up a post will not normally be payable except in special circumstances to be agreed by negotiation. Staff shall be entitled to one day's paid leave for removal; up to one day a year.

## 19. DISCIPLINARY PROCEDURES

Details of the disciplinary procedures are given in the staffing policy document which accompanies this statement.

## 20. GRIEVANCES

In the event of the member of staff having any grievance, they should complain to (**). A complaint can be made either in writing or by speaking to the person concerned personally. Details of the procedures under which the grievance will be dealt with are given in the staffing policy document which accompanies this statement.

## 21. EQUAL OPPORTUNITY EMPLOYERS

*(name of organisation)* is an equal opportunity employer. All employees shall be afforded equal opportunities in the employment context, irrespective of their nationality, ethnic or national origin, age, colour, creed, disability, gender, marital status, HIV status, race, or sexual orientation. A copy of the *(name of organisation)*'s Equal Opportunities Policy may be obtained from (**). The Equal Opportunities Policy contains details of a special grievance procedure that staff may use where they consider that they

have been discriminated against or harassed in breach of the Equal Opportunities Policy.

It is a term of the contract of employment that the employee will comply with the Equal Opportunities Policy of the employer as amended from time to time, and a breach of that Policy by discrimination or harassment will amount to gross misconduct in the circumstances set out in the Equal Opportunities Policy and may lead to dismissal.

22. **RELIEF ALLOWANCES**
In certain circumstances staff may be entitled to the payment of an allowance for undertaking additional work or responsibility. A paper setting out this policy may be obtained from (**).

23. **REDUNDANCY**
The *(name of organisation)* has a redundancy agreement, a copy of which may be obtained from (**).

24. **FIXED-TERM CONTRACT** (delete as appropriate)
This is a fixed-term contract of two years or more and the employee hereby agrees that on the expiry of the term without its being renewed, a claim for unfair dismissal or redundancy payment is excluded under the provisions of the Employment Protection (Consolidation) Act, 1978, Section 142.

**SIGNED:**     (Employee)

**SIGNED:**     (For *(name of organisation)*)

**DATED:**

# Booklist

ACAS codes of practice:

1: **Disciplinary practice and procedures in employment**, HMSO, £1.25

2: **Disclosure of information to trade union officials for collective bargaining purposes**, HMSO, 45p

3: **Time off for trade union duties and activities**, HMSO, £2.50

**Accountancy services for voluntary organisations**, National Council for Voluntary Organisations (1992), £6.00

**Code of good practice on the employment of disabled people**, Employment Service (1993), free

**Contributions Agency leaflets** (free):
  **A guide to maternity benefits** (NI17A) (6/94)
  **National Insurance for employees** (CA01) (2/94)
  **Quick guide to NI contributions Class 1A, SSP and SMP contributions** (CA27) (4/94)
  **Statutory Maternity Pay manual for employers** (CA29) (6/94)
  **Statutory Sick Pay: check your rights** (NI244) (6/94)
  **Statutory Sick Pay manual for employers** (NI270) (4/93; supplement 4/94)
  **Statutory Sick Pay small employers' relief** (CA33) (4/94)
  **Voluntary and part-time workers** (FB26) (6/94)

**The employment handbook: a good practice guide for housing coops**, *Tony Bloor, Genevieve Macklin and Peter Lush*, CATCH, £17.50

**Employer's further guide to Pay As Your Earn** (IRP7), Inland Revenue (1994), free

**Employment law: an adviser's handbook**, Legal Action Group (1994), £17.50

**Equal opportunities for lesbians and gay men: guidelines to good practice in employment**, Lesbian and Gay Employment Rights (1993), £2.50

**Equal opportunity in employment: a guide for employers**, Commission for Racial Equality (1990), free

**Example form of a written statement of employment particulars** (PL700), Employment Department (1994), free

**Just About Managing?**, *Sandy Adirondack*, London Voluntary Service Council (1992), £12.45

**A practical guide to PAYE for charities**, *Kate Sayer*, Directory of Social Change (1994), £9.95

**We're counting on equality: monitoring equal opportunities in the workplace in relation to sex, race, disability, sexuality, HIV/AIDS and age**, City Centre (1993), £12.50

# Chapter 5:
# Health and safety

The **Health and Safety at Work Act, 1974** (HASW) provides a comprehensive framework for health and safety in the workplace. The Act not only covers the health and safety of employees but also extends to others using an organisation's premises and equipment, for example members of the public, trainees, volunteers and committee members.

*The Government has accepted the Charities and Voluntary Organisations Deregulation Task Force's recommendation that clarification is needed about which health and safety regulations apply to premises where a significant amount of the activity is conducted by volunteers, such as village halls and hostels, and that the Health and Safety Executive should produce guidance to enable voluntary organisations to understand what is required in the way of assessment.*

Under HASW, regulations have been introduced for six specific areas:

- the management of health and safety;
- health, safety and welfare in the workplace;
- manual handling, for example lifting;
- display screens;
- provision and use of work equipment;
- personal protective equipment.

The Health and Safety Executive has published codes of practice and guidance recommending how the regulations should be implemented.

This chapter describes the general duties placed on employers under HASW and looks at the six regulations in more detail. It then considers other legislation relating to health and safety that affects voluntary organisations. For further details of all health and safety legislation see *Essentials of health and safety at work.*

## General duties

Organisations have a number of different responsibilities under HASW.

### Duties to employees

Organisations which employ staff owe a duty 'so far as reasonably practicable' to ensure the health, safety and welfare at work of all their staff.

This duty includes:

- providing and maintaining machinery, equipment, appliances and systems of work that are safe and without risks to health;

- having arrangements for ensuring the safety and absence of risk to health from use, handling, storage and transport of any articles and substances;

- providing information, instruction, training and supervision as necessary to ensure the health and safety of staff;

- maintaining any place of work in a condition that is safe and without risk to health;

- maintaining the access to and exit from the workplace so that it is safe and without risk to health;

- providing and maintaining a working environment that is safe and without risk to health and adequate as regards arrangements for welfare.

### 'Reasonably practicable'

The obligations on employers do not extend to guaranteeing total protection against accidents because this would be impossible. Essentially employers have to balance the needs of their organisation to achieve their objectives against the risks staff face and measures that can be taken to reduce or avoid the risks.

### Duties to non-employees

Any organisation which employs staff also has a duty to run the organisation and its activities in such a way as to ensure 'so far as reasonably practicable' that people who are not employees but who might be affected by its activities are not exposed to health or safety risks.

This duty will be owed to trainees, volunteers, committee members, consultants, users and members of the public.

### Duties to users of premises

All organisations with control over premises or access to or exit from premises have a responsibility to anyone using those premises for work or as a place where they use machinery, equipment, appliances, articles or substances provided for their use. Reasonable measures must be taken to ensure 'so far as reasonably practicable' that the premises, their access and exit, together with machinery, equipment, appliances, articles or substances used are safe and without risk to health. Owners of premises and, in most cases tenants under the terms of the lease, have responsibility for repairs and for the health and safety of people using the premises. Organisations with a licence for their premises should clarify their responsibilities for health and safety (see chapter 6).

This duty will also be owed to trainees, volunteers, committee members and consultants who use the premises, to anyone sharing the premises and, in some cases, to anyone hiring the premises.

## Other responsibilities placed on employers

### Health and safety policy

HASW requires that employers have a written health and safety policy and procedures for putting the policy into practice. The policy and procedures must be reviewed and revised regularly. All staff must be informed of the policy and procedures and of any revisions.

### Safety representatives

Any recognised trade union may appoint safety representatives. Wherever possible, the representatives must have worked for the organisation for at least two years or have had at least two years' experience in similar work.

HASW requires that employers consult safety representatives when drawing up their health and safety policies to ensure cooperation between the organisation and staff in developing good health and safety practice and monitoring the effectiveness of health and safety measures.

Safety representatives have the following responsibilities:

❏ to investigate potential hazards and dangers and examine the causes of accidents;

❏ to investigate complaints by staff relating to health, safety or welfare;

❏ to submit proposals and suggestions to the employer on any matters relating to health and safety at work and in particular about steps to be taken relating to complaints, hazards and accidents;

❏ to carry out inspections of the workplace;

❏ to represent employees in dealings with health and safety inspectors;

❏ to receive information from inspectors about matters identified by them during inspections;

❏ to attend meetings of safety committees where these have been set up (see below).

An employer must allow safety representatives to take reasonable time off with pay to carry out their responsibilities and for health and safety training. For further details see *Safety representatives and safety committees.*

Employers must allow safety representatives to inspect the workplace or any part of it:

❏ at least once every three months;

❏ where there has been any substantial change in the conditions of work, for example when new machinery has been introduced, or new guidance has been issued by the Health and Safety Commission relating to that type of work or workplace;

❏ where there has been a serious accident, a dangerous occurrence or a notifiable disease.

Before carrying out the inspection, the safety representative must give the employer reasonable notice. The employer must provide reasonable assistance to the safety representative for carrying out the inspection, including facilities for independent investigation and private discussion with employees.

An employer must also allow the safety representative to inspect and take copies of any documentation relating to health and safety. There are exceptions which include:

❏ an employee's health records where the employee can be identified;

❏ information which the law prohibits from being disclosed (for example under the Data Protection Act, 1984, see chapter 9);

❏ information relating to any individual unless he or she has consented;

❏ other information which would cause 'substantial injury ' to the employer's business.

## Safety committees

Any two safety representatives can require an employer to set up a safety committee whose function is to review measures taken to ensure the health and safety of staff. The employer must consult the safety representatives and recognised trades unions when setting up the committee and inform all staff of the names of committee members. The committee must be set up within three months of the request being made.

## Paying for health and safety measures

An employer is prohibited from charging staff for any health and safety measures, for example protective equipment or training.

## Responsibilities on staff

HASW imposes a duty on each member of staff to take reasonable care for their own health and safety and that of any person who may be affected by anything they do or fail to do. Staff are also placed under an obligation to cooperate as far as necessary to enable employers to comply with their responsibilities.

# Enforcement

The Health and Safety Executive, through its inspectors, and local authority environmental health officers, are responsible for enforcing the responsibilities under HASW. They have wide powers to enter and inspect premises, test equipment, take measurements, photographs and samples and, if necessary, remove equipment for testing or preserving. They can also require staff or committee members to answer questions on health and safety matters.

If an organisation is not complying with the law, inspectors can serve an 'improvement notice' or a 'prohibition notice' or they can prosecute the organisation. An improvement notice sets out the steps the organisation must take, with a timescale, to comply with the law. A prohibition notice will be served only if there is an immediate danger; it can require the organisation to stop one or all of its activities until health and safety measures are implemented. Failure to comply with either type of notice is a criminal offence.

In addition, the inspector can prosecute an organisation for failing to carry out its responsibilities. This is likely to happen only if an accident occurs in which someone is seriously injured or killed, or if an organisation:

❏ has failed to address health and safety issues;

❏ is considered to be unwilling to implement health and safety measures or is believed to be deliberately delaying them;

❏ has ignored obvious and immediate risks.

Any person who is injured because of a failure by an organisation to comply with health and safety law will be able to make a claim for compensation. An organisation must have insurance to cover such claims. Those employing staff must have employers' liability insurance. Public liability insurance should also be taken out to cover claims by others, including volunteers, trainees and consultants (see chapter 7 for further details about insurance).

# Responsibilities of committee members and staff

Committee members of all voluntary organisations must ensure that the organisation complies with health and safety at work legislation. HASW states that where an organisation has failed to comply with the law and has committed an offence, then that offence has also been committed by any individual who has failed in his or her individual responsibilities. This will *always* include committee members, and in many organisations will also include senior staff who have been given health and safety responsibilities.

Committee members and senior staff should therefore be aware that if they do not individually ensure that the organisation carries out its responsibilities, they could be committing a criminal offence and could be prosecuted and fined. The committee cannot rely on staff to ensure their own health and safety nor on trades union safety representatives to alert them to dangers. The legal responsibility rests with the committee.

# The management of health and safety at work

The **Management of Health and Safety at Work Regulations, 1992** are the first in the set of six regulations dealing in more detail with the way in which organisations should comply with their responsibilities under HASW.

The regulations deal with the following matters. Full details can be found in *Management of health and safety: approved code of practice.*

## Risk assessment

The regulations require that every employer must:

❑ make an assessment of risks to the health and safety of employees to which they are exposed whilst at work;

❑ make an assessment of risks to the health and safety of others (for example volunteers, committee members, consultants and members of the public) arising from the organisation's activities;

❑ review and revise the assessment whenever necessary.

The regulations require a systematic examination of an organisation's activities. This must involve identifying hazards arising from activities (whether from the type of work or other factors, for example the condition of the premises) and then evaluating the extent of the risks, taking into account any precautions already taken.

Employers should also read health and safety publications.

There should be regular reviews of the assessment of risk as well as a continual process of monitoring health and safety. If a new area of work is developed, or an organisation moves into new premises or buys new equipment, further risk assessments will be needed.

There are no fixed rules on how a risk assessment should be undertaken. In small organisations with few hazards, the assessment could be carried out by a non-specialist staff or committee member. In larger organisations or where there are special hazards, an overall assessment could be carried out by a non-specialist followed by a specialist assessment of particularly hazardous activities. In organisations with several workplaces, some risks will be common and can be included within an overall assessment, but each site and the equipment within it will need to be assessed separately.

It is important that the risk assessment takes account of what *actually* happens in the workplace rather than what is *supposed* to happen. If staff ignore safety or other instructions, for example on the use of equipment, the risk that results should be included within the risk assessment and a decision made on what action to take.

Particular attention should be paid to those who may

be especially at risk, for example inexperienced or new staff or volunteers, people with disabilities, and those who have difficulty understanding written or spoken English.

The risk assessment should take account both of existing precautionary measures and of the extent to which they are actually being used and are effective.

Organisations with five or more staff must produce a record of the significant findings of the assessment. It is good practice for all organisations to do so. The record should include:

❑ significant hazards identified;

❑ existing control measures and the extent to which they control, minimise or eliminate the risks;

❑ the people who are at risk.

## Preventative and protective measures

The regulations require that every employer must have arrangements in place for effective planning, organisation, control, monitoring and review of preventative and protective measures and, where there are five or more employees, must record these arrangements in writing.

The Health and Safety Commission suggests that:

❑ it is best to avoid risk altogether if possible;

❑ risks should be combatted at source rather than mitigated, for example it is better to design an item so there is no risk rather than put up a warning notice;

❑ wherever possible work should be adapted to the individual, for example design of workplaces, choice of work equipment and methods of work;

❑ organisations should take advantage of technological and technical progress which often enables work to be done more safely;

❑ risk prevention measures need to be part of a coherent policy and approach and aim to minimise progressively risks that cannot be prevented or avoided altogether;

❑ priority should be given to those measures that affect the whole workplace and so yield the greatest benefit;

❑ workers, including trainees and volunteers, must understand what they need to do;

❏ the avoidance, prevention and reduction of risk needs to be an accepted part of the approach and attitude at all levels of the organisation, ie there needs to be a 'health and safety culture'.

## Health surveillance

Apart from the responsibilities for health surveillance under specific regulations, for example asbestos and other dangerous substances, this regulation requires all employers to introduce health surveillance where it is needed. The Health and Safety Commission recommends it is introduced where the risk assessment shows that:

❏ there is an identifiable disease or some health condition relating to the work carried out;

❏ techniques are available to detect indications of the disease or condition;

❏ there is a reasonable likelihood that the disease or condition may arise in the work environment;

❏ surveillance will improve protection for the staff against the disease or condition.

## Getting advice

The regulations require that employers appoint at least one competent person to help them carry out the risk assessment and take necessary preventative and protective measures. The assessor, who may be a member of staff, must have appropriate training, experience and knowledge and must be given all the necessary information including details of anyone working on short-term contracts.

## Emergency procedures

All employers must have appropriate procedures to follow in the event of serious and imminent danger to people at work, and nominate enough competent staff to implement the procedures to evacuate premises in an emergency.

The procedures must ensure that all members of staff exposed to serious and imminent danger are informed of the nature of the hazard and of the steps to be taken to protect them. They must also enable people to stop work and leave the danger area if exposed, and not to return until it is safe to do so.

The risk assessment should identify the likely events that will lead to the implementation of emergency procedures, for example fire, bomb alert or building collapse.

The procedures should set out the limits of any steps required of employees in an emergency, for example when to fight a fire and when to evacuate, whether to notify emergency services, shut down machinery or secure essential documents, and how the emergency procedures will be activated.

## Information to staff

The regulations require that employers provide all staff with understandable and relevant information on risks identified, preventative and protective measures, emergency procedures and the names of those responsible for evacuation. Employees must also be told about risks identified by any other employers using the same workplace.

Special consideration should be given to the needs of staff who have difficulties with communicating in written or spoken English, for example by producing information in different languages, braille or on tape.

## Cooperation between employers

If two or more employers share a workplace, they must cooperate on health and safety matters. Each employer must provide information on the risks to the other employers' staff arising from the notifying employer's activities. Wherever possible, employers must coordinate their health and safety measures. Cooperation may involve carrying out a joint risk assessment for the whole premises as well as a more limited assessment for each employer's activities. The Health and Safety Commission recommends that either one employer, for example the owner or tenant, takes responsibility for the premises, or that a health and safety coordinator is jointly appointed.

## Visiting employees

Employers have a responsibility to visiting employees and self-employed people working within the organisation or on its premises. They must notify self-employed people and the employer of anyone working on their premises of any health and safety risks and of the precautionary measures taken. They must also provide instructions and understandable information about any risks to the self-employed person or visiting employee.

Examples of situations where this rule will apply include cleaning and service contracts, the employment of agency staff and consultants.

## Capabilities and training of staff

Employers must ensure that the capabilities of staff regarding health and safety are taken into account when allocating work, and that adequate health and safety training is provided both when staff are recruited and when they are exposed to any new or increased risks. Training should be repeated periodically and take place during working hours.

## Temporary workers

Anyone employed on a temporary fixed-term contract (of whatever length) must be given understandable information on any special qualifications or skills required to carry out work safely and any necessary health surveillance before they begin work. The same information must be provided to agency staff.

# Workplace health, safety and welfare

The **Workplace (Health, Safety and Welfare) Regulations, 1992** apply to any workplaces used for the first time after 31 December 1992. From 1 January 1996 the regulations will apply to all workplaces. Until that date, the **Office, Shops and Railway Premises Act, 1963** still applies to workplaces used before 1 January 1993. As the new regulations have similar requirements to the 1963 Act they are described here.

Full details of the regulations can be found in the *Workplace (health, safety and welfare): approved code of practice.*

## Premises and equipment

Premises and equipment must be kept in a good state of repair, in proper working order and must be properly maintained. Defects should be rectified immediately or steps taken to protect anyone who might be at risk, for example by preventing access. Where a defect makes equipment unsuitable for use but causes no danger it can be taken out of service until repaired. There should be a suitable servicing and maintenance system which identifies potentially dangerous defects and ensures they are remedied. A record should be kept of defects which arise and maintenance carried out so that monitoring can take place.

## Ventilation

There must be effective and suitable provision for ventilation. This may simply involve windows that open. Any air conditioning or mechanical ventilation provided must be cleaned, tested, maintained and serviced, and must operate effectively. Recycled air must be filtered.

## Temperature

A reasonable temperature must be maintained in the workplace. It must be neither too hot nor too cold. The employer must provide a sufficient number of thermometers to enable people to establish the temperature inside any workplace. Unless there are special reasons for lower temperatures the minimum acceptable temperature is 16° C in most cases.

## Lighting

Every workplace must have suitable and sufficient lighting. As far as practicable, this should be natural lighting. Emergency lighting must also be provided if anyone working in any part of the premises would be in danger if normal lighting was defective. The light should be sufficient for people to work and move safely around without eye strain. Stairs should be well lit and without shadows on treads. Where necessary, lighting should be provided to individual workstations and at places of particular danger. Windows and sky lights should be cleaned regularly if possible.

## Cleanliness and rubbish disposal

Workplaces, furniture and fittings must be kept clean and there should be additional cleaning if there is a spillage or soiling. Surfaces of floors, walls and ceilings should be capable of being kept clean. Rubbish should not be allowed to accumulate except in rubbish receptacles. The standard of cleanliness should be adapted according to the workplace or area use.

## Workspace

Workrooms should have enough space to enable staff to get to and from workspaces and move within the room easily and safely. This will depend on how much space is taken by furniture and fittings and on the layout. A worker should normally have an absolute minimum of 11 cubic metres of space, discounting any height above three metres. This minimum area may be insufficient if a high percentage of this space is taken by furniture.

## Workstation design

A workstation is the place where an individual works, for example a desk, chair, computer, immediate shelving and drawers. It must be suitable for the individual for whom it is provided as well as for the work he or she is required to do. It should be protected from the weather and be designed so that a person can leave it quickly in an emergency. It should also be designed to ensure that an individual will not slip or fall. A suitable seat and footrest should be provided where necessary. Work equipment and materials should be within easy reach without undue bending or stretching. The workstation should take account of the specific needs of any member of staff with a disability.

## Floors and internal traffic routes

These must be suitable for their purpose without any dangerous holes or slopes, or slippery or uneven surfaces. Floors should have drainage where necessary. Handrails and guards should be provided on all staircases except where they would obstruct a traffic route.

## Preventing people and objects from falling

Suitable and effective measures should be taken to prevent anyone being injured through falling or by being hit by a falling object. Any area where there is a risk should be clearly indicated. Wherever possible any place where someone could fall and injure themselves should have fencing.

Objects should be safely stored and stacked so as not to cause injury by falling on someone. Storage units should be strong and stable enough for their task and not be overfilled. The height of stacking should be limited and checks made on the safety of stored objects.

## Windows

All windows and other transparent areas should be made from material which does not cause danger, for example making them robust enough not to break or using glass which does not shatter. Transparent surfaces should be marked so that they are apparent.

Windows, skylights and ventilators should be easily reachable so that they can be safely opened and closed. There should be controls so that people cannot fall out of any window.

It should be possible to clean windows and skylights safely, for example through having pivoting windows or using ladders.

## Vehicular traffic

Steps should be taken to ensure that pedestrians are not put in danger from vehicles. Traffic routes for pedestrians and vehicles should be clearly marked, and if possible separated. Particular attention should be paid to the safety of people with visual disabilities or in wheelchairs.

## Doors and gates

These should be suitably constructed. Sliding doors should have a device to prevent them from being derailed, and upward opening doors a device to prevent them falling back. Powered doors must have features preventing them from trapping anyone and enabling them to be overridden if power fails. It should be possible to see through doors that open both ways.

## WCs

There must be suitable WCs which are adequately ventilated and lit and kept clean and tidy. Separate facilities should be provided for men and women unless each WC is in a separate room with a lockable door. There should be at least one women-only WC for every 25 women and one men-only WC for every 25 men.

## Washing facilities

Suitable and sufficient washing facilities must be provided if they are required by the nature of the work or for health reasons. They should also be provided in the immediate vicinity of each WC and changing area. There must be hot and cold or warm water, soap and towels. The rooms must be ventilated and properly lit and kept clean and tidy. Separate facilities should be provided for men and women unless they are provided in a room with a lockable door and the facilities in each room are intended to be used by one person at a time.

## Drinking water

There must be regularly accessible and marked places where drinking water can be obtained. Cups or drinking vessels should be provided unless the water comes in a jet.

## Storage and changing facilities

Where staff need to change for work secure storage facilities for home and work clothes must be provided — two areas if it is necessary to keep the two types of clothes separate for hygiene or health reasons. They should include facilities for drying clothing.

If changing requires privacy, there should be separate facilities for men and women.

## Rest and eating facilities

Workplaces should have suitable rest facilities at

convenient places. If food cannot be eaten in the workplace, separate eating facilities should be provided. There must be suitable arrangements to protect non-smokers from discomfort caused by tobacco smoke. Facilities should also be provided to enable pregnant women and nursing mothers to rest.

# Personal protective equipment

Full details of the **Personal Protective Equipment at Work Regulations, 1992** can be found in the *Personal protective equipment at work regulations 1992: guidance on regulations*. The regulations do not apply if there are more specific regulations dealing with particular activities, for example in the woodworking industry there are regulations which deal with the use of cutting machinery.

Personal equipment and clothing must be provided to protect staff against the weather and risks to their health and safety, unless risks are controlled by other equally effective means.

The regulations include, for example the provision of helmets, gloves, rainwear, high visibility jackets, aprons, eye protectors, life-jackets and safety harnesses.

Protective equipment and clothing must:

❑ be appropriate for the risks involved and the place where the risks may occur;

❑ take account of the practicality of its use and the state of health of the person using it;

❑ be capable of fitting the wearer correctly;

❑ be effective in preventing or controlling the risks involved.

The equipment provided must be readily available.

Employers must carry out an assessment of the suitability of protective equipment before they supply it and if more than one piece of personal protective equipment is required, employers must ensure the equipment is compatible.

Employers must also ensure that equipment is well maintained, in good working order, replaced when necessary and that there are storage facilities for equipment not in use.

Employers must provide staff with clear information, instruction and training to enable them to know:

❑ the risks which the equipment will avoid or limit;

❑ the purpose of the equipment and how to use it;

❑ steps the employee should take to maintain the equipment properly.

Employers must take reasonable steps to ensure that protective equipment is used. In turn, employees must use the protective equipment and report defects in or loss of the equipment.

# Work equipment

Details of the Provision and Use of Work Equipment Regulations, 1992 can be found in the approved code of practice.

The general requirements of the regulations are now in force, whilst more specific requirements relating to machinery will not apply to machinery in use before 1 January 1993 until 1 January 1997. The regulations apply immediately to any equipment first used on or after 1 January 1993.

The regulations impose a duty both on an employer and on any organisation controlling premises where people work and where machinery is used. An organisation which shares its premises and equipment will owe a duty to the employees of those sharing the premises as well as to its own staff.

## Suitability and maintenance of equipment

Employers must ensure that work equipment is suitable for the purpose for which it is used. When selecting equipment, they must take into account working conditions, existing risks and any additional risk posed by the equipment.

Employers must also ensure that equipment is in good repair, and its maintenance should be recorded in a log book.

## Specific risks

If any equipment is likely to involve a specific risk to health or safety, the employer must ensure that its use is restricted to specifically authorised staff.

## Information and instruction

Employers must ensure that all those who use work equipment, and their managers, have adequate understandable health and safety information and, where appropriate, written instructions on its use. Instructions should include details of:

❑ how the equipment should be used;

❑ possible problems and the action to be taken if they occur, for example likely faults;

❑ comments from those with experience of using the equipment.

## Training

Employers must ensure that everyone using equipment, together with their managers, has received adequate health and safety training which includes:

❑ methods of using the equipment;

❑ possible risks from its use;

❑ precautions to be taken.

## Other requirements

More specific requirements apply to machinery covering:

❑ dangerous parts of machinery;

❑ protection against specific hazards;

❑ high or very low temperatures;

❑ controls and control systems including emergency stop controls;

❑ isolation from sources of energy;

❑ stability;

❑ lighting;

❑ maintenance operations;

❑ markings;

❑ warnings.

Further details can be found in the code of practice.

# Manual handling

Full details of the **Manual Handling Operations Regulations, 1992**[1] can be found in the *Manual handling operations regulations: guidance on regulations.*

## General duties on employers

Employers should, wherever possible, avoid the need for staff to undertake manual handling which involves a risk of injury. If a task cannot be avoided,

employers must assess the risks involved against a series of factors set out in the regulations. These include:

❑ tasks involved in the handling;

❑ type of load;

❑ working environment;

❑ individual capability;

❑ other factors.

The guidance provides a model checklist that can be used for making the assessment.

# Display screen equipment

Full details of the **Health and Safety (Display Screen Equipment) Regulations, 1992** can be found in the *Health and safety (display screen regulations), 1992: guidance on regulations.* This document provides useful guidance on safe methods of using display screens including diagrams of seating arrangements.

The regulations impose duties on employers only in relation to employees who use display screen equipment as a significant part of their normal work. The Code of Practice gives examples of staff who are likely to be included and excluded by the regulations.

## Analysis of workstations

Employers must carry out a thorough analysis of workstations to assess the health and safety risks. The assessment must be updated as often as necessary. Risks that are identified must be reduced to the lowest extent reasonably practicable.

## Requirements for workstations

All workstations established on or after 1 January 1993 must meet the requirements set out in the schedule to the regulations. Workstations in use before 1 January 1993 must comply with these requirements by 1 January 1996.

The requirements relate to:

❑ the display screen, for example size and legibility of characters, brightness and contrast;

❑ the keyboard, for example whether it can be tilted, spacing, legibility;

❑ the work desk, for example it should be non-reflective with a document holder;

---

[1] See note at beginning of chapter about Task Force recommendations

❏ the work chair, for example adjustability, stability and height (a footrest should be supplied if requested);

❏ the environment, for example space, lighting, glare, noise, heat, radiation and humidity;

❏ the interface between computer and worker, for example ease of use and suitability of software.

## Daily work routine for users

Employers must plan the work routine of staff using display screens to ensure that there are periodic breaks according to the nature and demands of the job.

## Eyesight tests

Any user of display screen equipment can request an eyesight test at the employer's expense. Further tests should be provided at regular intervals, and especially if the user is experiencing visual difficulties. An employer must provide special corrective appliances if required.

## Training

All users of display screen equipment must receive health and safety training in the use of their workstations. Further training must be provided if a workstation is modified.

## Information

Staff must be provided with information on all aspects of health and safety relating to their workstations, together with the measures taken by employers to analyse risks and to comply with the regulations. Employers must also provide information about the steps they are taking to ensure breaks in use of equipment and the training they are providing.

# Other health and safety laws

## Electrical apparatus

The **Electricity at Work Regulations, 1989**[2] set out requirements for the construction and use of electrical systems in all workplaces. Further information is contained in *Memorandum of guidance HS(R) 25.*

The regulations impose a general duty on employers to ensure that so far as is reasonably practicable:

❏ systems are constructed to prevent danger;

❏ systems are maintained to prevent danger;

❏ use is made in a manner to prevent danger arising.

The regulations also have specific requirements about earthing and types of connectors, and require that users must be properly trained and supervised to avoid injury.

## Hazardous substances

The **Control of Substances Hazardous to Health Regulations, 1988** as amended (COSHH)[2] require employers to identify hazardous substances and assess risks to employees. A hazardous substance would include photocopier toner. The assessment must be reviewed whenever necessary. Exposure to substances identified must then be prevented or controlled, or protective equipment issued. Any protective equipment or control methods must be regularly tested.

Both the assessment and the maintenance tests must be recorded and these records must be kept safely and made available for inspection.

Further guidance on COSHH can be found in *A step by step guide to COSHH assessment* .

## First aid

Under the **Health and Safety (First Aid) Regulations, 1981,** workplaces must have first aid provision, the form of which depends on various factors, including the number of employees. The Health and Safety Executive (HSE) booklet *First aid at work* (COP 42) contains an approved code of practice and guidance notes.

### First-aiders

Organisations with fewer than 50 employees have no legal obligation to have a trained first-aider on the premises, but it is good practice to have at least two people with first aid training.

### Training

First-aiders must have undertaken training and obtained qualifications approved by the HSE. First aid certificates are valid for three years; refresher courses must be started before certificates expire, otherwise a full course will need to be taken.

### Appointed person

Organisations which have no trained first-aiders must make sure there is an appointed person who is authorised to take charge of the situation (for example to call an ambulance) if there is a serious injury or

---

[2]  See note at beginning of chapter about Task Force recommendations

illness. Emergency first aid training should be considered for all appointed persons.

## First aid boxes

First aid boxes and kits should contain only the items that a first-aider has been trained to use. They should not contain medication of any kind.

For further information about first aid see *First aid needs in your workplace: your questions answered.*

## Duties relating to premises

The **Occupier's Liability Act, 1957** states that reasonable care must be taken to see that all those using the premises with permission will be reasonably safe. This includes staff, committee members, guests, and people delivering goods or mending appliances.

The **Occupier's Liability Act, 1984** applies to trespassers (for example children who come onto a site when closed). There is in all circumstances a duty to take reasonable care to avoid the risk of people being injured or killed; for example if a site is dangerous to unsupervised children you may have a duty to see that it is securely fenced, particularly if you are aware that children are coming onto the site without your permission.

# Public health laws

Public health legislation is very detailed, broad in scope, and includes many local bylaws. It is therefore important to meet an environmental health officer, preferably on site, to discuss your obligations. The main scope of public health legislation is detailed below.

## The quality of the air

Any building in which people work or meet must have proper ventilation. The property must be free from pollution, for example from a badly maintained boiler or the burning of rubbish. Noise pollution and vibration are also controlled by law.

## The quality of housing

If a group is running hostel accommodation or has a resident worker, further public health laws, concerned with housing, come into force. Environmental health officers have powers to insist on standards of cleanliness, fire precautions, the provision of lavatories, hot and cold water supplies, heating, rubbish disposal and proper repairs. Their exact powers will depend on whether the building is classified as having a single tenant or as being a house in multiple occupation.

Ask for advice about your responsibilities from a law centre, housing aid centre or any other advice centre specialising in housing work, or contact the local authority environmental health department.

If residential care is provided, accommodation will have to be registered with the local social services department under the **Registered Homes Act, 1984.** The department has powers to set detailed standards relating to the accommodation and the level of care provided.

## Drainage and refuse disposal

Any faults in drainage and refuse disposal systems can create serious health risks, and the environmental health officer will look carefully at the systems provided. Organisations can be prosecuted if they burn rubbish or allow it to accumulate. It may be necessary to pay for trade refuse to be removed.

## Infectious diseases

Under the **Food Hygiene (Markets, Stalls and Delivery Vehicles) Regulations, 1966** and the **Food Hygiene (General) Regulations, 1970** employees in contact with food have a duty to inform the employer at once if they are suffering from or have been in contact with certain illnesses, such as typhoid or salmonella poisoning. If any staff member suffers from these diseases the environmental health department must be informed immediately.

## Pests and vermin

If pests such as rats, mice or cockroaches are found on the premises, contact the environmental health department immediately. After an outbreak, review the arrangements for cooking, cleaning, and storing food. Regularly inspect the premises for cleanliness, especially behind boilers and pipe runs and under floors. Call in a specialist firm to carry out a complete spring clean if necessary.

If there are young children on the premises look out for head lice and bugs. Contact the health visitor or nurse from the district health authority if you find any.

## The quality of food

The **Food Hygiene (General) Regulations, 1970** cover the provision of any food served on the premises, for example pensioners' lunches and refreshments at socials. A large number of regulations also govern certain aspects of food, for example its nature, substance, quality, transport, storage and handling; and food hygiene, particularly the state of kitchens. This is discussed in more detail in chapter 9. The *Health Education Council* and many local authority environmental health departments publish guides to the regulations.

## Public entertainment

Premises used for public entertainment have to meet particular conditions, especially on fire precautions, ventilation and sound insulation. A group will usually need a licence (see chapter 9); the licensing magistrates, fire officers and environmental health departments will provide details of the requirements.

# Fire precautions

Strict rules on fire precautions govern all buildings used by the public. They are enforced by the local authority and the fire brigade. The main regulations cover:

- ❑ means of escape;
- ❑ fire alarms;
- ❑ fire fighting equipment;
- ❑ access for firefighters.

## Means of escape

Means of escape refers to the design of the building. The management committee has a legal duty to see that adequate escape routes are provided and that they are kept clear from obstructions. The routes must be planned so that any person confronted by a fire can turn away from it and walk to a protected staircase or exit. Also ensure that the means of escape are accessible to people with disabilities. Extra work may be needed if a building is used for public entertainment. Consult the fire brigade before making any alterations.

## Fire alarms

It is a legal requirement to provide a fire alarm in many premises. The type of system needed depends on the size of the building and how easy it would be to hear an alarm; for example in premises with only a few rooms, a handbell would be enough so long as everyone could hear it. Employers should also consider installing alarms with flashing lights to alert deaf people. The *Disabled Living Foundation* has details of such alarms.

In a larger building an electric fire alarm, with call points at each of the exit doors, must be installed. If there are more than six call points or if people sleep on the premises, the electric system should have a secondary power supply so that if the power fails during a fire the alarms can still go off. Fire alarms must be tested at regular intervals. Smoke detectors may also be required. Fire prevention officers will advise on different fire alarm systems.

## Fire fighting equipment

Extinguishers and fire blankets are needed; these are particularly important if there is a kitchen with a risk of a fat fire. You may also need sprinklers or foam inlets. Fire extinguishers should be inspected regularly. Again, ask the fire prevention officers for advice.

## Access

Try to arrange parking space so that a fire engine could get right up to the building, and make sure that emergency exits are kept clear. Dry riser mains and sprinklers must also be kept clear at all times.

# Accidents

An employer has a legal duty to keep an accident book and to record fatal accidents or those which result in three or more days' absence from work. It is good practice to keep a record of all accidents. The date, time and circumstances should be noted and steps taken to ensure the incident does not happen again.

# Health and safety policies

## Good practice

Health and safety legislation generally is designed to protect only employees. As a matter of good practice voluntary organisations should develop health and safety policies to cover trainees and volunteers as well as paid employees. Volunteers and trainees could be invited to join the safety committee.

## Implementing a health and safety policy

The following checklist provides the steps needed to implement a policy.

### Organisation

- ❑ Ensure that the management committee decides who is responsible, and if necessary delegates decision making powers; for example will responsibility lie with the whole committee, a subcommittee or a particular officer?

- ❑ Appoint staff members to be given overall responsibility for health and safety and for implementing the policy on a day to day basis, for example the director may take overall responsibility but an administrator could be given day to day responsibility.

❑ Set up a safety committee including those committee members and staff members with responsibility for health and safety, together with trades union representatives and other staff and volunteers.

❑ If premises are shared try to organise with other employers a joint risk assessment and appoint a coordinator.

❑ Ensure the health and safety requirements are included in the annual budget.

## Information and training

❑ Obtain necessary advice and publications, for example from the Health and Safety Executive, the local authority and trades unions.

❑ Identify the training needs of committee members and staff with health and safety responsibilities and design a training programme.

## Assessment

❑ Carry out a preliminary risk assessment of the workplaces and activities in consultation with staff and trades unions. Before starting, list the headings covered by the health and safety regulations and by COSHH. Assess the risks to users and members of the public as well as to staff.

❑ Carry out a thorough inspection of workplaces to identify the steps required to comply with the workplace regulations.

❑ Carry out a thorough inspection of work and display screen equipment to identify any steps required to comply with regulations.

❑ Assess any manual handling operations using the checklist in the guidance on Manual Handling.

❑ Arrange external expertise if this is needed to complete the assessment.

❑ Make a written record of the assessment and discuss the findings with the members of the safety committee and other staff.

❑ Decide on a review date for the assessment.

For further details see *5 steps to risk assessment*

## Preventative and protective measures

❑ Identify preventative and protective measures that can be taken to reduce or avoid any risks. These may include providing personal protective equipment, health surveillance, eye tests and regular servicing of equipment.

❑ Identify the modifications to display screen and work equipment and the workplace necessary to comply with the regulations.

❑ Establish the costs of preventative and protective measures and any necessary modifications and draw up a timescale for their implementation in consultation with the safety committee.

## New premises and equipment

❑ Ensure that a risk assessment is made before acquiring new premises or equipment and that the costs of removing any risks are identified.

## Emergency procedures

❑ Draw up emergency procedures to deal with risks identified during the assessment and identify those responsible for evacuation and other tasks in the event of an emergency.

## Training, instructions and information for staff

❑ Inform staff of the risks identified, the steps they should take to reduce the risks and the steps the employer will be taking.

❑ Ensure that all staff are properly trained and instructed in the use of all protective equipment, work and display screen equipment and on safe manual handling techniques.

❑ Ensure new and temporary staff are given necessary health and safety information.

❑ Pay particular attention to staff who may be more vulnerable to accidents, for example inexperienced or young staff and people with disabilities.

❑ Ensure the cost of staff induction, training and instruction are included in the annual budget.

## Accidents

❑ Establish a policy that all accidents and near accidents and their causes are recorded and reported to the safety committee.

❑ Establish procedures for dealing with accidents and ensure that there are sufficient staff with first aid training.

## Monitoring and review

❑ Ensure that those responsible for health and safety are regularly provided with updated information and training.

❑ Monitor the implementation of the policy at regular intervals in consultation with the safety committee, and revise the assessment and targets as necessary.

❑ Revise the assessments and the steps required whenever circumstances change, including new kinds of work, new premises, new equipment or changes in good practice.

## A framework

Implementing a health and safety policy may appear daunting and, certainly in larger organisations, involves a substantial amount of work. One way of producing information in a manageable form is to use a series of columns headed:

❑ **hazard identified**, for example shelves overloaded, floor slippery;

❑ **risk**, for example items may fall, person may slip;

❑ **priority**, for example high, medium or low;

❑ **preventative or protective steps required**, for example new shelving in neighbouring room, new floor covering;

❑ **costs** involved;

❑ **timescale for completion of steps** identified;

❑ **information and training** required for staff;

❑ **timescale** for completion of training and information.

A similar format can be used to identify the steps required to comply with work equipment, workplace and display screen equipment regulations. Details of new hazards, for example from new equipment, can be added as necessary.

Information presented in this way enables monitoring and reviews to take place easily. It can be simple to see whether the steps and training required have been delivered within the agreed timescale. If a particular hazard has become more urgent, for example if it proves to be more dangerous than envisaged, the priority can be changed and the timescale revised.

## Booklist

**5 steps to risk assessment**, Health and Safety Executive, free

**A step by step guide to COSHH assessment** (HS(G)97), Health and Safety Executive (1993), £5.00

**Display screen equipment at work: guidance on regulations** (L26), Health and Safety Executive (1992), £5.00

**Essentials of health and safety at work**, Health and Safety Executive (1994), £5.95

**First aid at work: general guidance for inclusion in first aid boxes**, Health and Safety Executive (1987), £4.50 for 50

**First aid needs in your workplace: your questions answered**, Health and Safety Executive (1992), free

**First aid at work: Health and Safety (first aid) Regulations, 1981 — approved code of practice and guidance**, Health and Safety Executive (1990), £3.00

**Health and safety law: what you should know**, Health and Safety Executive (1989), £3.50 for 50

**Management of Health and Safety at Work Regulations, 1992: approved code of practice** (L21), Health and Safety Executive (1992), £5.00

**Manual handling: guidance on regulations** (L23), Health and Safety Executive (1992), £5.00

**Memorandum of guidance on the Electricity at Work Regulations 1989**, Health and Safety Executive (1989), £4.00

**Personal Protective Equipment at Work Regulations, 1992: guidance on regulations** (L25), Health and Safety Executive (1992), £5.00

**Provision and use of work equipment regulations, 1992: approved code of practice** (L22), Health and Safety Executive (1992), £5.00

**Safety reps and safety committees**, Health and Safety Executive (1988), £2.50

**The VDU factpack — a guide to safer VDU operation**, City Centre, £6.00

**VDU work and the hazards to health**, London Hazards Centre (1993), £6.50

**Workplace health, safety and welfare: approved code of practice and guidance** (L24), Health and Safety Executive (1992), £5.00

# Chapter 6:
# Your responsibilities for premises

This chapter starts by looking at the advantages and disadvantages of the different types of tenure. It then discusses factors that need to be considered when making the decision about taking on premises. The following section describes planning permission. Subletting and hiring out premises are then examined, and the final section describes how to dispose of property. A model hiring agreement and a model deed of trust for appointing holding trustees are given at the end of the chapter.

Health and safety is dealt with in chapter 5, insurance in chapter 7 and the licensing of activities in chapter 9.

**Buying or renting property is a major step and involves considerable responsibilities for both staff and management committees. Always get legal advice before taking on property.**

# Form of tenure

There are three main forms of tenure: ownership of a freehold or a long leasehold, renting on a lease or tenancy, or taking property on a licence. The options are discussed below. Make sure the management committee understands the implications of each form of tenure.

When an unincorporated association or a trust buys property or holds a lease, the property will often be put into the names of a few individuals as trustees (often called **'holding trustees'**). In this case it is usually advisable to draw up a separate trust deed setting out holding trustees' and management committee members' rights and obligations. This is discussed further later in the chapter.

## Buying property

There are two ways of buying property: buying a **freehold** or buying a **long leasehold**. As a freehold gives absolute ownership, the only controls on the property are the rules on planning permission and building regulation approval, which apply to all buildings. Some properties may also be subject to special restrictions known as **'restrictive covenants'**, which a solicitor will identify.

A leasehold interest in a property involves paying a capital sum to acquire a long lease of, for example 99 years, together with an annual rent, which is usually minimal. Such a lease provides long-term security of

tenure. Because long leases generally have few restrictions they offer a certain amount of freedom in managing the property. It is crucial to obtain advice from a solicitor and surveyor before signing a lease or mortgage agreement. Remember that a named individual may have to stand as a guarantor for any mortgage a group raises.

## Advantages and disadvantages

The advantages of buying a freehold or a long leasehold are long-term security and independence, although leaseholders will have some restrictions and obligations and will have to pay a small rent. However, these options are available only to groups with a substantial capital sum.

## Leasing or renting premises

Leasing or renting premises for a short period usually involves paying a market (or near-market) rent and

QUICK - CHECK THE LEASE TO SEE WHETHER THE REMOVAL OF THE PREMISES BY A GIANT GORILLA IS THE LANDLORD'S RESPONSIBILITY....

provides an exclusive right to occupy a property. A lease (or tenancy) imposes obligations on both the landlord and tenant.

Before signing a lease, make sure everyone involved fully understands the effects of all the clauses and the costs of complying with the obligations. If in any doubt, get advice from a solicitor and, where necessary, a surveyor before signing the lease.

## Advantages and disadvantages

The **Landlord and Tenant Act, 1954** gives security to tenants in business premises: property rented by voluntary groups usually falls within this category. Landlords can serve notice only under the terms of the Act. Even if they serve a notice of termination, tenants can ask a court to grant a new tenancy. Landlords can oppose applications on certain specified grounds, for example that the rent has not been paid, or that they need the premises for themselves. If the landlord does not oppose the application, the court will probably grant a new tenancy.

Some tenancies are exempt from the Landlord and Tenant Act. These include:

❏ those granted for less than six months, where either the tenant has been in occupation for less than 12 months or there is no provision for extension or renewal;

❏ those where both parties, with the agreement of a court, have decided not to apply the Act. Many landlords will only lease premises to groups who are prepared to make a joint application to the court to exclude the Act.

Taking on a lease involves risks. For unincorporated associations (see chapter 1) these are considerable. Since such organisations have no distinct legal existence, they cannot acquire property in their own right. The trustees or members of the management committee must therefore hold property on behalf of the group. Unless the lease specifically excludes trustees from personal liability (which is unlikely) they become personally liable for meeting the terms of the lease if the group is unable to do so.

The risks are less for incorporated organisations as they have a distinct legal existence and therefore can hold property in their own right. However, some commercial landlords will still expect an individual to be a named guarantor for a lease.

## Holding a licence

Unlike a lease, which gives an exclusive legal interest in the property, a licence grants only a personal permission to occupy the premises and is generally a temporary agreement.

A licence will spell out the obligations of both the landlord and licensee in a simpler form. Before signing a licence, organisations should still obtain legal advice and ensure that they have the financial resources to meet their obligations under the terms of the licence.

### Advantages and disadvantages

The main advantage of holding a licence is that a group can usually surrender the licence to the landlord and generally has no obligation for repairs or insurance. Also, many local authorities do not consider licensees to be occupiers for the purposes of non-domestic rates, so the financial responsibilities for organisations with licences can be considerably less onerous than for those with leases. However, licensees may still be responsible for water charges.

Properties held under licence are not protected by the Landlord and Tenant Act so the licensee has very little security. A licence will usually be either for a fixed period (for example one year) or will continue indefinitely but have a fixed notice period. Once the notice has been given and expired the occupant must leave. If the licence continues on a weekly or monthly basis and no notice period is mentioned in the licence, the law would imply that the licensee would be entitled to reasonable notice.

The advantages of a licence must be set against the lack of security. The ultimate decision may depend on a group's finances.

# Finding premises

Groups may rent their premises from local authorities, other voluntary groups, commercial landlords and, occasionally, private individuals.

One place to start looking for new premises is the local authority. The estates department keeps a record of available council premises.

The local authority may charge a commercial rent but include an equivalent amount in a group's grant, or it could charge a peppercorn (nominal) rent. It may state as a condition of tenure that a group must use the premises only to carry out the activities for which it is being funded. If the group changes its activities without permission, it could then be evicted.

Local estate agents have lists of property belonging to commercial and private landlords, who will charge market rents. Landlords may be willing to negotiate the terms of a lease. For example it may be possible to persuade them to reduce the rent, agree to a rent-free period, redecorate the premises or pay for repairs. Any concessions need to be balanced against the possibility of future rent increases.

The local council for voluntary service, churches, community centres and housing associations may know of vacant premises. London Voluntary Service Council often advertises offices wanted and to let in *Voluntary Voice*, its monthly magazine.

When looking for premises, consider:

❏ proximity to public transport;

❏ access for people with disabilities and those with children;

❏ the immediate locality and whether members would be happy attending activities in the premises. For example a building down a dark alley would not be suitable for a pensioners' club, as members might feel unsafe going home;

❏ the neighbours. A youth club running discos every night would not be popular next door to sheltered accommodation;

❑ whether goods can easily be delivered. This is particularly important if the group is running a bar or workshop;

❑ any planning permission granted on a property.

# People with disabilities

The **Chronically Sick and Disabled Persons Act, 1970** requires employers running offices, shops or factories to make practicable and reasonable provision for the needs of people with disabilities regarding the following:

❑ means of access to the premises;

❑ means of access within the premises;

❑ parking facilities;

❑ sanitary conveniences.

The organisation's equal opportunities policy should cover this provision.

# Making the decision

An organisation may wish to delegate decisions about premises to a subcommittee. Before doing so check whether the constitution will allow this.

The committee or trustees of an unincorporated association or trust may be personally liable for complying with the terms of any lease or licence. It may therefore be more appropriate for all the committee to participate in the final decision once they have all the relevant information.

When negotiating to take on premises ensure there is sufficient time for informed decision making. Although groups may want to move into premises quickly so that services can be provided, it is important to consider the risks of taking on an inappropriate lease and allow time to ensure committee members understand their responsibilities.

## Checking a lease or licence

The following outlines the points that need to be considered when negotiating a lease or licence. Many landlords are currently desperate to rent out premises, so you may be in a very strong negotiating position.

### The duration

Leases can be weekly, monthly or for a fixed period. There may be an option to renew a fixed-term lease at the end of a specific time. The duration of a lease is particularly important because an organisation must meet its obligations for the whole period of a fixed-term lease, even if it no longer uses the building. The trustees of unincorporated associations and trusts will be personally liable for the rent for the full term of a lease even if the organisation has run out of funds and ceased to exist.

There are two possible ways for an organisation to overcome this; either to surrender or assign the lease. In both cases the lease must allow such options. **Surrendering a lease** means handing it back to the landlord or giving notice to quit. **Assigning a lease** means selling it or giving it to new tenants, who must be financially viable, otherwise you could be responsible for their debts. Charities have to go through certain formalities before surrendering or assigning a lease (see 'Disposing of premises', below).

Trustees can avoid or reduce their own personal liability by ensuring that the organisation can assign or surrender the lease. They can avoid liability completely if they can persuade the landlord to include a clause in the lease which excludes any personal liability for the rent. However, experience shows that few commercial landlords are prepared to accept such clauses.

### The amount of the rent and payment periods

Always check whether the rent is inclusive or exclusive of VAT. Most leases give landlords the option to introduce VAT at any stage during the period of the lease. Also, note the payment period; leases often require rent to be paid quarterly in advance.

### Rent review

Longer leases often include a clause allowing the landlord to review the rent periodically. In such cases, it would be wise to negotiate a break clause so that you could surrender the lease (see above) if you could not afford the higher rate.

### Service charges

Many leases of shared premises include a clause requiring the tenant to pay service charges in addition to the rent. Check the lease carefully to see what these service charges will cover. If, for example a building needs a new roof a tenant could end up having to pay a proportion of the cost even if the lease is short-term, for example one year.

Although it is appropriate for organisations taking on short-term leases to pay a contribution, for example towards heating and lighting of communal parts, they should ensure that they do not have responsibility for paying service charges towards long-term maintenance and repair obligations.

There are two ways in which a lease may be amended to protect a tenant:

❏ ensure the service charge provision makes it clear it cannot include maintenance and repair costs, or major structural repairs and maintenance costs;

❏ specify a fixed amount for service charges or impose a top financial limit on repair and maintenance costs during any financial year. A fixed sum could be written in as the contribution for repairs and maintenance or added to the rent.

## Responsibility for repairs

Tenants have to maintain property to a reasonable standard. This may include painting. It is important to define this responsibility and clarify any other obligations for repairs. Where possible, have the property inspected by a surveyor and discuss the likely costs of minor repairs and the possibility of encountering major ones.

The surveyor should also draw up a **schedule of condition** describing the state of the property before the tenant moves in, which must be agreed by the landlord and tenant. When the tenant moves on, the landlord may ask for another survey and expect the tenant to pay for any repairs needed to put the property back into the original state. Just as the organisation or its trustees are responsible for the rent throughout the duration of the lease, the organisation or its trustees will also be responsible for putting the property back into the original condition once the lease expires.

## Insurance

Most leases require either that the tenant insures the premises or, more usually, pays the premium to the landlord, who will arrange insurance. A lease will require the tenant to have public liability insurance and insurance for fixed glass, for example shopfronts. Insurance is discussed further in chapter 7.

## Rates and water charges

Tenants will usually be responsible for non-domestic rates and water charges. Always check with the local authority the exact amount of rates payable on occupation. Rates are dealt with in more detail later in the chapter. Regardless of its size, an organisation will have to pay water charges in full unless the landlord agrees to meet these charges under the terms of the lease.

## The costs of drawing up the lease

Most commercial leases impose a requirement that the tenant pays the landlord's legal costs in drawing up the lease. Landlords' solicitors often charge substantial amounts for this; the costs may well exceed £1,000. Before entering into detailed negotiations ensure there is a top limit placed on the landlord's legal costs.

## Permitted activities

Check whether any activities are restricted under the terms of the lease. Some set out what the premises can be used for; make sure this includes your intended uses. There may be other restrictions, for example on dancing or drinking. Try to ensure that the lease allows a sufficiently wide range of uses so that it is easier to assign if necessary.

## Subletting and use by others

Most leases do not allow subletting. However, hiring out rooms or allowing other groups to share the premises would not normally amount to a subletting. If necessary negotiate an amendment if you wish to share.

## Alterations to the structure of the building

Most leases do not permit structural alterations without the landlord's consent. If alterations are necessary try to get the landlord's permission before signing the lease.

## Is the lease or licence right for you?

Before making a decision to take on a lease or licence an organisation must:

❏ understand all the provisions of the agreement and its obligations, particularly those that will involve incurring expense;

❏ obtain all the necessary advice about its obligations and likely expenditure (especially from a solicitor and surveyor);

❏ have funds to meet the likely expenditure, including rent, VAT, insurance, service charges, non-domestic rates, water charges, repairs, decorations and structural alterations, and to cover health and safety requirements (see chapter 5);

❏ obtain planning permission for use of the premises and make sure there are no covenants in the lease preventing the organisation from using it in the way desired;

❏ have building regulation approval for any intended alterations;

❏ ensure there is a way of bringing the lease to an end if it runs out of money; this is particularly important for unincorporated associations and trusts;

❏ have the landlord's consent for proposed adaptations.

# Signing the lease

Check the constitution for any provisions relating to the signing of leases or other documents.

## Incorporated organisations

The organisation itself (as opposed to individuals) can be a named party to a lease. For companies, a lease can be sealed with the company seal (if it has one) in the presence of the company secretary and one, or two, committee members. Alternatively it can simply be signed on behalf of the company by the same people. An industrial and provident society must attach its seal in the presence of the secretary and two committee members.

## Unincorporated associations and trusts

There are a number of ways in which unincorporated associations and trusts can enter into legal documents relating to premises:

❏ in the case of a licence, signature by one person: only appropriate where one person can be authorised to sign the licence on behalf of the organisation;

❏ appointment of holding trustees: constitutions may either **require** or **allow** holding trustees (see 'Form of tenure', above) to be appointed by the committee. If this option is used, the committee should agree a trust deed, with the holding trustees clearly setting out their responsibilities and obligations.

A model trust deed is given at the end of this chapter. Although not all the provisions may be necessary they should still be considered;

❏ the third option is set out in the **Charities Act, 1993** and is available only to charities with a constitution that does **not** require the appointment of holding trustees. Under this option the committee can pass a resolution which authorises at least two members to enter into legal documents on behalf of the committee. Any such document must then contain a specific clause stating that it has been executed in pursuance of **Section 82** of the **Charities Act, 1993** by people signing on behalf of the charity, who are then deemed to have signed on behalf of the whole committee.

There are two advantages of using this method. It is unnecessary to enter into a separate deed of trust between the committee and the holding trustees and it does not place two or three individuals in a more risky position than the whole committee.

## Checklist of formalities

Before entering into a lease or licence or before buying property a group should:

❏ check its constitution (if a charity) to see whether it has to appoint holding trustees or whether it has the option of passing a resolution under Section 82 of the Charities Act, 1993;

❏ pass a resolution appointing signatories;

❏ agree the terms of any trust deed if appointing holding trustees.

# Planning and building regulations

Planning laws govern many aspects of a building and its surroundings and can restrict a group's activities, regardless of tenure. The relevant law is the **Town and Country Planning Act, 1990**. Its detailed planning regulations, often called **development control**, are enforced by the local planning authority through granting or refusing planning permission.

## Development

Some minor developments are given automatic permission by the **Town and Country Planning General Development Order, 1988** as amended, and certain changes of use are also allowed (see below). Temporary developments may also be possible without planning permission, for example land used for any purpose for a period not exceeding 28 days in any calendar year.

Planning permission is needed for:

❏ certain changes in the use of buildings and land;

❏ major changes to the external appearance of a building;

❏ changes to the internal appearance of listed buildings;

❏ erection of new buildings.

## Use of buildings and land

The **General Development (Use Classes) Order, 1987** sets out 16 different classes of use, collected into four groups, for land and buildings. It is permissible to change the use of land or a building from one purpose to another provided the use remains in the same class.

The four basic uses are:

❏ **class A:** retail shops, financial and professional services and food and drink shops;

❏ **class B:** industrial and commercial uses;

❏ **class C:** residential, including houses, hotels, hospitals and residential institutions; hostels are *not* included;

❏ **class D:** public places, including churches, schools, libraries, art galleries, cinemas, nurseries and arts centres.

The subclasses of particular relevance to voluntary organisations include:

❏ class A1: shops - this would include charity shops;

❏ class A2: financial and professional services - this could apply to advice centres;

❏ class A3: food and drink - relates to the sale of food or drink to be consumed on the premises or hot food to be taken away;

❏ class B1: business - includes office premises used by charities; could include small manufacturing processes such as making poppies or Christmas cards;

❏ class B8: storage and distribution - includes warehousing and storing the products of small manufacturing processes (see class B1, above);

❏ class C2: residential institutions - residential accommodation with care;

❏ class C3: dwelling houses - includes houses providing accommodation for not more than six residents living together as a single household, including those where care is provided for residents;

❏ class D1: non-residential institutions - for example creches, day centres, arts centres and educational uses.

## The appearance of a building

Permission is not required for painting or repairs, but is needed for a major change in a building's appearance, for example:

❏ installing a shopfront;

❏ building an extension over a certain size;

❏ erecting a garage.

The **Town and Country Planning (Control of Advertisements) Regulations, 1992** govern planning permission for advertisements. Illuminated and hanging signs usually need planning permission whereas non-illuminated signs do not. Check with the local authority's planning department if in doubt.

## Listed property

If a building is in a conservation area or listed as being one of special architectural importance, extra restrictions are imposed. Controls are extended to internal alterations in the highest grades of listings. Again, if in doubt check with the local authority.

## New buildings

Every new building needs planning permission. The first step is to submit an outline application to the planning department of the local authority setting out the general plans for the site. If planning permission is granted, a more detailed application must be made.

## Obtaining planning permission

If a group is buying, or moving into a building, its solicitor should check on the need to apply for planning permission as part of the searches. Groups wishing to make alterations to the building they already occupy should contact the planning department in the local authority. Staff will need to know:

❏ the address of the premises;

❏ the floors being occupied, if applicable;

❏ what the premises are (or have been) used for;

❏ what new activity is intended;

❏ any alterations being considered.

## Making an application

All planning applications must be submitted on a form provided by the local authority's planning department, together with a simple plan showing the location of the premises and a drawing of any proposed alterations or extensions.

When considering alterations to the building always take into account the needs of people with disabilities, both as members or potential members of staff and as members of the public using the building.

The planning department can advise about implementing the *Code of practice: Access for the disabled to buildings.*

Most local authorities notify the neighbours about applications. Check whether this is going to happen, and if an application might be seen as controversial explain to the neighbours what is actually involved.

### If permission is refused

Permission could be refused altogether, or special conditions imposed, such as restricting the hours of certain activities. There is a right of appeal against refusal or restrictions but appeals can take a long time. It is however possible to agree to lease or buy premises subject to obtaining planning permission. For help contact *Planning Aid for London* or *The Association of Community Technical Aid Centres.*

## Building regulations

These regulations apply to new buildings and extensions or major structural changes to existing property. The law in general controls:

❏ the materials used, which must meet certain standards;

❏ the preparation of the site;

❏ the building's structural stability;

❏ means of escape in the event of a fire;

❏ measures to prevent fire spreading;

❏ sound insulation;

❏ heat insulation and conservation;

❏ stairs and ramps in all new buildings;

❏ light, ventilation, drains, hygiene, fireplaces, food storage and refuse disposal;

❏ access both to and within the building for people with disabilities.

The regulations are enforced by the district surveyor who must check the work as it progresses. The builder will usually make the arrangements. The public health department and fire brigade may also need to be consulted, depending on how the property is to be used.

# Non-domestic rates and water charges

Both non-domestic rates and water charges are payable by the occupiers of premises. Although non-domestic rates are usually referred to as 'business rates' they are payable on any premises which are not used as a dwelling and so will include all those occupied by voluntary organisations. Organisations which occupy premises under a lease or licence will normally be the occupiers and will therefore be liable for both non-domestic rates and water charges. However, a licence to occupy premises may state that the landlord is still in occupation and will therefore be responsible for non-domestic rates: check the terms of your licence. In unincorporated organisations the management committee will be the occupier.

## Mandatory rate relief

Registered charities, and organisations which do not have to register as charities (very small charities, industrial and provident societies with charitable rules and friendly societies), are entitled to 80% relief on non-domestic rates.

## Discretionary rate relief

Under **Section 47** of the **Local Government Act, 1988** local authorities have the discretion to grant additional relief to charities on non-domestic rates, up to a maximum of 100%.

They also have the discretion to grant rate relief up to 100% in the case of properties occupied wholly or partly by a range of non-profit making bodies. This would include organisations whose main objects are concerned with such purposes as social welfare, religion or recreation.

## Applying for rate relief

All groups should consider applying for relief from non-domestic rates. Discretionary relief can only be backdated to the beginning of the rating year in which the local authority agrees to grant relief (1 April to 31 March). Once relief is given it can continue automatically each year but this decision is up to the local authority. Mandatory relief can be backdated to 1 April 1990.

There is no statutory requirement for charities to submit applications for rate relief but it is advisable for all voluntary organisations to inform the rating authority immediately they begin to occupy premises, and ask for relief. Also, as charity law requires trustees to safeguard the organisation's assets, spending them unnecessarily on rates could be seen as a breach of trust.

If the end of the rating year is close it may be necessary to ask for relief in advance.

# Sharing other organisations' premises

One way of obtaining premises is to share property belonging to or rented by another organisation, either as a sub-tenant or (more likely) a licensee. Although the arrangements between the two organisations need not be too formal they must be clear from the start. Therefore the following points should be clarified in writing:

❑ the areas a group will have for exclusive use (for example an office) and those it will be allowed to share (for example kitchen, WCs and meeting rooms);

❑ whether furniture or equipment will be provided;

❑ use of resources such a photocopier and fax, and charging policies;

❑ whether adaptations to the premises are permitted;

❑ responsibilities for security arrangements;

❑ that insurance companies will be notified of plans to share premises;

❑ responsibilities for cleaning;

❑ other rules and regulations, for example regarding non-smoking;

❑ how use of shared facilities will be organised.

# Sharing premises on a long-term basis

Renting or licensing parts of your premises for longer periods can be a useful way of raising funds. The points made later in this chapter relating to security and safety for hiring out premises apply equally to any sharing arrangements. In addition, the following points need to be considered.

## Subletting

If an organisation sublets any part of the premises to another organisation it may create a business tenancy and be unable to regain the right to use the whole premises. Just because a document is called a 'licence' rather than a 'tenancy' or 'lease' does not necessarily prevent it creating a sub-tenancy.

A tenancy or lease can be created only if the occupant has exclusive use of some part of the premises. This can be avoided by retaining the right of access for regular cleaning or to equipment or property held in that part of the building, or by providing the organisation with the right to share the whole premises.

Always check the terms of your lease before entering into any arrangement with another organisation; it may prohibit subletting.

## Other restrictions in the lease

Check whether other restrictions in the lease might prohibit the sharing of premises with other organisations. For example some leases contain a provision making clear that the tenant is the only organisation entitled to use the premises. A landlord may be prepared to waive that requirement provided it is clear that no sub-tenancy is being created.

## Avoiding disputes

Consider the points made under 'Sharing other organisations' premises', above. It is in the interests of both landlord and tenant for the matters listed to be clarified. Also consider whether to enter into a formal agreement which includes some of the provisions contained in the model hiring agreement at the end of this chapter.

## Legal advice

Always take legal advice before making any arrangement for the continuous use of any part of the premises by another group.

# Hiring out parts of premises

Hiring out rooms for meetings and functions can be a useful way of raising funds as well as providing a community facility.

The key points to consider when other groups are using your premises are:

❑ complying with the law;

❑ security;

❑ safety;

❑ retaining control.

## Legal requirements

The relevant legal requirements to consider include:

❑ restrictions imposed by the lease or licence, for

example some leases state that the premises cannot be used by other groups, or that music must not be played;

❏ licensing laws if alcohol is to be sold;

❏ planning laws, for example a condition may be that the building cannot be used after 11 pm;

❏ noise limits under the **Environmental Protection Act, 1990**;

❏ whether corporation tax is payable: even charities may be required to pay corporation tax on rents and licence fees; if in doubt check with the Inland Revenue or an accountant.

It is worth stating in the hiring agreement that alcohol must not be provided on the premises in circumstances which require a licence unless one is obtained (for details see chapter 9).

## Security

The following security precautions should be considered when the building is in use by the hirer:

❏ checking the identity of those entering (in large buildings identity passes may be necessary);

❏ locking internal doors to private areas (but remember that doors allowing escape in case of fire must remain unlocked);

❏ warning staff to take special care of their belongings when other people will be in the building;

❏ providing secure storage for personal belongings;

❏ locking away cash, cheques and other valuables;

❏ securing expensive office equipment;

❏ storing confidential information in a locked filing cabinet.

Remember that security includes protecting staff from possible attack by intruders who may gain access to offices unchallenged. This is especially important if staff work in the evening.

The following precautions should be taken after people have left the building:

❏ ensure responsibility for locking up is clear. This could involve appointing a caretaker, worker or management committee member to lock up after use and set the burglar alarm, or ensure the hirer has done so;

❏ adopt procedures for ensuring that everyone has actually left the building before it is locked up.

It is essential to inform the insurance company that the premises will be hired out. The insurance company may impose additional conditions on your policy which must be met if the insurance is to be effective.

## Safety

The group letting out the building is likely to be responsible for any injury or damage suffered by visitors caused by the state of the premises. It may also be responsible if someone is injured because the fire fighting apparatus is not functioning or a fire escape is blocked. Some, but not all, of these responsibilities may be transferred to the hirer by a specific clause in the hiring agreement. The agreement should certainly require the hirer to ensure that fire escapes are not blocked (see the model agreement at the end of the chapter).

Whether or not hirers are made responsible for safety you should take out public liability insurance to cover injury or loss suffered by visitors and others (see chapter 7). Again make sure that the insurance company is told that the building will be hired out. The cost of this can be passed on to the hirers through the hiring charges.

## Retaining control

Obtain legal advice before making arrangements for the continuous use of any part of the premises by another group because they may create a sub-tenancy (for further details see 'Subletting', above).

# Disposing of premises

Organisations can dispose of their premises in a number of ways including:

❏ selling;

❏ leasing or creating sub-tenancies;

❏ transferring a lease;

❏ giving the lease back to the landlord (surrendering the lease or giving notice to quit).

Always obtain legal advice before disposing of premises and, if appropriate, obtain advice from the Charity Commissioners.

## Charities

The **Charities Act, 1993** sets out certain requirements that must be followed by charities in some cases before they can dispose of their premises. However, if a charity wishes to sell or lease its premises to another charity at a price lower than the market price, and this is permitted under the terms of its constitution, it may be possible for a charity to:

❑ assign a lease to another charity at no cost;

❑ transfer property it owns to another charity free or for a reduced price;

❑ lease or sublet its premises to another charity at a peppercorn or reduced rent.

## Requirements under the Charities Act, 1993, Sections 36-39

The provisions discussed below do not apply to a friendly society or to an industrial and provident society with charitable rules.

### Leases

If a charity plans to let or sublet for seven years or less, before entering into the lease the committee has to obtain advice from a person who has the necessary ability and practical experience. The committee then has to be satisfied that, having considered that person's advice, the proposed terms are the best that can be reasonably obtained in the circumstances.

### Other disposals

A charity's trustees or management committee members have to obtain written advice from a qualified surveyor (using the letters FRICS, ARICS, FSVA or ASVA) if it is proposing to:

❑ sell its property;

❑ enter into a lease for more than seven years;

❑ transfer its property or lease to another organisation; or

❑ surrender its lease to the landlord.

Again, the committee has to be satisfied that the proposed terms are the best that can reasonably be obtained. In addition, the property for sale or lease must be advertised publicly unless the surveyor has advised that it would not be in the best interests of the charity. The Charity Commissioners have the authority to waive the requirements.

### Premises held on trust

There are certain restrictions on disposal of property where the document under which the premises were given or sold to the charity specifically states that the premises are to be used by the charity for the purposes or a particular purpose of the charity. In such cases the trustees must give at least one month's public notice of their intention to dispose of the premises, in order to allow people who may be affected to give their views.

These rules do not apply if:

❑ the property disposed of will be replaced with other property; or

❑ the premises are being let for two years or less; or

❑ the Charity Commissioners have said that the rules should not apply to the charity generally, or to the particular disposal in question.

## Documentation

The **Charities Act, 1993** sets out requirements for specific clauses that must be included in any document disposing of a charity's property. Legal advice should be obtained when these documents are drawn up.

# Booklist

**Code of practice: Access for the disabled to buildings**, British Standards Institute (1979), £30.50

**Managing your community building: a practical handbook for people running buildings in local communities**, *Peter Hudson*, Community Matters (1993), £13.95

**Accessible offices**, Women's Design Service (1993), £7.00

# Example:
# Community Centre hiring agreement
(NB The size of deposits in this agreement are suggestions only)

(NAME OF ORGANISATION)
ADDRESS

Application to hire the meeting hall

I                                                                     ('the Hirer')
living at
                                                                      (Address)

                                                                      (Phone: day)
                                                                      (Phone: evening)

on behalf of                                                          (Organisation)
for the purpose of holding                                            (Type of event)

apply for the use of the meeting hall on behalf of the above organisation. I am authorised on behalf of the committee of the above organisation to agree to abide by and observe the conditions of hire required by the *(name of organisation)* of which I have been provided with a copy.

Date of hire:
Number of people attending:

From         am/pm
To           am/pm
We do/do not intend to serve alcohol in circumstances that require a licence.

We intend to apply for an Occasional Licence for the sale of alcohol. The name and address of the licensee will be as follows:

                                                                      (Name)
                                                                      (Address)

I undertake to supply a copy of the licence to the *(name of organisation)* at least three days before the hiring commences.

Signed                                                                Hirer


FOR OFFICE USE

Scale of fees:                                                        Cost
Deposit (25%)                                                         Date      Receipt No
Balance                                                               Date      Receipt No
Cleaning deposit (£7.50)                                              Date      Receipt No
Cleaning deposit returned                                             Date

Additional information and comments:

# CONDITIONS OF HIRE OF THE *(NAME OF ORGANISATION)*'S MEETING HALL

1. The person named in the application shall be the Hirer and shall be personally responsible for ensuring that these conditions are complied with in all respects.

2. The management committee of the organisation referred to in the hiring application shall be jointly and severally liable with the Hirer for complying with this agreement.

3. The premises to be hired are part of the *(name of organisation)* and consist of meeting hall, kitchen, bar area, toilets and entrance hall. Tables, chairs, cooker, fridge and sound equipment are provided by the *(name of organisation)*.

4. THE HIRER AGREES:

   a) To pay a deposit of 25% of the hiring charges upon the acceptance of the hiring application by the *(name of organisation)*.

   b) To pay the full hire charge not less than two weeks before the date of hiring.

   c) To ensure that he or she or some other person authorised in writing by him or her is present throughout the period of hire.

   d) To ensure that the responsible person does not leave the premises at the end of the period of hire until the caretaker attends to secure the premises.

   Note: The hirer may provide the *(name of organisation)* in advance with a list of those persons who will be responsible during the period of hire.

   e) To ensure that the premises are not used for any purpose other than that stated in the hiring application.

   f) To ensure that members of the committee or staff of the *(name of organisation)* are allowed access to the premises at all times during the period of hire.

   g) To accept full responsibility for and to indemnify the *(name of organisation)* against all costs, charges and claims in respect of injury to any person using the premises except such as may be caused by the negligence of the *(name of organisation)* or its staff or agents.

   h) To compensate the *(name of organisation)* for any damage caused during the period of hire or as a result of any breach of this agreement to the building or to any apparatus, chattels or appliances belonging to the *(name of organisation)* or its staff.

   i) To compensate the *(name of organisation)* or any member of its staff should any theft occur of any items during the period of hire or as a result of a breach of this agreement.

   j) To ensure that the fire apparatus on the premises is not interfered with.

   k) To ensure that at no time during the period of hire is any emergency exit from the premises locked or obstructed.

   l) To ensure that all persons using the premises are aware of the site of fire appliances and emergency exits.

   m) To take all proper precautions for the prevention of accidents to any persons on the premises during the period of hire.

   n) To allow no more than 200 people to attend the premises at any one time.

o) Not to issue tickets or tokens to any function on the premises less than two hours prior to the commencement of the hiring.

p) Not to issue tickets or tokens on the premises or in the area of the premises prior to or during the period of hire.

q) To take proper steps to control admittance to the function and ensure that there is no intrusion or hindrance to any other event or function taking place elsewhere in the community centre.

r) To ensure that no music is played on the premises after 11pm.

s) To ensure that the activities for which the premises are hired cease in sufficient time before the time stated for completion of the hire in the application form to enable all people to leave the premises and all apparatus concerned with the hire to be removed and the premises cleaned and tidied by the time of completion of the hire.

t) To ensure that all facilities used are left in a clean and tidy condition.

u) To ensure that all noise, including music, is kept within the level set by the local authority, details of which can be obtained from the environmental health department.

v) To ensure that any licences, including liquor or music and dancing licences required for the function, are obtained from the relevant authority and that the premises are not used for any activities that require a licence unless the appropriate licence has been obtained.

w) That no public announcement of any function proposed to be held shall be made until the hiring charge has been paid in full and the application accepted by the *(name of organisation)*.

x) That employees and members of the committee of the *(name of organisation)* are not authorised by the *(name of organisation)* to assist the hirer in the organisation of any function held on the premises or to accept responsibility for the safe custody of any money or goods.

y) That he or she has inspected the premises and that they are suitable for the purposes for which they are hired.

z) To ensure that the noise level during the arrival or departure of people attending the premises is not such as to cause a nuisance or inconvenience to occupiers of neighbouring property.

5. The *(name of organisation)* reserves the right of entry to the premises at all times during the period of hire of its committee and staff.

6. The *(name of organisation)* shall not be responsible or liable for any damage to or loss of property, articles or objects placed or left on the premises by the Hirer or any other person.

7. The *(name of organisation)* reserves the right to allow the use of other parts of the community centre during the period of hire and to allow the common use of the entrance hall and toilets.

8. The *(name of organisation)* will provide cleaning materials.

9. The *(name of organisation)* will deduct £7.50 from the deposit for cleaning charges if condition 4(t) is not complied with.

10. The deposit paid on acceptance of the hiring is payable in addition to the hiring charge and shall be held by the *(name of organisation)* as security for any damage to property belonging to the *(name of organisation)* during the course of the hiring or any other breach of this agreement.

11. In the event of any breach of the above conditions or in the event of any misstatement in the form of application or any material omission from the form whenever discovered, the hiring may be cancelled

without prior notice in the absolute discretion of the *(name of organisation)*, and any charges paid, including the hiring charge, may be forfeited.

12. If the full hiring charge is not paid as required by condition 4(b) the *(name of organisation)* may, without prior notice, cancel the hiring and forfeit the deposit unless the *(name of organisation)* is satisfied in its absolute discretion that there is good reason why the full charges were not paid or unless the *(name of organisation)* receives another application for hiring covering the same period and suffers no loss of income.

13. Staff and committee members of the *(name of organisation)* have delegated authority from the *(name of organisation)* to act on the *(name of organisation)*'s behalf in relation to matters under this agreement.

14. The *(name of organisation)* reserves the right to cancel this agreement for any good reason beyond its control and in that event to return all fees paid to the Hirer.

# Example: Deed of trust setting out terms of appointment of holding trustees

NB: Usually, holding trustees will be committee members when they are appointed. As long as they continue to be members of the committee, they will be part of the management of the organisation and will therefore be informed of financial developments. However, committee membership changes. The model deed makes clear that anyone who is acting as a trustee has the right to financial information and to be heard at any meeting making decisions which affect their responsibilities even if they are no longer members of the committee. This provides a safeguard for trustees in respect of the additional responsibilities they are taking on.

This is a Deed of Trust made on the day of 19 BETWEEN:

1. The Committee of Management of *(name of organisation)* acting by *(enter name and position of the person to sign on behalf of the Committee, for example the Secretary)*; and

2. *(names and addresses of holding trustees)* *(in this agreement referred to as 'the Trustees')*

Background to this Agreement

1. *(name of organisation)* is an unincorporated association (or charitable trust) with a constitution.

2. *(name of organisation)* proposes to enter into a lease of premises at *(address)*.

3. Clause *(enter number)* of the constitution states that the title of all real and personal property which may be acquired by or for the purposes of *(name of organisation)* may be vested in Trustees appointed by the Committee of Management. That clause also requires that such Trustees shall enter into a Deed of Trust or such other document as may be appropriate.

4. At a duly convened meeting of the Committee of Management of *(name of organisation)* held at *(place)* on *(date)* it was resolved that the Trustees named above should be appointed to hold the title to the premises at *(address)* for the purposes of the *(name of organisation)* and *(enter name of person authorised to sign on behalf of the Committee)* was authorised to sign this Deed on behalf of the Committee of Management.

AGREEMENT
The following is agreed:

1. *(name of organisation)* appoints the Trustees to act as Trustees of *(name of organisation)* for the purposes of holding the lease due to be completed in respect of *(premises)*.

2. The Trustees jointly and severally agree to hold the said lease in trust for the purposes of *(name of organisation)*.

3. The Trustees agree to act in respect of *(premises)* only in accordance with the lawful and reasonable instructions of the Committee of Management of *(name of organisation)*.

4. The Committee of Management hereby jointly and severally indemnifies the Trustees against all the costs, claims and liabilities incurred or to be incurred under the terms of the proposed lease.

5. *(name of organisation)* will use its best endeavours to obtain the release of the Trustees or any of them from the terms of the lease in the event that any Trustee wishes to resign from his or her post prior to the determination of the lease.

6. Whether or not the Trustees are members of the Committee of Management of *(name of organisation)*, they shall have the following rights during their term of office as Trustees, or until such time as the lease has been determined and all the obligations of the Lessee under the lease have been discharged, whichever is the longer:

a) the right to receive notification of any meeting of the Committee of Management of *(name of organisation)* as if they were members of that committee;

b) the right to receive notification of any general meeting of members of *(name of organisation)* as if they were members;

c) the right of access upon demand to inspect the books of account of *(name of organisation)* including cash books, vouchers, bank statements, cheque books and other similar documents (including the right for their advisers to inspect such books) and the right to take copies of those documents upon payment of a reasonable fee;

d) the right to attend and speak at any meeting of the Committee of Management or any general meeting of the members of *(name of organisation)* on any matter relating to the proposed lease or finances of *(name of organisation)*;

e) the right to receive from time to time the names and addresses of all members of the Committee of Management of *(name of organisation)* and to be kept informed of any changes;

f) the right to receive copies of any internal memoranda, financial reports or assessments and accounts and balance sheets produced for the treasurer, Committee of Management or any subcommittee of *(name of organisation)*;

g) the right to require immediate payment of any liability outstanding under the terms of the proposed lease.

7. The Trustees agree:

a) to notify the Secretary or Treasurer of the Committee of Management of *(name of organisation)* of all correspondence or other communication in respect of *(premises)*;

b) to act in accordance with all lawful and reasonable decisions made by the Committee of Management of *(name of organisation)* in respect of *(premises)* but not otherwise.

Signed and delivered as a Deed
by *(name)* on behalf of the
Committee of Management of *(name of organisation)*
acting under their authority by resolution on *(date)*
in the presence of:

Signed as a Deed
by *(first trustee)*
in the presence of:

Signed as a Deed
by *(second trustee)*
in the presence of:
(and so on for each trustee)

# Chapter 7: Insurance

This chapter starts by discussing general rules about insurance. It then looks at the types of insurance that are compulsory and suggests other forms of insurance which organisations could take out. The final section describes how to make a claim.

Insurance can be bought either directly from an insurance company or through a broker. The *British Insurance Brokers' Association* has a list of registered brokers for each area. It may be worth asking other voluntary groups and local businesses if they can recommend an insurance company.

## General rules

In insurance contracts, an application for insurance is a **proposal** and the person or organisation taking out the insurance the **proposer.**

When taking out insurance the proposer owes a duty of the 'utmost good faith' to the insurance company. This means that the company can refuse to pay out on any insurance claim if, when making the proposal (usually by filling in an application form) the proposer has:

❑ failed to disclose a **material fact** (see below); or

❑ misrepresented a material fact.

## Material facts

A material fact affects the degree of risk the insurance company is accepting. Examples affecting all types of insurance are:

❑ previous refusals of similar insurance;

❑ special conditions imposed on previous insurance;

❑ previous claims on similar insurance.

Examples for specific types of insurance are given below.

### Theft insurance

❑ criminal convictions of staff or management committee members;

❑ use of the premises by other organisations or the public.

### Fire insurance

❑ defective fire equipment;

❑ regular blocking of fire access by parked cars;

❑ use of the premises by other organisations or the public.

### Motor insurance

❑ age of drivers;

❑ road traffic convictions of any drivers;

❑ the use of vehicle(s).

## The extent of the duty

The proposer must disclose all material facts until the proposal is accepted. As this may be several months after the application is submitted, additional material facts may arise. If this is the case the proposer must inform the insurance company.

The obligation to disclose material facts includes providing information which could be discovered by making reasonably prudent enquiries.

### Renewals

The obligation to disclose all material facts arises each time the insurance is renewed, even though no additional proposal form is completed. The proposer must volunteer additional information even if not specifically asked to do so.

### Exclusions

All insurance policies contain a list of circumstances which are excluded from cover. Make sure you are clear about them before taking out a policy.

### Conditions

The list of conditions in the policy set out the requirements that have to met when making a claim. For example, it may be necessary to report a theft to the police, or make a claim within a limited period. Before making an insurance claim read the conditions carefully. If you fail to meet them, the insurance company can refuse to pay the claim.

## Completing the proposal

It is essential that whoever is responsible for completing a proposal on behalf of an organisation (whether staff or committee member) is aware of the consequences of making a mistake. If an insurance broker completes the proposal form, make sure all the information recorded is accurate, all the necessary information has been recorded and that the organisation receives a copy. If a material fact is not disclosed or the application form is inaccurate, the insurance company may be able to refuse payment of a claim. If the insurance company refuses to pay a claim for negligence, the management committee members of an unincorporated association may be personally liable to pay compensation. Leaving a blank space on a proposal form is taken to mean that no material fact exists in reply to that particular question: if in any doubt give the insurance company too much rather than too little information.

Keep at least two copies of all information supplied: keep one copy away from the premises to refer to in case papers stored on the premises are lost through fire or theft.

# Types of insurance

## Compulsory insurance

There are five types of insurance which may be compulsory. In each case organisations should consider obtaining cover above the legal minimum.

## Employer's liability insurance

Under the **Employer's Liability (Compulsory Insurance) Act, 1969** all employers have a duty to insure against any claims by workers for injury or disease. The insurance must be for at least £2 million to cover any one claim, and the insurance certificate must be displayed in the workplace.

This insurance does not cover management committee members, trainees, consultants, self-employed people doing work for the organisation, volunteers or service users. Public liability insurance will therefore be needed to extend this cover (see below).

## Road traffic insurance

Under the **Road Traffic Acts** all organisations with vehicles used on the road must insure the drivers against third party risks — injury or death caused to other road users. The certificate of insurance must be readily available.

Third party insurance does not cover theft of or damage to the vehicle. It is therefore worth taking out further insurance, either third party, fire and theft (in this case damage to the insured vehicle is still not covered except by fire) or comprehensive, which includes damage.

Insurance companies must be informed of the purposes for which the vehicle will be used and who is likely to be driving it.

In some organisations, staff and/or volunteers use their own cars to carry out the organisation's work. In this case the organisation must either have road traffic insurance which covers staff or volunteers' use of their own cars, or ensure that the staff's or volunteers' insurance policies cover business use. NB: An organisation cannot take out insurance to cover damage to cars belonging to staff, only against injuries or damage caused to others (third party insurance).

It is essential to ensure cover is adequate because an organisation may be liable for personal injury or damage to property as a result of a traffic accident in the course of work. Check the following:

❑ the insurance is current;

❑ it covers the employee or volunteer for use in connection with their work;

❑ the nature of the work has been accurately disclosed to the insurance company;

❑ the insurance company has been notified of any particular risks associated with the kind of use to which the vehicle will be put, for example where it will be used to carry service users, or for unusual activities such as off-road driving.

If an employee or volunteer uses a car owned by someone else, for example their partner, make sure the insurance covers the employee's or volunteer's business use, since this is quite unusual as a term of an insurance policy.

## Buildings insurance

An organisation which leases a building may, under the terms of the lease, have an obligation to insure the premises for the costs of rebuilding, and to cover the rent if the premises cannot be occupied whilst they are being rebuilt. The lease may allow the landlord to state which insurance company must be used, the amount of cover and the risks to be insured against. Normally the landlord insures the building and the tenant contributes towards the cost, in which case the tenant should have a right under the terms of the lease to inspect the insurance policy.

Organisations are under no explicit legal obligation to insure premises they own. However, the committee would be negligent and could be in breach of trust if it left any building uninsured. It is usual to insure for the cost of rebuilding the premises if completely destroyed, including architects' fees. It is also worth considering cover for the cost of temporary, alternative accommodation whilst the rebuilding takes place.

## Insurance for plate glass windows

Leases of property with shopfronts often require tenants to insure any plate glass windows against breakage, either accidentally or by vandals.

## Public liability insurance

This covers injury, loss or damage caused to any person as a result of an organisation's negligence. It would include injury suffered by someone using the organisation's premises as a result of a breach of the duty under the **Occupier's Liability Act, 1957** (see chapter 5).

Leases often require tenants to take out insurance to cover against injuries suffered as a result of defects in the premises. It would be sensible to extend the insurance to cover all types of public liability, as the cost is often very small when the policy is taken out in conjunction with another type of insurance.

Management committee members, volunteers, trainees and consultants are not covered for accidents they suffer under the terms of the employer's liability insurance policy. To protect itself against such claims, an organisation must therefore ensure it has adequate public liability insurance. It is important to inform the insurance company of the nature of the organisation's work and the fact that it uses volunteers, trainees and consultants.

Because an organisation might be liable for the negligence of people acting as consultants, it is essential to ensure that consultants are adequately insured themselves where there is any element of risk, for example through giving professional advice of any kind, and to make this a condition of appointment.

## Discretionary insurance

Organisations should consider the following types of insurance, depending on the nature of their activities and the extent of their property.

## Contents insurance

This normally covers the contents of a building for theft or damage by, for example fire, but usually excludes accidental damage caused directly by individuals (for example by dropping a typewriter), and theft by the organisation's employees (for this, the organisation would need fidelity insurance: see below). The insurance will also exclude property while it is out of the organisation's building unless there is provision covering the property during a move to other permanent premises (see 'All risks insurance', below).

Insurance companies must be told about the likely users of a building. They may impose conditions on the policy, for example restrict cover to loss after a break in or insist on additional locks or burglar alarms. If the policy is to cover theft of cash, the insurance company may require the purchase of a safe.

It is especially important to inform the insurance company if volunteers carry out any work or the premises are used by other organisations.

## All risks insurance

This is usually an extension of the contents insurance but also covers property when it is outside the building. It is especially useful for organisations which shift around expensive equipment to different venues, for example theatre or music groups.

## Equipment failure

It is possible to insure major equipment, such as boilers and lifts, against damage and breakdown. Most policies then require regular maintenance checks and services.

## Employees' dishonesty (fidelity insurance)

Organisations dealing with large amounts of cash should consider insuring against employees' dishonesty. The insurance company would want details of any conviction against employees.

Some organisations may wish to consider insuring against dishonesty by members of the management committee. This is not a standard type of insurance, but an insurance company might supply it as an extension to a policy covering employees' dishonesty. Again, members would have to disclose any previous convictions.

## Loss of documents

It is possible to obtain insurance against loss of documents, including computer records. This can be important for organisations relying on large amounts of documentary information, for example those providing advice or other professional services.

## Loss of fees

It is possible to obtain insurance against loss of fees resulting from damage to the office or its contents.

## Professional indemnity insurance

Groups that advise the public or other organisations, or provide other professional services, should take out this type of insurance, which covers claims resulting from incorrect advice or services which cause damage or injury to the client.

Professional indemnity insurance can be extended to cover defamation (slander or libel: see chapter 9). There are always risks of this occurring if an organisation represents people or writes letters on their behalf.

## Insurance for accidents, medical care and assault

Insurance is available against staff sickness, covering the cost of sick pay. Other policies will pay out standard sums to staff for specific injuries at work, for example loss of a limb. It is also possible to take out policies to cover staff who have suffered injuries through being assaulted. You will need to negotiate extending this to volunteers and committee members.

## Legal expenses' insurance

This is often added onto other forms of insurance, for example professional indemnity or accident insurance, to cover the cost of legal fees incurred in taking action against those responsible for any loss or injury.

## Trustees' indemnity insurance

This covers the trustees of an organisation (including a committee of an unincorporated association or company limited by guarantee) against liability for acting in breach of trust or against the committee of a company or industrial and provident society for any liability for wrongful trading. It sometimes includes other types of insurance (professional indemnity, fidelity and/or loss of documents, for example).

However, there are restrictions on the circumstances in which an organisation can take out this form of insurance. Because it covers trustees rather than the organisation, there is a potential conflict of interest between the individuals and the organisation they are managing.

A charity's constitution must specifically allow for this type of insurance. If it does not, the organisation would have to amend its constitution with the consent of the Charity Commissioners before it could take out the insurance.

*The Government has accepted the recommendation of the Charities and Voluntary Organisations Deregulation Task Force that the law should be amended to allow charities to take out indemnity insurance. This is unlikely to be in force until 1995 at the earliest.*

If such insurance is constitutionally possible, the trustees or committee must set aside their own interests and decide whether it is in the charity's interest to take out the insurance. The Charity Commissioners have stated quite clearly that it would never be appropriate for the insurance to cover:

❏ breach of trust where the trustees knew there was a breach of trust or duty;

❏ breach of trust where the trustees ought to have known that there would be a breach of trust or duty and where there was a reckless disregard of whether or not it was a breach of trust or duty.

Given these exclusions, the only circumstances which are likely to be covered by the insurance are where the trustees have entered into an arrangement having made an honest but reasonable mistake.

As explained in chapter 1, the court has power to release trustees from personal liability for breach of trust if they have acted honestly and reasonably.

In most of the cases that can be covered by insurance, it is likely that the court would exercise its discretion to release the trustees. However, this can be never be established with certainty in advance.

An organisation that wants to obtain indemnity insurance for its committee should approach the Charity Commissioners for advice and, where necessary, consent for any necessary changes to the constitution. The Commissioners have a standard wording which they will want to have included in the insurance policy.

They will also want the organisation to justify the need for insurance, taking account of the nature of the group's activities, the degree of risk, the number of committee members, the amount of cover required and the likely insurance premium.

The Charity Commissioners will be prepared to allow charitable companies to take out insurance cover to protect committee members against claims for 'wrongful trading' (see chapter 10), provided it does not cover deliberate insolvent trading or doing so recklessly. Again, it would only cover the committee if they made an honest and reasonable mistake.

Trustees must understand that trustees' liability insurance does not cover them for losses or debts arising from contracts. It does not, for example, cover inability to pay bills or meet redundancy costs.

# Being covered for the right amount

In all types of insurance it is essential to be covered for the right amount.

## Property insurance

There are usually two possibilities: to be insured for the value of the property or for the actual cost of its replacement. This is applicable to buildings, contents and all risks insurance.

For example, with buildings insurance the premises can be insured for the market value if sold, or the cost of rebuilding (including surveyors' and architects' fees and possibly the cost of alternative accommodation). It is advisable to insure for the replacement cost of buildings, which may be considerably more than the market value.

When deciding on contents and all risks insurance bear in mind replacement costs. Obviously the secondhand value of a three-year-old photocopier is less than the price of a new one. It may be more sensible to pay higher premiums and insure for replacement cost; this is often called 'new-for-old' cover.

## Other insurance

For other types of insurance, work out the likely maximum claim that might be made against the organisation. Public liability insurance is usually in the region of £2 million. Road traffic insurance is unlimited.

Professional indemnity policies are geared to large professional practices and premiums are charged to match. Many voluntary organisations give advice but the maximum claim that could be made against them may be small in any one case. It might be worthwhile getting together with similar groups to persuade an insurance company to produce a tailor made package to meet your needs. This should reduce the premiums.

## Underinsurance

A policy usually states that the organisation has to insure for a sufficiently large sum to cover any claim. If the organisation is underinsured, some policies allow the insurance company to refuse to pay out at all. Other policies (which are usually more expensive) operate an average clause. This means that the insurance company pays out only a proportion of any loss. For example if a building valued at £200,000 is insured for only £50,000, the insurance company would pay only one quarter of any claim made, however small. If a claim is made for £4,000 worth of damage to a roof during a storm the insurance company would only pay £1,000.

# Who should be covered by insurance?

Any action, or the failure to perform any action by an organisation is, in practice, the responsibility of an individual within that organisation. That person will usually be a worker or management committee member but could also be a volunteer or member of the organisation. It is therefore advisable to cover staff, management committee members, volunteers and ordinary members for any liability that they may incur carrying out the work of the organisation. This would include cover by professional indemnity insurance, public liability insurance and road traffic insurance (if they are driving the organisation's vehicles).

Merely taking out insurance in the name of the organisation may not be enough. Specific extensions may be necessary. Remember that most insurance companies design their policies for individuals or businesses. Their standard policies may cover staff but usually do not cover volunteers or unpaid management committee members.

## Incorporated organisations

Incorporated organisations can take out insurance in the name of the organisation.

## Unincorporated organisations

Unincorporated organisations should take out insurance in the name of the committee of the organisation but the proposal form should be signed by one individual who is specifically stated to be taking it out on behalf of the management committee. If that individual leaves the organisation the insurance must be transferred to someone else's name.

# Making a claim

Immediately you are aware that there may be a possible claim under an insurance policy check the conditions to ensure that you comply with them. There may be preconditions to a claim, for example reporting the matter to the police, or a claim may need to be submitted within a specific period. It is therefore essential that you are able to get hold of the relevant policy quickly.

Contact the insurance company as soon as possible giving full details and quoting the policy number. If a claim involves a question of legal liability (such as the degree of responsibility for an accident) obtain legal advice before making any contact with the other party; some policies may cover this cost.

Never admit responsibility for an accident, however obvious it is that you are at fault. Many policies allow the insurance company to refuse to pay out if you have accepted liability.

# Booklist

**Trustee liability insurance: is it for you?**, *Tim Gill and Kate Kirkland*, National Council for Voluntary Organisations (1993), £3.00

**Short guide to the Employer's Liability (Compulsory Insurance) Act** (HSE4), Health and Safety Executive, free

**Insurance protection: a guide for voluntary organisations**, National Council for Voluntary Organisations (1992), £5.00

# Chapter 8: Financial management

All voluntary groups should keep accounts and in most cases it is a legal requirement to do so. Accounts will also help to show funders, members and the public that an organisation is operating effectively. In addition, keeping well-organised records will help a group to manage its activities by showing how actual income and expenditure compares with budgeted figures.

This chapter begins by outlining the legal requirements and the duties of the committee and the treasurer, then gives some general rules on drawing up budgets, handling money and maintaining financial records. The final sections describe the procedures involved in auditing the accounts. A glossary of accounting terms and a summary of accounting regulations for charities under the **Charities Act, 1993** are given at the end of the chapter.

## Legal requirements

Regulations governing accounting records, statements of account and auditing requirements vary according to an organisation's legal status (see chapter 1) and annual income and expenditure.

**Throughout this chapter reference is made to Part VI of the Charities Act, 1993. This is not currently (August 94) in force, but is likely to be implemented during the 1995/96 financial year. If in doubt, contact the Charity Commission.**

**Note:** the Government has accepted in principle the Charities and Voluntary Organisations Deregulation Task Force's recommendation to harmonise reporting requirements under the Charities Act, 1993, the Companies Acts and Industrial and Provident Societies Acts. At time of writing (August 94) this had not been implemented.

### Charities Act, 1960

This section describes the regulations in force at time of writing (August 94). These will be amended by Part VI of the Charities Act, 1993. The new regulations are described in the following section. If in doubt about which Charities Act applies, contact the Charity Commission.

Under the **Charities Act, 1960** all charities are required to:

❑ keep proper books of accounts, which must include an income and expenditure account and cover no more than a 15 month period;

❑ prepare consecutive statements of accounts;

❑ send statements of accounts to the Charity Commissioners on request.

**Endowed charities** must submit annual statements of accounts to the Charity Commissioners.

Unless required by funders or the constitution, **charitable associations** and **charitable trusts** do not currently have to have their accounts audited. It is, however, common practice to have annual accounts independently examined or audited, and this may enhance an organisation's public credibility.

Charities which are registered as **companies** have to prepare accounts in accordance with **Part VII** of the **Companies Act, 1985**.

### Charities Act, 1993

**Part VI** of the **Charities Act, 1993** governs accounting, reporting and auditing rules for charities. The details given below include the recommendations of the Charities and Voluntary Organisations Deregulation Task Force.

Under the Charities Act, 1993 all charities will be required to:

❑ maintain financial records;

❑ produce up to date accounts annually; and

❑ make their most recent annual accounts available to the public.

Registered charities with an annual income of more than £10,000 will have to submit annual accounts and reports to the Charity Commissioners; those whose annual income is £10,000 or less will only have to submit annual accounts and reports on special request.

### Trustees' annual report

Charity trustees will have to prepare an annual report, within ten months of the end of the financial year.

The trustees' report of **charities with an annual income of more than £10,000** must describe the charity's principal objectives, explain any changes in objectives and activities which have occurred in the previous year, review the year's activities and provide any other information required by the regulations. The trustees' report, together with the statement of accounts or audited/examined accounts and auditor's/examiner's report will have to be submitted to the Charity Commission within ten months of the end of the charity's financial year.

**Charities with an annual income of £10,000 or less** need only prepare a simplified trustees' report, which will not have to be submitted to the Charity Commission unless requested. At time of writing (August 94) the content of the simplified report had not been defined.

**Charitable companies** have to prepare a trustees' annual report according to the above requirements. Although this is not the same as a directors' report (prepared under the Companies Act, 1985) it is possible to combine the two by ensuring the report fulfils the requirements of both Acts. Companies must include a copy of their accounts prepared under **Part VII** of the **Companies Act, 1985**, together with the auditor's report or compilation report, with the trustees' report.

**Exempt charities** and **excepted, non-registered charities** need not prepare a trustees' annual report.

## Public access to accounts

Anyone will be able to ask any charity to provide them with a copy of its most recent accounts on payment of a reasonable fee. The copy must be provided within two months of a written request.

# Accounting records

Committee members of all charities have a duty to ensure that accounting records are kept which record the financial transactions — money spent and received — on a day to day basis, and in particular show the nature and purpose of each transaction and record all assets and liabilities.

Although records do not have to be updated each day, accounts must be able to show the financial position of the charity on any particular date in the past.

**Charitable companies** must maintain records to the same standard, under the **Companies Act, 1985.**

Although companies limited by guarantee need only keep records for three years, many funders may require records to be kept for longer periods and it is good practice to keep them for at least six years from the end of the financial year.

**Unincorporated charities** must keep accounting records for at least six years from the end of the financial year to which they relate. This applies even if the charity folds before the end of six years.

# Accounting requirements

The **Companies Act, 1985** governs the requirements for the preparation of charitable companies' annual accounts; industrial and provident societies are governed by the **Friendly and Industrial and Provident Societies Act, 1968** and unincorporated charities by the **Charities Act, 1993**. The figures quoted below can be altered by the Home Secretary.

**Unincorporated charities with a gross annual income of £100,000 or less** may prepare a receipts and payments account and a statement of assets and liabilities, or a full set of accounts.

**Unincorporated charities with an annual income of over £100,000** must prepare a full statement of accounts for each financial year, in accordance with regulations issued by the Home Secretary.

**All charitable companies** are required, under company law, to prepare a full set of accounts. An abbreviated version can be produced by small or medium-sized companies; however, the full accounts must be filed with the Charity Commissioners.

## SORP 2

The Statement of Recommended Practice on Accounting by Charities (SORP2), laid down by the Accounting Standards Committee, is a set of recommendations designed to help those involved in preparing charity accounts and annual reports. It is not part of law and so charity trustees can choose whether, and to what extent they will follow the recommendations. However, as the recommendations are regarded as good practice, charities would be expected to follow them. If they do not, funders, and the public, may query why this was the case.

At time of writing (August 94) a revised SORP was being finalised and was due to come into effect at the same time as new charity accounting regulations. For further details contact the Charity Commissioners.

## Auditing or examining accounts

Legal requirements are given below; the audit process is described in the final section of the chapter.

### Companies limited by guarantee

**Non-charitable companies with a turnover of less than £350,000** and **charitable companies whose gross income is less than £250,000** need not have an audit if they have assets of less than £1.4 million, unless required by the membership.

However, **non-charitable companies with a turnover of between £90,000 and £350,000**, and **charitable** companies with a gross income of between £90,000 and £250,000 have to produce a 'compilation report'. This involves a less detailed examination of the accounts by a qualified practising accountant, and the accountant's certificate does not need to certify that the accounts give 'a true and fair view' of the company's financial position. It will therefore be cheaper to have a compilation report prepared than to pay for a full audit.

Members of a company can require an audit. To exercise this right at least 10% of the membership has to give notice in writing, no later than one month before the end of the financial year in question, to the registered office.

The regulations bringing the new rules on company audits came into effect on 10 August 94. Companies which had their accounts approved by the committee before that date can take immediate advantage of the new rules, even if their financial year ended before the regulations came into force. Any organisation whose financial year ended 31 March 1994 should consider whether it wishes to take advantage of the new rules.

Two points to note. A company's articles may require an audit. If this is so they could be amended to enable the organisation to take advantage of the new rules. If any funders require a full audit the organisation would not be able to take advantage of the new rules.

## Unincorporated charities

The requirements under the **Charities Act, 1993** are given below. They are likely to come into force during the 1995/96 financial year.

**Exempt charities** do not have to have their accounts audited or examined under the Charities Act, but may have to under other legislation.

**Charities with an annual income of £10,000 or less** do not have to have their accounts audited or examined.

**Charities with gross income _and_ total expenditure of between £10,000 and £250,000** in the current financial year and each of the two previous financial years need only have their accounts examined by an 'independent examiner' — ie 'an independent person who is reasonably believed by the trustees to have the requisite ability and practical experience to carry out a competent examination of the accounts'. This includes people such as bank managers. They must, if the constitution or funders so require, have a full audit.

**Charities with a gross income _or_ total expenditure of more than £250,000** in the current financial year or either of the two previous financial years will have to have their accounts audited by a qualified auditor. At time of writing (August 94) 'qualified auditor' had not been defined, but is likely to include people eligible under the Companies Act, 1989, including members of the Institute of Chartered Accountants in England and Wales and many members of the Chartered Association of Certified Accountants (qualified auditors use the initials CA, ACA, FCA, ACCA or FCCA after their name).

If the audit is not carried out within ten months of the end of the financial year the Charity Commissioners will have the right to order an audit and make the trustees jointly and individually liable for the costs, or recover the costs from the charity's funds. The Commissioners also have the power to order an audit by an eligible auditor if they are not satisfied with an independent examiner's report.

## PAYE

Organisations employing staff must keep records showing income tax deductions under Pay As You Earn (PAYE), national insurance (NI) contributions and statutory sick pay payments (see chapter 3).

An organisation must register with the Inland Revenue for PAYE if it pays workers, even on a casual basis who:

❑ earn more than the minimum national insurance (NI) threshold (£57/week in 1994/95); or

❑ work in another job as well (even if they earn less than the NI threshold in either or both jobs).

Tax and NI deductions must be made from the earnings of workers who earn more than the thresholds and organisations must pay the tax and NI (both employees' and employer's contributions) to the Inland Revenue every month. PAYE records must be kept for at least three years, although it is advisable to keep them for at least six years (for further details of PAYE see chapter 4).

## Value Added Tax

If an organisation's turnover from sources other than grants, donations and investments exceeds the annual threshold (£45,000 in 1994/95) it may need to register for Value Added Tax (VAT) and keep detailed records. It may also need to charge VAT on goods and services.

An organisation will need to register for VAT if:

❑ at the end of any month, the value of taxable supplies (goods or services provided which are liable to VAT either at the standard rate or at the zero rate) in the past 12 months has exceeded the annual threshold; or

❏ at any time, there are reasonable grounds for believing that the value of taxable supplies in the next 30 days will exceed the annual threshold.

There is one month in which to register, by completing registration form VAT1 (available from the local VAT office — listed in the phone book under Customs & Excise). Customs & Excise will stipulate a date from which an organisation is registered and provide a VAT number. It is unlawful for an organisation to charge VAT before it is registered. Once registered, VAT invoices must be provided and kept. Quarterly returns will be sent automatically and must be completed and returned within one month of the end of the quarter. Organisations which have been registered for at least a year and whose annual taxable supplies excluding VAT are £300,000 or less may be able to submit annual returns. Contact the local VAT office for details.

There are substantial penalties for failing to register for the purposes of VAT or registering late. It is therefore essential to keep a regular check on the level of turnover to see whether the annual threshold will be reached. Remember that income from grants, donations and legacies does not generally count towards the threshold for VAT purposes.

Customs & Excise will provide details of the current threshold, advise on registration and record keeping and help with the assessment of taxable turnover (not all income-generating activities by charities are regarded as 'sales').

Registration for VAT may bring some benefits and in some cases it is possible to register even if the level of taxable turnover is below the threshold. Although you would have to charge others VAT on goods or services provided, you can recover VAT on goods or services purchased, and this may result in an overall saving. However, the process does involve a lot of work.

VAT is a complicated subject, particularly for charities, and cannot be covered in full in this book. For further details contact your accountant or auditor and the local VAT office, and see *A practical guide to VAT for charities.*

## Income tax

Charities are generally exempt from income tax provided that the income from each source is used only for charitable purposes, subject to certain conditions and activities. Charities are therefore able to recover basic rate income tax on covenanted and some one-off payments made by donors out of taxed income.

Non-charities may have to pay income tax and should take advice from their accountant or auditor.

## Corporation tax

Charitable companies are exempt from corporation tax in the same way that other charities are exempt from income tax. Grants and donations are not subject to corporation tax but charitable companies which receive income from other sources, such as trading or property rents, may have to pay.

Non-charitable companies may be subject to corporation tax and should take advice from their accountant or auditor.

## Covenants

Charities which reclaim tax on covenanted donations (see chapter 9) must also keep special records of income received. Further information is available from the *Inland Revenue Charities Claims Branch.*

# Duties of the committee

All committee members have a duty to see that the organisation is being properly managed and funds are spent correctly. Committees of charities have a statutory duty to ensure that funds are being spent appropriately for charitable purposes. Committees of companies limited by guarantee must conform to the requirements of the Companies Acts.

In a registered charity the members of the committee are usually the charity trustees. Responsibility for all the organisation's money and property lies with all the trustees and cannot be delegated to the treasurer. If trustees fail to carry out their duty properly they may be liable for any losses caused by their breach of trust.

The main financial responsibilities of the committee are to:

❏ comply with legal requirements — these will vary according to the legal structure of the organisation;

❏ approve and monitor budgets;

❏ ensure that proper control is exercised over income and expenditure;

❏ oversee fundraising policy and activities and trading activities;

❏ ensure tax affairs are managed effectively;

❏ ensure that the organisation's funds are used in accordance with its constitution, committee decisions and funders' conditions;

❏ ensure funds are spent for the purpose for which they were given and the committee is not acting 'ultra vires' (spending funds on activities outside the remit of the constitution).

Day to day control and supervision of finances can be delegated to the treasurer or finance worker(s); however, committee members still remain responsible for the overall management of the finances.

In any organisation the members of the committee must make sure that the treasurer is carrying out the job properly. This means satisfying themselves that the treasurer is honest and competent.

There are several ways in which the committee can minimise risks. For example, it can:

❑ make sure that anyone who stands for election as treasurer has some experience of handling money and accounts;

❑ arrange additional training for the treasurer if necessary;

❑ appoint a finance subcommittee to oversee day to day management of finances and meet regularly to examine the accounts;

❑ require the treasurer to make regular financial reports to the committee;

❑ have careful procedures for handling cash, involving at least two people;

❑ require two signatures on cheques and ensure that blank cheques are never signed, for any reason. No cheque should ever be signed without documentation, for example an invoice, explaining the expense;

❑ ensure that all expenses are authorised by the treasurer, manager or other authorised person, no one can authorise expenses paid to his or herself, and all expenses are paid by cheque rather than in cash;

❑ employ a bookkeeper to carry out all transactions.

# Duties of the treasurer

In a small group, the treasurer may deal with all aspects of financial management including keeping records. In organisations with paid staff the treasurer's job can be time consuming. In such cases the day to day management of the finances could be delegated to a paid finance worker or another staff member, who would report to the treasurer.

However, in all cases final responsibility for financial matters always rests with the committee as a whole.

The treasurer's responsibilities may include the following:

❑ general financial oversight;

❑ managing income — funding, contracts, fundraising and sales;

❑ financial planning and budgeting;

❑ financial reporting;

❑ banking, bookkeeping and record keeping;

❑ control of fixed assets and stock.

Use the following checklist to decide which tasks should be carried out by the treasurer or finance staff and which need the involvement of the finance subcommittee or whole committee.

## General financial oversight

This covers broad responsibility for the organisation's financial decision making and may include:

❑ ensuring workers and committee members know enough about financial administration, bookkeeping and the accounts to make decisions for which they are responsible;

❑ advising on financial policies, for example what expenses can be claimed and the procedures for claiming them, financial implications of new activities, or the organisation's policy on charging for its services;

❑ advising on contracts of employment and other contracts;

❑ making day to day financial decisions on behalf of the committee, if given delegated authority, and reporting such decisions to the committee;

❑ liaising with the bank or other financial institutions;

❑ preparing accounts for audit and liaising with the auditor;

❑ deciding on measures to ensure security of cash and cheques.

## Managing income

This involves ensuring the organisation has enough money to carry out its activities. The sources of income can be divided into **funding** (grant aid), **contracts** or **service agreements** (to provide activities or services — see chapter 9), **fundraising** (for example membership drives, appeals, jumble sales or special events undertaken to raise money for the organisation), and **sales of goods or services**.

Responsibilities include:

❑ developing and implementing an income-generating strategy;

❑ coordinating fundraising activities;

❑ collecting information on funding sources;

❑ completing, submitting and coordinating funding applications;

❑ liaising with funding agencies;

❑ drawing up tenders or proposals for contracted services;

❑ running fundraising activities;

❑ ensuring money received for special projects is spent for that purpose and if necessary is separately accounted for;

❑ ensuring goods or services to be sold are priced appropriately.

## Financial planning and budgeting

This includes:

❑ preparing budgets and cashflow forecasts (see below), in consultation with workers and funders;

❑ presenting budgets to the committee for approval;

❑ keeping track of how actual income and expenditure compares with budgeted income and expenditure and adjusting financial forecasts as appropriate;

❑ in the case of cashflow problems, deciding priorities for paying and negotiating for late payment if necessary.

## Financial reporting

The treasurer is responsible for ensuring the committee has enough information to make its decisions. This means:

❑ reporting regularly, in writing, to the committee on the organisation's financial position;

❑ preparing and presenting financial reports and accounts when required;

❑ presenting the end of year financial report (draft annual accounts) to the committee;

❑ presenting the audited or examined accounts to the annual general meeting (AGM);

❑ ensuring members at the AGM understand the annual accounts and the budget for the current year.

## Banking, bookkeeping and record keeping

The treasurer is responsible for:

❑ advising which banks or other financial institutions the organisation should use and the type of bank accounts it should have (every decision to open, close or change bank or other accounts must be approved by the committee);

❑ serving as a signatory for the organisation's bank accounts (all changes of signatory must be approved by the committee);

❑ ensuring there are proper systems for receiving and paying out cash and cheques;

❑ setting up appropriate bookkeeping and petty cash systems, and ensuring related documentation is kept;

❑ ensuring membership records are kept and subscriptions collected;

❑ ensuring other money due to the organisation is collected, that there are procedures for non-payment and that such action is taken if required;

❑ ensuring all bills are paid and receipts are received for all payments;

❑ ensuring payment of wages, income tax, national insurance, statutory sick pay, pensions and maternity pay and that records are kept of these payments;

❑ ensuring everyone handling money for the organisation keeps appropriate records and documentation.

## Control of fixed assets and stock

The treasurer has broad responsibility for ensuring proper control of **fixed assets** (major equipment, vehicles, buildings and other property owned by the organisation), its **materials** or **supplies** (goods required for running the organisation) and its **stock** (goods such as publications waiting to be distributed or sold). This responsibility includes:

❑ ensuring the organisation keeps records of material and supplies used;

❏ establishing systems for stock control and reorders;

❏ undertaking or overseeing regular stock checks;

❏ ensuring the organisation keeps records of its equipment and vehicles, including date of purchase, supplier, value, model and serial number (sometimes called an inventory);

❏ ensuring the organisation has all necessary insurances and keeps them up to date (see chapter 7).

# The budget

Each year a group needs to draw up a budget — an estimate of how much it expects to pay out in expenditure and receive in income during the financial year. The budget should be used to monitor income and expenditure during the year. It is also useful to produce a longer term financial plan covering, for example three years, which will include any planned new developments.

It is essential to estimate costs as accurately as possible and include these in any funding application. Funders are realistic and want to see a viable proposal. The recent shift from grant aid to service level agreements or contracts between voluntary groups and statutory authorities (see chapter 9) makes accurate estimates even more important. A group which contracts to provide a service for a fixed price could be in breach of contract if it cannot complete the work because it runs out of funds.

When preparing a budget allow for the following:

❏ salaries and future salary increases including annual increments, overtime, if paid, and use of temporary staff;

❏ statutory sick pay;

❏ employer's national insurance contributions;

❏ employer's pension contributions, if paid;

❏ recruitment costs;

❏ staff, volunteer and committee training;

❏ travelling;

❏ capital expenditure;

❏ heating, lighting, water, telephone and fax;

❏ office expenditure such as stationery, post and printing;

❏ auditor's fees, legal fees, bank charges and bookkeeping charges;

❏ building costs, including rent, rates, repairs, service charges, maintenance and insurance;

❏ equipment costs, including rent, rates, repairs, maintenance and insurance;

❏ any other costs (if they are not fixed make an allowance for inflation).

Other matters to take into consideration are:

❏ inflation;

❏ how staff and the treasurer will be involved;

❏ timing — allow time for presenting the budget to the committee.

Think carefully about the headings used in the budget, as the same headings should be used in financial records and accounts (see below).

The budget must be presented to the full committee for approval. Committee members must ensure they understand what is being presented and ask the right questions:

❏ do I understand where the income comes from?

❏ do I understand the headings used for expenditure?

❏ do the figures balance?

❏ are estimates and assumptions made reasonably justified?

A balanced budget is one in which anticipated income equals anticipated expenditure. If anticipated income is greater than anticipated expenditure the excess may be shown as 'surplus transferred to reserves' to balance the budget. If the reverse is true, the difference will be shown as a deficit. If this is the case, the committee needs to know how the organisation will cover it.

The treasurer should report at least quarterly on the organisation's income and expenditure and whether it is in tune with budget. If the organisation has more than one project the report should cover these separately. Such reports are called **management accounts** and are the best way to enable groups to anticipate any financial problems.

# General rules on handling money

Always issue receipts for money received and obtain receipts for all expenditure. Ensure that all money received is entered into the books before it is used to pay outgoings. It is good practice to pay all cash received into the bank, and to draw the amounts required separately. Keep detailed records and notes of transactions.

Never keep more cash than is necessary on the premises; pay any surplus into the bank as soon as possible. Keys to the safe should be held only by authorised people, with duplicates kept at the bank.

# Bank accounts

To open an account in the name of an organisation the committee needs to pass a resolution, the wording of which is set out on a form supplied by the bank (the **Form of Mandate**) which must be completed by officers of the organisation. Attached should be a copy of the group's constitution. Those officers authorised to draw cheques on behalf of the organisation must be named on the form.

The constitution will usually include rules on cheque signatories. Many organisations choose to have three or four signatories and state that cheques must be signed by at least two of them. If an organisation has paid staff it may be convenient for one of them to be a signatory. As most groups need to withdraw small amounts for cash, it is possible to arrange that cheques below a certain amount require the signature of only one committee member. Cheques should never be signed blank; any committee member who signs a blank cheque might have to pay the organisation back for any loss that resulted.

Organisations that have extra cash should consider opening a deposit account to accumulate interest. Registered charities do not generally have to pay tax on interest earned in a deposit account.

Bank charges vary and can add a significant amount to a group's expenditure. It is worth spending some time talking to bank managers in order to get the best deal. Always get written details of how charges are calculated.

# Looking after cash

Organisations that handle cash should take extra precautions, to safeguard against theft by outsiders, staff, volunteers or committee members. An insurance company may require certain precautions to be taken for cash covered by insurance, for example the purchase of a safe (see chapter 7).

Remember that staff may be more vulnerable to attack if there is cash on the premises. Wherever possible ensure that two people are involved in the management of cash.

# Record keeping

Financial responsibility involves keeping records ('accounts' or 'books') of how much money has come into the organisation, where it has come from, and how it has been spent. This process is called **bookkeeping**. Along with the books you must keep documentation, such as invoices and receipts, to prove the money was spent in the way shown. The books and proofs will be used to draw up regular accounts (monthly and/or quarterly), financial reports (sometimes called **management accounts**) and the **annual accounts**.

It is a legal requirement for unincorporated charities to keep the books and financial documentation for six years: it is good practice for all voluntary organisations to do so.

The treasurer should aim to keep only those books of records necessary to maintain adequate financial control and the information the committee needs. For most small groups two books are sufficient:

❑ the **cash analysis book**: to record **money paid into** and **out of the bank** (this includes cheques, standing orders and direct debits);

❑ the **petty cash analysis book**: to record incidental expenses made in cash.

Subsidiary records are used to record additional detailed information that would be impossible to enter into the cash analysis book (for example membership subscriptions).

Analysis books can be purchased from large stationers. They are available with a number of different columns, so check the number of columns you need before making a purchase.

Brief descriptions of these books are given below; for more detailed information, including worked examples, see *How to manage your money if you have any.*

## Cash analysis book

The **cash analysis book**, often known as the **cash book**, is an organisation's most important financial record. Entries should be made as soon as possible after every transaction (ie money paid into the bank, cheques drawn or standing orders or direct debits paid).

If an organisation receives income from a number of sources it may be advisable to have two books — one to record income and one to record expenditure. An alternative is to use one book and record income and expenditure on alternate pages.

Cash analysis books use a number of columns to analyse each transaction. Each column is given an appropriate heading, for example, 'stationery', 'rent', 'travel', but it is up to the treasurer and committee to decide what these should be. If all income is recorded in one column, this should be headed 'income'. It is convenient to use budget headings to enable actual and anticipated expenditure to be compared.

For each transaction you should record:

❏ the date;

❏ cheque number, SO (standing order) or DD (direct debit) if a payment; receipt number if income;

❏ to whom a cheque was payable and for what, or where income came from and what it was for;

❏ the amount of the transaction under the appropriate column heading.

It is good practice to issue receipts to those who give money to the organisation. Receipt books, in duplicate, can be purchased with numbered pages. The receipt number should be entered in the cash book.

## Bank statements and bank reconciliation statements

A bank statement is the bank's record of the organisation's finances. This record may not agree exactly with that in the cash book(s) because it can take a few days for credits and debits to appear in a bank account.

Bank statements should be checked immediately against the cash book(s) and a **bank reconciliation statement** should be prepared along the following lines and kept at the back of the cash analysis book:

---

### Bank reconciliation statement @ 31.7.94

|  | £ |
|---|---|
| Balance shown on bank statement | 1958.32 |

Less uncleared cheques (those recorded in the cash book but not yet appearing on the bank statement):

| cheque no | amount | |
|---|---|---|
| 243881 | 346.22 | |
| 243884 | 92.44 | |
| 243888 | 100.00 | |
| total of uncleared cheques | | 538.66 |
| | | 1419.66 |

Add credits not shown on statement (those recorded in the cash book but not yet appearing on the bank statement)

| date paid into bank | amount | |
|---|---|---|
| 25.7.94 | 250.00 | 250.00 |
| **True balance at bank** | | **1669.66** |

Balances shown in cash book

| | | |
|---|---|---|
| Total receipts paid into bank | 3495.24 | |
| Less total payments from bank | 1825.58 | |
| **Balance as per cash book** | | **1669.66** |

---

If the two figures do not balance, check the entries in the cash book:

❑ have all payments and receipts been entered? (standing orders, direct debits and bank charges might be on the statement but not yet in the cash book);

❑ have they been entered correctly?

❑ has a cheque issued some time ago not been cleared?

❑ has the cash book be added up correctly?

❑ are there any unexplained items in the bank statement?

## Special accounts

If a grant is received for a special project (for example a summer playscheme) it is not necessary to open a new bank account. Extra bank accounts only complicate bookkeeping and can create additional bank charges. All that is usually needed to be able to account for a special grant is an additional analysis column on both the income and expenditure sides of the cash book. A brief comment should be made in the details column explaining the entries (for example 'playscheme').

## Petty cash analysis book

A common method for recording small cash transactions is the **'imprest'** or **'float'** system. You estimate how much you are likely to need each month (say £50) and draw that amount from the bank account to start up the float. When most of the money has been spent (say £45), it is topped up by drawing cash from the bank equal to the expenditure (ie £45).

Cash transactions should be kept to the minimum; use cheques wherever possible. All petty cash transactions must be recorded on petty cash vouchers and in the petty cash analysis book, and analysed under appropriate headings (for example 'travel expenses', 'postage'). Whenever possible a receipt should be obtained and stapled to the petty cash voucher, which should be numbered. Always record full details of the transaction — the amount, what it was for and the voucher number.

The amounts entered in the columns in the cash book should be included in the organisation's accounts.

## Other financial records

Other records an organisation may keep include those relating to PAYE and VAT, a sales invoice book, purchase order book, purchase invoice book and covenanted income.

# Financial reports

A **financial report** or **management account** is any statement which informs committee members of the current financial situation. For most small organisations an appropriate financial report for the committee would be presented quarterly and would include:

❑ receipts and payments for the period, showing the balance in hand (amount left at the end of the period);

❑ a statement of how much money was owed to the organisation at the end of the financial period, and for what;
❑ a statement of how much money the organisation owed and for what;

❑ a comparison with the budget to date showing variances and a projection to the end of the financial year;

❑ an indication of any actual or potential financial problems or situations needing a decision by the finance subcommittee or committee.

The system does have its drawbacks. Although a receipts and payments account gives an accurate statement of money received and paid out by an organisation it does not show its true financial position. It does not include expenditure committed but not yet paid or payments made in advance, nor income due but not yet received or income received in advance.

## Receipts and payments account

This is the form of report favoured by most small voluntary organisations, mainly because of its simplicity. A summary of the cash book, it presents a simple statement of money received and paid out:

**balance brought forward** + **receipts**
(amount held at the beginning      (money received
of the accounting period)          during the period)

=

**payments**                      + **balance in hand**
(money spent                       (amount left at the
 during the period)                 end of the period)

## Income and expenditure account

This is based on the receipts and payments account but is adjusted to include money owed to and by the organisation. It gives a more accurate surplus/deficit position but requires some bookkeeping knowledge.

## Balance sheet

A **balance sheet** is designed to show how much the organisation is worth on a particular day (normally the last day of the financial period). It includes **assets** (everything the organisation owns) and **liabilities** (what it owes). A balance sheet shows the organisation's **net worth** at a particular point; it does not show what happened over a period. It shows the solvency of the organisation.

For further information, including worked examples, see *How to manage your money if you have any*.

## Forecasts

A forecast revises the organisation's anticipated income and expenditure by taking into account developments since the budget was drawn up, and helps the committee make financial decisions. Ideally forecasts should be produced every quarter, and at least every six months. They can also be built into the financial reports/management accounts (see above).

When examining forecasts, committee members should consider the following:

❏ do the forecasts for income or expenditure need to be adjusted, either upwards or downwards?

❏ what are the implications of any adjustments?

❏ do they take account of inflation or changes in interest rates?

❏ does the organisation need to take steps to ensure future budgets are more accurate?

### Cashflow forecasts

Cashflow means just that — the flow of money (cash and cheques) into and out of the organisation. A cashflow forecast shows, usually on a monthly basis, when in the year payments are made and income is received. It is therefore a useful method of warning committee members when a cash shortage may result.

#### Cashflow and other financial problems

If an organisation has a short-term cashflow problem, an arranged overdraft will ease the crisis, but constant overdrafts are not a good form of financial control. They are expensive, which can make the financial situation even worse, and the bank will probably want security for the overdraft, in the form of collateral (the organisation's assets) or personal guarantees from committee members. Overdrafts can also be called in at any time.

**Committee members who give personal guarantees become personally responsible for the overdraft if the organisation cannot pay it.**

**In unincorporated organisations they will always be responsible.**

If the organisation does not have a reasonable prospect of ever being able to pay its bills it needs to seek advice urgently from a qualified accountant or auditor. If the organisation is unincorporated, committee members could be held personally liable for its debts.

If the organisation is a company limited by guarantee it may be unlawful under the **Insolvency Act, 1986** for it to carry on operating. The company's accountant or auditor should be contacted immediately. If it carries on despite being in such financial difficulty, individual committee members could lose their limited liability and be held personally liable for the organisation's debts.

# The auditing or examining process

Each year the annual accounts may have to be audited or examined; this should be carried out before the annual general meeting (AGM) so that members can be given a report about the accounts. Some organisations include a clause in their constitutions requiring an audit to be done and financial reports circulated a specified period before the AGM. Limited companies, industrial and provident societies and friendly societies are required by law to circulate audited or examined accounts to members 21 days before the AGM. It is good practice for all organisations to do the same.

The requirement for conducting an annual audit will often be laid down by a grant giving body, which may also state that a qualified auditor must be used.

## Responsibilities of the auditor

The main duties of an auditor are to:

❏ check that the organisation has spent money within the terms of its constitution or aims and objectives, committee decisions, agreed accounting policies and funders' requirements;

❏ check that all money received and spent has been entered in the books;

❏ verify that vouchers (such as receipts, used cheques or cheque stubs) and subsidiary records exist to back up the entries in the cash book;

❏ verify that the receipts and payments account (or income and expenditure account plus balance sheet) gives a true picture of the organisation's financial position and transactions;

- advise on ways in which the controls and record keeping systems could be improved, if necessary;

- report the findings to the organisation's members and issue a written statement saying that proper books of accounts have been kept (assuming this is the case);

- verify that the treasurer has followed the committee's and officers' instructions.

## Appointing an auditor

Many constitutions include a clause stating that the auditor must be appointed by the AGM. Some also state that the AGM must set the fee or delegate responsibility for this task.

Before employing a professional auditor get quotations. It may be useful to seek advice or recommendations from the local council for voluntary service, community accountancy project or bank manager before arranging an audit (some bank managers will arrange for one of their staff to carry out the audit free of charge or for a minimal fee). Also refer to *Accountancy services for voluntary organisations.*

## Records the auditor needs

The items the auditor may require to carry out an end of accounting year audit are:

- a copy of the constitution (or memorandum and articles of association);

- cash analysis books;

- petty cash analysis book;

- bank reconciliation statements;

- bank paying in book;

- bank statements;

- cheque book stubs, and used cheques if returned by the bank;

- written confirmation by the bank of the balance in the bank account;

- purchase invoices;

- all vouchers, including receipts obtained for money paid out and the duplicate receipt book (which should contain carbon copies of receipts for money received);

- details of wages and salaries, and written evidence of salary changes;

- PAYE records;

- any subsidiary records kept;

- VAT records;

- conditions of grants from funders;

- the receipts and payments account (or income and expenditure account and balance sheet) for the previous year;

- the receipts and payments account (or income and expenditure account and balance sheet) for the period being audited;

- all legal documents signed during the year;

- a copy of the organisation's written financial procedures, if any;

- list of debtors;

- list of opening balances;

- list of liabilities including items contracted but not yet paid for and unpaid purchase invoices;

- committee minutes authorising financial decisions (for example salary increases).

# Glossary

**Accruals**

Expenses that have been incurred in an accounting period, but have not yet been paid. They should be entered on the balance sheet as money owed.

**Accumulated funds**

Money a group may accumulate year by year through not spending all its income. If the group spends more than it receives it will end up with an accumulated deficit.

**Audit**

The annual check of the accounts by an independent person (the auditor).

**Accounting year**

The 12 month period of financial operations. The most commonly used period for voluntary groups is 1 April to 31 March.

**Balance sheet**

A record of the group's assets and liabilities.

**Bank reconciliation**

A method of making the figures in the cash book(s) match those on the bank statement.

**Bookkeeping**

The process of keeping records of how much money has come into an organisation, where it has come from, and how it has been spent.

**Budget**

An estimate of how much an organisation expects to pay out in expenditure, and receive in income during a financial year.

**Cash analysis book**

A detailed summary of monies received and paid out (also known as the cash book).

**Cashflow forecast**

Statement showing when in the year payments are made and income received.

**Current assets**

These include the money in the bank and in the petty cash box; any money owed to the organisation; stocks of goods for sale; and prepayments (see below). They are called current assets because they can, in theory, be converted into cash within a year.

**Current liabilities**

Money owed, including bank overdrafts and accruals.

**Depreciation**

A method for spreading the cost of a piece of equipment over its useful life. For example a minibus may last for five years. If it cost £7,500 it is more realistic to show £1,500 of depreciation in each of these five years' accounting rather than one large sum every so often. There are many different methods of accounting for depreciation; for example an equal amount each year, or a percentage reduction each year. Whichever method is used should be stated in the notes to the balance sheet.

**Financial report**

Any statement which informs committee members of the current financial situation. Also called management accounts.

**Fixed assets**

Items that have a longer life than one year, for example buildings, vehicles and equipment. Each year a proportion of their value can, if appropriate for the item concerned, be charged as an expense in the income and expenditure account as depreciation. So, by the time the item needs replacing, it no longer has a value in the book.

**Imprest book**

A record of cash spent (a form of petty cash book).

**Income and expenditure account**

A statement of the organisation's finances showing outstanding debts and money owed.

**Management account**

See 'Financial report'

**Petty cash analysis book**

The day to day listing of petty cash paid out.

**Prepayments**

Items paid in advance. They are deducted from the income and expenditure account and shown on the balance sheet as money owed to the organisation.

**Receipts and payments account**

A statement of actual income received and expenditure made by the organisation in a fixed period (not adjusted as it is for an income and expenditure account).

**SORP2**

Statement of Recommended Practice on Accounting by Charities — a set of recommendations for preparing charity accounts and annual reports: not part of the law.

**Taxable supplies**

Goods or services provided which are liable to VAT either at the standard rate or at the zero rate when the goods are supplied by a trader registered for VAT.

**VAT**

Value Added Tax

# Summary of accounting regulations under Part VI of the Charities Act, 1993

At time of writing (August 94) Part VI of the Charities Act was not yet in force: it is likely to be implemented during the 1995/96 financial year.

*See chapter 1 for definitions of legal status*

## Unregistered very small charities

❑ do not have to submit accounts to the Charity Commission;

❑ do not have to prepare a trustees' annual report;

❑ must provide a copy of their accounts within two months of a written request; a reasonable fee can be charged.

## Registered very small charities

Very small charities which are voluntarily registered must comply with the requirements for unincorporated charities with income up to £10,000.

## Unincorporated charities: annual income £10,000 or below

❑ must draw up annual accounts, which can be a receipts and payments account and a statement of assets and liabilities, or a full set of accounts;

❑ must have accounts audited or independently examined;

❑ must prepare a simplified trustees' annual report, in line with Charity Commission guidance;

❑ do not have to submit annual accounts or a trustees' report to the Charity Commission, unless specifically required to do so;

❑ must provide a copy of their accounts within two months of a written request; a reasonable fee can be charged.

## Unincorporated charities: annual income between £10,000 and £100,000

❑ must draw up annual accounts, which can be a receipts and payments account and a statement of assets and liabilities, or a full set of accounts;

❑ must have their accounts examined by an independent examiner or audited by a qualified auditor;

❑ must prepare a trustees' annual report;

❑ must submit the trustees' report, together with the examined/audited accounts and examiner's/auditor's report to the Charity Commission, within ten months of the end of the charity's financial year;

❑ must provide a copy of their accounts within two months of a written request; a reasonable fee can be charged.

## Unincorporated charities: annual income between £100,000 and £250,000

❑ must prepare a full set of accounts;

❑ must have their accounts examined by an independent examiner or audited by a qualified auditor;

❑ must prepare a trustees' annual report;

❑ must submit the trustees' report, together with the examined/audited accounts and examiner's/auditor's report to the Charity Commission, within ten months of the end of the charity's financial year;

❑ must provide a copy of their accounts within two months of a written request; a reasonable fee can be charged.

## Unincorporated charities: income or expenditure over £250,000

❑ must prepare a full set of accounts;

❑ must have their accounts audited by a qualified auditor;

❑ must prepare a trustees' annual report;

❑ must submit the trustees' annual report, together with the audited accounts and auditor's report to the Charity Commission, within ten months of the end of the charity's financial year;

❑ must provide a copy of their accounts within two months of a written request; a reasonable fee can be charged.

## Charitable companies

❑ must prepare a full set of accounts in accordance with company law;

❑ must have their accounts audited or reported on under company law;

❑ must prepare a directors' annual report as

required under company law and a trustees' annual report as required under charity law (these reports can be combined, but must fulfil both sets of requirements);

❑ must submit the trustees' annual report, together with the full accounts and auditor's or other report to the Charity Commission, within ten months of the end of the charity's financial year;

❑ must make their accounts and reports available to the public as required under company law.

### Excepted unregistered charities

❑ must prepare annual accounts depending on income (see above);

❑ must, if required as specified above, have their accounts independently examined or audited by an independent examiner or auditor;

❑ do not have to prepare a trustees' annual report unless required by the Charity Commission;

❑ do not have to submit the trustees' report or annual accounts to the Charity Commission unless specifically required to;

❑ must provide a copy of their accounts within two months of a written request; a reasonable fee can be charged.

### Excepted registered charities

Must comply with the above, according to income and expenditure levels.

### Exempt charities

❑ must prepare annual accounts under appropriate legislation;

❑ if not required by any other legislation, must prepare an income and expenditure account and statement of assets and liabilities at least every 15 months;

❑ do not have to prepare a trustees' annual report;

❑ must provide a copy of their accounts within two months of a written request; a reasonable fee can be charged.

# Booklist

**A practical guide to VAT for charities**, *Kate Sayer*, Directory of Social Change (1992), £9.95

**How to manage your money if you have any: an accountancy handbook for community organisations**, Community Accountancy Project (1992), £3.50

**Accountancy services for voluntary organisations**, National Council for Voluntary Organisations (1992), £6.00

**Planning for the future: an introduction to business planning for voluntary organisations**, *Nicholas Martin and Caroline Smith*, National Council for Voluntary Organisations (1993), £10.95

**Financial reporting for charities**, Croner Publications (1994), £84.75 plus £34.50 update service

**How to assess the financial health of your organisation**, Voluntary Action Camden (1994), free

**Income tax and corporation tax: clubs, societies and associations** (IR46), Inland Revenue (1991), free

**Tax reliefs for charities** (IR75), Inland Revenue, free

# Chapter 9: Any other business

This chapter starts by describing the legislation that affects activities provided by voluntary organisations. The first section looks at the law and good practice concerning equality of opportunity in the delivery of services. Following sections examine the legal implications of campaigning, organising meetings and marches, running festivals and street parties, and looking after people. The next two sections describe defamation and the Data Protection Act. The following two sections look at the legal aspects of fundraising and the implications of taking out contracts to provide services. Finally, the implications of leasing equipment under contract are examined.

## Equal opportunities

It is easy to believe that voluntary sector services are there for anyone to use. However, this pre-supposes that everyone knows what is available, feels confident about approaching the organisation, and believes the services offered are appropriate to their needs. Groups should therefore examine their services and take positive measures to make sure that they are accessible and relevant to all.

The following sections describe both the legal requirements and good practice in the delivery of services.

### Legal requirements

The **Sex Discrimination Act, 1975 (Section 29)** generally prohibits discrimination against men or women in the supply of goods or services. There are two major exceptions for voluntary groups. These are:

❑ where a charity has as its main object the provision of services to one sex **(Section 43)**;

❑ where an organisation restricts its membership to one sex and provides services only to its members **(Section 34)**.

The **Race Relations Act, 1976 (Section 20)** generally prohibits discrimination in the provision of goods and services on the basis of race. If a group has more than 25 members, the Act also prohibits discrimination against an applicant for membership unless the group's main object is to enable members of a particular racial group, defined without reference to colour, to enjoy the benefits of membership **(Sections 25 and 26)**.

An organisation's constitution may limit the people for whom it provides services. For example registered charities are sometimes restricted to supplying services to specific people. If an organisation decides to extend its services because of equal opportunities objectives, it may have to amend its constitution (see chapter 2).

Check the conditions attached to your grant. If any clauses are potentially discriminatory, negotiate with the funder to have them removed. Many funding agencies now require organisations to implement an equal opportunities policy as part of the terms and conditions of grant aid.

### Good practice

Organisations should draw up an equal opportunities policy relating to its service provision which extends beyond the legal requirements. The policy should prohibit all discrimination on grounds of race, sex, disability, HIV status, age, trade union membership or activity, and sexuality. It should also identify ways in which services can be monitored and, if necessary, adapted so that they are relevant to all sections of the community. Measures to consider are given below.

Think about the image of the organisation. If it is seen as a predominantly white, middle class group, many people may be deterred from using its services. One way of changing the image to appeal to more people is to encourage representatives from groups facing disadvantage to sit on the management committee (see chapter 2); another is to ensure that the composition of staff, at all levels of the hierarchy, and volunteers reflects the make up of the community (see chapter 3).

### Identifying needs

Find out about the needs of groups facing disadvantage and how services may be adapted to meet them by arranging conferences, open days and visits to your organisation. Recommendations made in this consultation process should be publicly available so that you can monitor and demonstrate your progress in making changes.

### Assessing services

Examine all the services currently provided to make sure that they do not discriminate against any minority group. Also consider how they may be adapted to tackle discrimination.

The promotion of equality of opportunity in every new piece of work should automatically be discussed and recorded by the management committee.

Before planning a new project to meet the needs of particular people, consider whether your organisation is the most appropriate one to deliver a service. It may be better to help the people concerned to set up their own services, or to establish a joint project with an existing group.

Before setting up a new project make sure that you have discussed the proposal with potential users. Also consider how the work is funded. If only short-term grant aid is available, it may be better to divert more secure funding from the organisation's existing resources to start the project. However, check the terms and conditions attached to your grant to make sure this is possible.

## Monitoring

Examine who uses your services to see how effective your organisation is in meeting the needs of everyone in the community. Explain why you are monitoring services and that participation is voluntary.

Introduce an equal opportunities perspective into programmes and targets and ensure that all lessons on the achievement or non-achievement of these goals are learned.

## Publicity

All written material should be free of jargon so that it can be more easily understood by people whose first language is not English and by those who have not had the opportunity to learn the jargon. Consider translating information into other languages, recording onto tapes and publishing in braille and producing material in large print. Many organisations will not be able to afford to translate all their written material. However, consider translating a pilot run to demonstrate to funders the need for such material.

Examine how activities are promoted. Contact organisations representing people who suffer from discrimination to publicise your services. Make sure such groups are invited to your annual general meeting, open meetings, courses, conferences and all other public events.

Add newspapers and journals written for groups facing disadvantage to your press list. The *Commission for Racial Equality* has a list of the Black and ethnic minority press.

## Accessibility

Think about where and when services are available, and the location and timing of special events. Consider how to make premises and other meeting places more accessible to people with disabilities (see chapter 6). Whenever possible provide creche or childminding facilities at public events, conferences and training courses. Arrange for drivers to bring people with limited mobility to these events; the local

dial-a-ride group may be able to provide transport. Remember that people with children and other dependents often find it difficult to attend evening meetings, and many women and elderly people do not like travelling after dark.

## Affiliation

Before deciding to affiliate or become a member of another voluntary organisation examine its commitment to equal opportunities. It may be necessary to help other organisations develop an equal opportunities strategy. Do not associate with organisations that have discriminatory practices and which are hostile to change.

## Complaints

Introduce a complaints procedure for people to use if they feel that they have been discriminated against. Make sure that the procedure is well advertised. Direct and indirect discrimination, victimisation and sexual harassment by a member of staff against any user should be a disciplinary offence (see chapter 4).

# Campaigning and political activities

## Restrictions on charities

There are some restrictions on political activity that charities can undertake (see chapter 1).

## Grant conditions

Funds from a public authority or a trust may be provided for a specific purpose or may include grant conditions which restrict the type of activities that you can carry out. Check that campaigning and other political activities are not prohibited.

Under the **Local Government Acts, 1986 and 1988** local authorities cannot fund or provide other support (for example subsidised premises) to organisations to publish material that appears to influence people's support for a political party.

In deciding whether there has been a breach of this rule the following factors will be considered:

❏ whether the material refers to a political party or a person identified with a political party;

❏ if the material is published as part of a campaign, the apparent purpose of the campaign;

❏ the contents and style of the material, the time and other circumstances of its publication, and the likely effect on the audience;

❑ whether the material promotes or opposes a point of view on a question of political controversy which is identifiable as the view of one political party.

**Section 28** of the **Local Government Act, 1988** prohibits a local authority from promoting homosexuality, or publishing material with the intent to promote homosexuality. In practice, however, local authorities can grant aid organisations which provide counselling and other services to gay men and lesbians.

For further details of how these laws affect voluntary organisations see *Publish and still not be damned*.

# Meetings and marches

## Meetings on private premises

Owners, and tenants with leases, can usually refuse to let a hall without giving a reason, as long as they do not discriminate on the grounds of race or sex. Similarly, those organising a meeting have the right to refuse admission, regardless of whether an entry fee is charged, without stating a reason. The only exception to this rule arises during elections, when some publicly funded organisations may be obliged to allow a meeting room to be used for a public election meeting. Contact the Returning Officer at the town hall if you are asked to allow such use.

People who force their way into a meeting are trespassing and can be evicted using reasonable force. If there is no admission charge, a person can be asked to leave at any time without warning. However, people who have paid an entrance fee can only legally be asked to leave if they are acting in such a disorderly way that the meeting cannot continue. Under the **Public Meeting Act, 1908** it is illegal to break up a meeting.

The police can attend meetings on private premises only if invited by the organisers or if they believe that there is likely to be a breach of the peace.

## Hiring out rooms

In legal terms, rooms are let on licences, and owners can lay down conditions for their use. If these are broken, the licensee may have to compensate the owner or can be asked to leave.

Conditions that may be imposed include:

❑ a ban on alcohol: this is quite common in church halls;

❑ a time by which the meeting must finish;

❑ a limit on the number of people allowed on the premises;

❑ the responsibility for any accidents or damage during the let of the hall to be taken by the hirer. It is possible to insure against this (see chapter 7).

For further details on hiring out premises see chapter 6.

## Meetings in a public place

The **Public Order Act, 1986** enables the police to control meetings of more than 20 people held in a public place in the open air. The police can in some circumstances direct:

❑ where the meeting may be held or where it should move to if it has already started;

❑ the duration of the meeting;

❑ the maximum number of people who may attend.

In addition, several local bylaws and local Acts of Parliament control public meetings in parks and open spaces and in some streets. Details are available from the local authority. The local laws may require notice to be given to the chief executive or local police.

The police can intervene during a meeting if they suspect a breach of the peace or an obstruction may occur, but since these terms are loosely interpreted by the courts, the police have a lot of discretion in the action they can take.

It is an offence to try to break up a meeting, although anyone has the right to heckle within reasonable limits. Stewards may not ask people to leave a meeting held on public property.

## Marches and processions

The **Public Order Act, 1986** also governs marches and processions. Seven days' notice must be given to the local police of any public procession which is intended to:

❑ demonstrate support for, or opposition to any views or actions;

❑ publicise a cause or campaign; or

❑ mark or commemorate an event.

The police must also be notified if there are any changes to a planned march. If the procession is organised within seven days, as much advance notice of the march as is reasonably practicable must still be given. Notice need not be given if this is not reasonably practicable or if the procession is one commonly or customarily held in that area.

The police can direct the route of a march or can prohibit a march from entering a specific public place.

If considering organising a march or procession obtain advice from a solicitor or the police about the detailed legal requirements for notice.

Marches and processions may also be covered by local bylaws or Acts of Parliament. Ask the local authority for details of the requirements.

In London the police have additional powers under the **Metropolitan Police Act, 1839** to prevent traffic congestion caused by demonstrations or meetings. While Parliament is in session, open air meetings and processions on the north side of the Thames within a mile of Parliament Square are banned. Carrying banners and placards, or handing out leaflets, is also prohibited within this area.

Special rules apply to meetings held in Trafalgar Square and major London parks. The Department of the Environment will provide the detailed regulations.

The Metropolitan Police issue a Code of Practice for organisers of marches, which covers arrangements for stewarding and agreeing the route. The Code is for guidance only, and is not legally binding.

### Loudspeakers

Local bylaws govern the use of loudspeakers, the details of which may be obtained from the local authority. It is usually necessary to give 48 hours' written notice to the police before using a loudspeaker for non-commercial purposes. Under the **Control of Pollution Act, 1974** loudspeakers are not allowed in public places between 9 pm and 8 am.

In London the **Metropolitan Police Act, 1839** governs what can be said through a loudspeaker.

# Festivals, parties and merry making

## Street parties

The police and local authorities may close streets only in an emergency or by going through a lengthy statutory procedure which is not designed to cater for street parties and festivals. But a group planning to hold an event on publicly owned space or in the street should inform the police, as well as the engineer's and housing departments of the local authority, to make sure there are no objections. The police can advise on certain aspects of organising an event such as safety, access and traffic problems. The engineer's department can advise on services such as gas, electricity and toilets. Temporary water supplies have

to be arranged through the water company, which will ask the group to sign an indemnity form, absolving the water company of any responsibility. The group must make sure it is adequately insured (see chapter 7).

## Selling food

The **Food Hygiene (Market Stalls and Delivery Vehicles) Regulations, 1966** as amended state that:

❑ a person allowing land to be used for food stalls must ensure that it is kept clean and that the stalls are clean and in proper repair;

❑ each stall must display the name and address of the person running it, or if it is an organisation, the name of the secretary;

❑ each stall must have a covered rubbish bin;

❑ food must be kept at least 18 inches off the ground, unless properly protected;

❑ all equipment in contact with food must be kept clean;

❑ servers' hands and clothing must be clean and any cut or graze covered with a waterproof dressing;

❑ stalls must have a first aid kit;

❑ wrapping paper must be clean, and food must not be kept in containers from which there is a risk of contamination;

❑ people serving or handling food must not smoke;

❑ food should be covered until sold. Stalls selling unwrapped food must have handwashing facilities with a supply of hot water;

❑ some foods must be kept below certain temperatures. However, there are exceptions for food which is to be sold within a short period;

❑ stalls serving unwrapped food must be covered unless the food is kept in a closed container before serving;

❑ a toilet must not open directly onto a food room and must have a notice advising servers to wash their hands after use.

The above regulations will be replaced in summer 1995 by the **Food Safety (General Food Hygiene) Regulations, 1994.** The new regulations contain the rules of food hygiene both for events where food is supplied on a temporary basis, for example stalls at a fete, and where groups supply food regularly, for example a café in a community centre.

For movable and temporary premises such as marquees, market stalls and premises used occasionally for catering, the following requirements must be met:

❏ premises must be sited, designed, constructed and kept clean and in good repair and condition in order to avoid the risk of contamination of food and harbouring pests so far as reasonably practicable. In particular, and where necessary:

- appropriate facilities must be available to maintain personal hygiene, for example washing and drying hands, and sanitary arrangements;

- surfaces in contact with food must be in sound condition and easy to clean and, where necessary, disinfect. Usually this will require smooth, washable, non-toxic materials;

- adequate provision must be made to clean and, where necessary, disinfect work utensils and equipment;

- adequate provision must be made for cleaning food;

- an adequate supply of drinkable hot and cold water must be available;

- adequate arrangements and/or facilities for the hygienic storage and disposal of hazardous and/or inedible substances and water must be available;

- food must be placed in order to avoid the risk of contamination so far as is reasonably practicable;

❏ transport and containers used to transport food must be kept clean and in good order and condition, to protect the food and must, where necessary, be capable of adequate cleaning and disinfection;

❏ containers must not be used for carrying anything other than food if this would risk contamination; food must be separated from anything which may contaminate it during transportation and must be carried and protected from contamination whilst being transported;

❏ all articles, fittings and equipment that come into contact with food must be kept clean and in good repair and condition so as to minimise the risk of contamination;

❏ if containers are reusable, they must be capable of being properly cleaned and, where necessary, disinfected;

❏ food waste must not be allowed to accumulate in food rooms and must usually be deposited in closable containers. Adequate arrangements must be made for removal and storage of waste;

❏ there must be an adequate supply of drinkable water available;

❏ where appropriate ice used should be made from drinkable water. If water used for heating or cooling is not drinkable, it must be kept separate from food and drinkable water to minimise the risk of contamination;

❏ anyone working with food must maintain their own personal cleanliness and wear suitable clean and, where appropriate, protective clothing;

❏ no person known or suspected to be suffering from a disease likely to be transmitted through food, for example infected wounds, sores, skin infections or diarrhoea can work with food;

❏ raw materials and ingredients must be kept in conditions which avoid deterioration and contamination;

❏ all food must be appropriately protected from contamination, and hazardous and non-edible substances must be kept separately and labelled.

The new regulations are designed to be less prescriptive than the old food hygiene regulations, allowing for more flexibility so that food hygiene arrangements can be adapted according to the type of food being supplied and the length of time food will be kept. Contact the local environmental health department for further details.

## The licensing laws[1]

Under the **Licensing (Occasional Permissions) Act, 1983** it is fairly easy to get an occasional licence to run a bar, by applying to the local licensing magistrates at least one month before the function. An organisation can, however, have no more than four occasional licences each year in one licensing area.

The organisers have legal powers to refuse to admit, or to eject people who are drunk, and may refuse to serve anyone, providing that they do not discriminate on the grounds of sex or race. It is an offence to serve alcohol to people aged under 18. Selling alcohol without a licence is illegal, as is the sale of raffle tickets in exchange for a drink.

---

[1] The Charities and Voluntary Organisations Deregulation Task Force recommended a comprehensive review of the licensing system for voluntary organisations, including liquor, theatre and cinema licensing. The Government has accepted this recommendation and therefore changes may be made.

An organisation planning to sell alcohol on a regular basis will need a licence or a registration certificate under the **Licensing Act, 1964**. Most voluntary groups would only need a registration certificate. If a group is registered as a charity it should consider setting up a separate organisation to run a bar, which may be able to covenant its profits to the charity and thus avoid income or corporation tax. For further details of the regulations contact *Community Trading Services Limited.*

Applications for a registration certificate are made to the local magistrates court, which will require a copy of the group's constitution and a plan of the premises. Copies of the application will be sent to the police, fire brigade and environmental health department, all of which may wish to inspect the premises. The application must also be advertised near the premises concerned or in a local newspaper.

Before applying for a registration certificate get financial advice on bookkeeping and accounts, and on liability for VAT and income tax. The liability for tax may affect the decision on whether to set up a separate organisation to run the bar.

Opening a regular bar is a big step to take and it is important to think about all the likely consequences. Among the points to consider are:

❏ the security precautions involved because of large quantities of cash; these will include precautions against theft by helpers behind the bar;

❏ the possibility of inconvenience to neighbours;

❏ whether volunteers will put all their energy into running the bar at the expense of other activities;

❏ the need for additional insurance.

## Films and plays

Organisations planning to show films regularly may need a licence, under the **Cinemas Act, 1985**.

There are exceptions. A licence is not required:

❏ to show films if they are for non-commercial exhibition and viewing is free or restricted to members;

❏ if film showings are restricted to six days per year, provided that the council, police and fire authorities are informed.

Organisations running a theatre will need a licence under the **Theatres Act, 1968**.

## Music and dance

Organisations providing entertainment involving music or dance will need a licence unless they are using premises already licensed for this purpose. Occasional licences can be obtained from the licensing authority (the local authority), which has power to waive fees for charities. The local authority will arrange inspection of the venue by environmental health officers and the fire brigade.

## Indoor sports

A licence is also required to hold an event involving indoor sports as the principal activity. Occasional licences can be obtained from the local authority, which will inspect the premises. If sport is not the principal activity, no licence is required.

# Defamation

If an organisation produces written publications, tapes or videos or if representatives give television, press or radio interviews or make public speeches, it is essential to ensure that no one is defamed.

Defamation covers both **libel** (involving the written word or any other permanent record such as a photograph or video) and **slander** (involving speech). For example a verbal accusation made in a speech at a meeting would be slander, and if recorded in the minutes would become a form of libel.

Anyone suing for defamation has to prove that his or her reputation has been damaged. This means that an untrue statement has been made to a third party, which tends to:

❏ lower the victim in the estimation of society; or

❏ make society view him or her with feelings of hatred, fear, ridicule, dislike or contempt.

Simply making one of the following accusations is likely to be defamatory:

❏ saying that someone has committed a criminal offence serious enough to be punished by imprisonment;

❏ alleging something calculated to disparage the person as to his or her office, trade or profession.

A general comment could be defamatory if:

❏ someone's name is mentioned in conjunction with damaging circumstances; for example 'Only criminals go to the XYZ club. Pat was seen there last week';

❏ someone could deduce a meaning by implication or innuendo, for example 'A person not a million miles away from Pat was seen handing money over to a police constable'.

Anyone defaming an unnamed person who is a member of a small identifiable group could be sued by each person in that group. So if six members of a management committee are accused of being dishonest, one or all of them could take action.

The five means of defence against an accusation of defamation are:

❏ proving that the statement was true;

❏ showing that the words were fair comment: correctly stated facts giving an opinion, not malicious, about a matter of public concern. This defence cannot be used against defamation of a person's moral character;

❏ privilege; this would include statements made by MPs in parliament or judges in court;

❏ qualified privilege; which covers people reporting fairly and accurately court cases, parliamentary proceedings and in some cases public meetings. It also includes reporting an allegation, when under a legal or moral duty, to an enforcement authority, for example social services or the police;

❏ innocent defamation, which claims that the statement was unintentional and reasonable care was taken to avoid making the mistake. An offer of amends, such as publishing a correction and an apology in a newsletter, should be made as soon as possible.

It is possible to insure against defamation (see chapter 7).

## The law on printed materials

Every printed publication must have an **imprint** — ie the name and address of the printer and publisher. The printer has to keep a copy, together with a record of who commissioned the work.

Material handed out in the streets of London must not be 'profane, indecent or obscene'. **The Public Order Act, 1986** states that leaflets must not be intended or likely to stir up racial hatred.

# Fundraising

## Subscriptions

Charging a membership fee is a useful, relatively easy method of raising a small amount of money. Provided it is permitted in your constitution, different fees can be charged for certain people, for example unwaged people and senior citizens could pay a reduced rate. Anyone willing to donate more than the standard amount could be given a title such as 'friend', 'patron' or 'life member'.

Before charging membership fees, consider the administration involved. The simplest method is to have a set membership period — the calendar year, financial year or the year starting from the annual general meeting — so that all reminders can be sent out at the same time. Depending on the amount of your subscription, reduced rates could be charged to members joining during the subscription year. Keep a record of members' names, addresses and dates of payment. If the membership is large it may be worth considering a computerised system of record keeping.

Companies, industrial and provident societies and friendly societies must keep a **register of members** (for details see chapter 2).

If a constitution does not allow a charge for membership, it is possible to alter it (see chapter 2). Alternatively membership could be free but a charge could be made for services, for example a newsletter.

## Deeds of Covenant

A Deed of Covenant is a legal agreement by a donor to make regular, usually annual payments, out of taxed income, to a beneficiary. Covenants can only be made to registered charities and have to be taken out for a minimum of three years. The advantage of receiving donations through covenants is that a charity can claim the donor's tax and so increase the amount given by at least the basic rate of income tax.

Arranging covenants is complicated but the *Charities Aid Foundation* provides a service at a reasonable cost.

## Legacies

A group may ask its supporters to remember it in their wills. This is a sensitive subject, so requests for legacies must be handled carefully.

Inform existing donors of the possibility of making a bequest, by including information and a legacy form in publicity material. It is also possible to advertise in journals such as the *Law Society's Gazette* or *Charities Digest*. It may be worth contacting local solicitors as they sometimes advise people on charitable bequests.

## Payroll giving

Individuals in work can give up to £900 (as at 1 April 94) in any one year to charities of their choice in a tax effective way: the money is taken out of their income before tax. Ask your supporters to use this method to make donations if their workplace operates such a scheme.

For further details contact *Give As You Earn*.

## Large donations

Individuals who make single donations of more than £250 (as at 1 April 94) to charity can obtain tax relief for each donation made up to a maximum of £5 million per year (as at 1 April 94) .

## Collections

Collections are a relatively simple, low cost way of raising funds. You do not need a permit to collect money on private premises but the owner's permission must be obtained. Under the **House to House Collections Act, 1939** and the **Police, Factories, etc (Miscellaneous Provisions) Act, 1916** there are strict rules governing house-to-house and street collections. Any group wishing to raise money in this way must apply at least a month in advance to the licensing authority (the Metropolitan Police or City of London Council in London and the district council elsewhere).

New rules relating to public collections are included in **Part III** of the **Charities Act, 1992**, which will replace the old legislation with new, integrated controls dealing with all public charitable collections. At time of writing (August 94) the Home Office was carrying out a consultation exercise in order to identify suitable practical arrangements before bringing these new provisions into force; the date of implementation was therefore unknown. For the time being, until advised otherwise, organisations concerned in operating the present legislation should continue on that basis. For further information contact the *Charity Law Section* of the *Voluntary Service Unit*.

Information requested will differ between authorities but they will usually need to know:

❑ the promoter's name;

❑ the purpose of the collection;

❑ where it is to be carried out;

❑ how many collectors there will be and whether or not they will be paid;

❑ the dates;

❑ whether the collection is for cash or goods.

The authority will also need to know whether a street or a house-to-house collection is planned as permits are usually granted for one or the other.

Some national charities have been granted a **Home Office Exemption Certificate** enabling them to make house-to-house collections anywhere in England and Wales at any time. All charities should, however, inform the local authority of their plans and try to avoid overlapping with collections being made by other charities.

If a licence is refused or revoked the charity can appeal to the Home Secretary within 14 days of receipt of written notice.

Once a permit has been received, permission is needed from London Regional Transport to collect outside London tube stations, and from British Rail for collections at overground stations.

The organiser of house-to-house collections is responsible for ensuring the following regulations are met:

❑ collectors must be aged 16 or over;

❑ each collector must carry a certificate of authorisation and a prescribed badge (from HMSO, PO Box 276, 51 Nine Elms Lane, London SW8) both signed by the organiser, which must conform to Home Office regulations;

❑ collectors must produce their badges on request and give their names to the police if asked;

❑ collectors must not cause annoyance to passers-by or house owners;

❑ collecting boxes must be numbered and sealed;

❑ envelopes must have a gummed flap;

❑ if neither boxes nor envelopes are used, receipts must be given from a receipt book with consecutively numbered pages;

❑ a record must be kept of each box, authorisation badge and permit issued.

After the collection, the boxes or envelopes must be opened in the presence of the organiser and a witness, unless the sealed box is taken to the bank. The contents should be recorded.

A statement of accounts must be sent to the licensing authority, showing the amount collected, the expenses incurred, the number of boxes distributed and whether they have all been returned.

The licensing authority can make rules covering street collections in its area. Contact the local licensing authority for details of local regulations.

In the Metropolitan Police District a group can make a collection at an open air meeting without a police permit, unless the event is in a park or a similar open space where bylaws may prohibit collecting. Check the position with the local authority.

Collection boxes can be purchased from *Angal Collecting Boxes and Devices Limited.*

# Lotteries and raffles

The **Lotteries and Amusements Act, 1976** governs the requirements relating to lotteries. Generally the law distinguishes between small and private lotteries, and public ('society') lotteries, which must be registered with the *Gaming Board for Great Britain*. Basic information is given below; for further details see *Lotteries and the law*, published by the Gaming Board, or ring them on 071 306 6269.

## Small lotteries

Small lotteries (or raffles) are those which are run for charitable, sporting or cultural purposes as part of an 'exempt entertainment'. This is defined in the Act as a 'bazaar, sale of work, fete, dinner, dance, sporting or athletic event or other entertainment of a similar character'. Section 3 of the Act gives full details of conditions to be observed, some examples are:

❏ proceeds must not be used for private gain;

❏ tickets can be sold only on the premises and during the course of the entertainment;

❏ no more than £250 can be spent on buying prizes;

❏ no money prizes can be awarded.

For further details see the Home Office briefing *Changes to the law on smaller lotteries: some guidance notes for local authorities and societies.*

## Private lotteries

A private lottery is one in which ticket sales are confined to either:

❏ members of one society; or

❏ people who work or live at the same premises.

Tickets must be printed with the price, together with the names and addresses of the promoter and must state that tickets can only be issued to members. The proceeds, less expenses, must go to the organisation or be used for prizes. The lottery can be advertised only on the organisation's or promoter's premises and tickets cannot be sent through the post. The promoter must be authorised to act by the governing body of the organisation.

## Society (public) lotteries

A society lottery is one promoted on behalf of an organisation wholly or mainly for one of the following reasons:

❏ charitable purposes;

❏ participation in or support of athletic sports or games or cultural activities;

❏ other purposes not for private gain or commercial undertaking.

An organisation wishing to promote a lottery must be registered either the appropriate local registration authority (usually the local authority) or the Gaming Board. Registration with the Board is essential if:

❏ the total value of tickets on sale in any one lottery is to exceed £20,000; or

❏ the total value of tickets on sale in any one lottery, added to the value of those already sold or put on sale in all earlier lotteries in the same calendar year is to exceed £250,000.

Under the **Lotteries and Amusements Act, 1976**, as amended, anyone running a lottery on behalf of a charity has to obtain a **Lottery Manager's Certificate** from the Gaming Board. This does not apply to a charity's employees or members.

For further details see *Lotteries and the law.*

Tickets must not cost more than £1 and all tickets must be the same price (so, for example it is not permissable to sell five tickets for the price of four). Every ticket must specify:

❏ its price;

❏ the name of the society promoting the lottery;

❏ the promoter's name;

❏ the date of the lottery;

❏ the fact that the society is registered with the Gaming Board for Great Britain or, if registered with the local authority, the name of the local authority.

Tickets cannot be sold to or by anyone aged under 16. They cannot be sold in any street, but can be sold door to door.

No prize may exceed £25,000 or 10% of the total value of the tickets sold, whichever is the greater. No more than 50% of the actual proceeds may be used to provide prizes. Prizes may be donated at a reduced cost or free of charge, but the value of any such single prize must not exceed the above limits.

For further details of rules on prizes see *Lotteries and the law*.

Where proceeds do not exceed £20,000, up to 30% may be used to meet expenses without reference to the Gaming Board.

Within three months of each lottery the promoter must submit a return to the Gaming Board or local authority, giving details of the proceeds, expenses and prizes, and showing how the balance of the amount raised was distributed. The returns must be signed by the promoter and another of the society's governing body. Under the **Lotteries and Amusements Act, 1976**, as amended, an organisation selling more than £100,000 worth of lottery tickets in any one year must submit audited accounts to the Gaming Board, together with a report prepared by a qualifying auditor.

Printing lottery tickets is a specialist job and a list of printers is available from *The Lotteries Council*.

Other types of lottery covered by the Act include sweepstakes, tombolas and games where tickets with a tear open window or scratch panel are sold and cash prizes are given. These will all fall into one of the above categories.

## Gaming machines

A gaming machine can be a good source of revenue but as some people object to them consult members before acquiring one. You will need to obtain a licence from the local magistrate. The machine can be used only by club members and must not be played if non-members are on the premises.
A notice from the firm renting out the machine must be displayed showing how much money can be won and how much is retained. Only authorised people can remove money from the machine; these would usually be committee members or club employees.

A gaming machine can be used with a licence at a bazaar, fete or social as long as it is incidental to the event and none of the proceeds are going to private gain.

Check with the clerk at the magistrates court if in any doubt about the legal position.

## Amusement machines

Amusement machines also require permits from the local authority. Coins or tokens can be won; the maximum pay out is £6 in tokens or £3 in coins.

## Bingo

The **Gaming Act, 1968** defines the following circumstances in which bingo can legally be played:

❏ if it is only one of a club's activities, there is no need to register or obtain a licence. The admission fee can be no more than 50p, although people may stake as much as they want. The game cannot be advertised to the public or played on premises to which the public is admitted;

❏ if more than 50p is charged for admission, the club must register with the licensing authority. A fee of up to £6 per person per day can then be charged, but the game still cannot be advertised to the public, and all takings must be distributed as prizes;

❏ if played to raise funds for a charitable or non-profit making organisation, bingo or whist drives may be held without a licence or registration. The games can be advertised and the public admitted. The stakes and fee must be no more than £3 and the total value of prizes cannot be more than £300;

❏ if bingo is the main event, the club must have a licence and obtain a **Certificate of Consent** from the Gaming Board.

## Use of professional fundraisers

From 1 March 1995 charities' use of professional fundraisers and commercial participators (a person, apart from a company connected with the charity, who encourages purchases of goods or services on the grounds that some of the proceeds will go to charity) will be regulated by **Part III** of the **Charities Act, 1992**. The regulations apply to fundraisers whose pay exceeds £5/day, £500/year or £500 for a particular fundraising venture. They do not apply to charities which undertake their own fundraising activities.

Under the new regulations professional fundraisers appealing for money on behalf of a particular charity must have a written contract with that charity which satisfies regulations laid down by the Secretary of State. Any request for funds has to be accompanied by a statement indicating who will benefit, the way in which the proceeds will be distributed and the method of calculating the fundraiser's remuneration.

Anyone who gives £50 or more in response to a radio or television appeal using a debit or credit card will be entitled to a full refund, less reasonable administration expenses, if they decide to cancel their donation within seven days. The fundraiser must notify all such donors of this right.

If a donor has received any goods, for example if an article has been purchased where 5% of the purchase price has been given to X charity, the refund is dependent on the return of the goods.

Breach of the above will constitute a criminal offence on the part of the professional fundraiser.

## Other fundraising ideas

### Sponsored activities

Events such as sponsored walks or bicycle rides can be financially rewarding. However, finding sponsors and collecting sponsorship money can take a lot of organisation. Keep a record of the names and addresses of everyone who is being sponsored. Include the following information on sponsorship forms:

❑ a description of the event;

❑ its purpose and date;

❑ the name, address and age (if under 18) of the sponsored person;

❑ each sponsor's name, address and amount pledged;

❑ the statement *'I certify that . . . has walked . . . miles/danced for . . . hours'*, followed by the organiser's signature and the date.

The organiser should keep a record of the value of the sponsorship on each form and whether the money has been handed in.

### Charity shops

Charity shops are often run for short periods on a licence (see chapter 6) in shop premises which would otherwise be empty. The rent charged is usually low, but a group is responsible for rates, water charges, overheads and staffing.

Charities are not allowed to trade regularly unless the activity directly furthers their objectives (see chapter 1). For example a workshop for blind people would

be allowed to sell its products. In other circumstances charities may have to form non-charitable subsidiaries for trading purposes. See *Charities, trading and the law*, or contact the *Charities Advisory Group*. Remember charities are liable for VAT on most sales. For further information contact the VAT Liability Division of the Customs & Excise (numbers are in the phone book).

### Community business

One structure voluntary organisations might choose to use for trading is that of a community business. The main characteristics of a community business are:

❑ it is run by an elected unpaid committee;

❑ any surplus funds are used for local social objectives;

❑ the business is community rather than worker led (ie it is not a workers' cooperative).

Community businesses can provide services as well as raising funds. Although it represents a considerable challenge it is possible for a community business to make profits which can be used for a voluntary organisation's social objectives.

For further information see *Community business and council estates*.

### Car boot sales

Under the **Local Government (Miscellaneous Provision) Act, 1982**, more than five cars or stalls constitute a market and therefore an application must be submitted to the local council at least a month before such an event. However, if all the proceeds of a car boot sale are for charitable purposes, or sales are carried out on private property with the owner's permission, the conditions imposed by the Act do not apply.

Regular events may require planning permission. If in doubt check with the planning department of the local authority.

## Minibuses and coaches

Organisations that own a minibus or coach may require a permit or licence from the *Operating Licensing Section* of the *Department of Transport* if they use the vehicle for 'hire or reward'. This includes any arrangement where there is payment for the trip, even if the charge includes other items such as a meal, or the payment is treated as a donation. The rules apply to vehicles adapted to carry more than eight passengers.

There is no need for a permit if the group does not charge passengers in any way.

For further information contact the *Department of Transport* which will advise on the requirements.

## Hiring to other organisations

If a permit is obtained there may be difficulties in an organisation allowing its minibus to be used by other organisations if they intend to charge the passengers. The group hiring the bus may need its own permit. The only way in which this can be avoided is for the driver to be appointed by the organisation owning the vehicle and holding the permit. Payment by the passengers must be made to the permit holder and not the hiring group. The hiring group could act as the collector of the money.

Whatever arrangement is made, remember to inform the insurance company. A standard vehicle insurance policy excludes use for 'hire or reward' so a special extension will be required.

# Looking after people

## Health and safety

An organisation which provides physical or emotional care or support of any kind will owe a duty to take reasonable care for the safety of its users. If it fails to do so and an accident occurs as a result, the organisation could have to pay compensation to the user. This would be covered by public liability insurance (see chapter 7) provided that the insurers have been informed of the activities undertaken.

Health and safety legislation requires an organisation to assess the risks to anyone, including users, affected by its activities. If an accident happens as a result of any failure to comply with health and safety requirements, the organisation and its committee members and senior staff could be prosecuted by the Health and Safety Executive (see chapter 5).

If failures to observe health and safety requirements result in the death of a user, the organisation could be prosecuted for manslaughter.

It is therefore essential for an organisation's health and safety policy to take into account the risks to users and include measures to avoid accidents.

## Physical restraint

Organisations that care for people who cannot always take responsibility for their own decisions may in some circumstances be under a legal obligation to restrain them physically in order to protect them from injuring themselves.

To ensure that the interests of both users and staff are protected make certain that:

❏ staff are given guidance on when physical restraint can be used and the degree of force that can or should be used;

❏ staff are given guidance on when physical restraint cannot be used and methods that cannot be used. They should also be given guidance on the circumstances in which use of physical restraint will amount to gross misconduct and lead to disciplinary action;

❏ staff are given guidance on the circumstances in which physical force should be used, including using appropriate methods and explaining reasons for restraint to the user;

❏ any decisions to allow users to take risks as part of a care plan are carefully recorded to prevent staff being subsequently criticised if accidents occur;

❏ consideration is given to providing: guarantees to staff, for example on legal representation if they follow policies but an accident occurs; training on safe techniques and ways of diffusing tense situations; first aid training; and ensuring that care plans will identify potential risks;

❏ consideration is given to obtaining insurance to cover any legal expenses incurred through possible criminal prosecution or an inquest;

❏ procedures are devised and implemented to minimise the need for physical restraint and in particular that careful consideration is given to ensure that users are treated with respect and dignity;

❏ safeguards are built into any procedures for using physical restraint including: records of use of and reasons for restraint; interviews with users and staff to establish facts; monitoring by senior managers of the use of restraint by individual staff and particular projects; discussion of each incident at staff meetings; disciplinary action in cases of obvious inappropriate use of restraint or excessive force; a 'whistle-blowing' service enabling any user or staff member who believes that restraint is being misused to report it to senior management in confidence.

## Data protection

Organisations using computers to hold personal data must register the use under the **Data Protection Act, 1984**. Personal data is defined as data relating to a living individual who can be identified, for example by a name or file number. This includes statements of opinion about that person but would exclude a record which was merely an organisation's intentions in relation to her or him.

Once registered, an organisation can hold only the class of data for which is it registered and must disclose information in line with the Act. If it wants to hold additional information, it will need to amend its registration.

The *Office of the Data Protection Registrar* produces information about the requirements of the Act. Registration packs are available from Wycliffe House, Water Lane, Wilmslow, Cheshire SK9 5AF .

# Contracting to provide services

Many local authorities, health authorities and government departments are now looking to the voluntary sector to provide services on a contract basis. Sometimes this will be for a one-off project (for example running a training course or carrying out a research project) but often it will be for a longer term service (for example providing day care or residential services for elderly people) and may involve contracts which last indefinitely.

The main types of agreements are formal contracts, agency arrangements and service level agreements. In each case, the nature and level of services to be provided will probably be set out in some detail by the authority.

In some cases, the contract will involve transferring a service previously run by a local authority to a voluntary group; in others the contract will replace grant aid. The local authority may have approached the voluntary organisation seeking a contract, or the services may have been put out to tender.

Entering into a contract to provide a defined service raises many questions for voluntary organisations, some of which are set out below.

## Should the organisation take on the service?

Before taking on a contract an organisation should consider the following questions:

❑ how does the proposed activity relate to the organisation's aims and objectives and is it allowed for within the constitution? (see chapter 1)

❑ is it advisable to become a company limited by guarantee before entering into a contract? (see chapter 1)

❑ will taking on the service have implications for charitable status? (see chapter 1)

❑ is there adequate insurance cover and if not, can the organisation afford it? (see chapter 7)

❑ do staff and committee members have sufficient training and expertise to manage contracts?

❑ can the quality of service be provided under the contract arrangements?

❑ will VAT or Corporation Tax have to be paid if the organisation enters into contracts? Check this with your accountant and Customs & Excise.

❑ will taking on a new service affect other providers, for example those in the statutory sector, or other voluntary groups active in the field?

❑ how will the organisation's other activities, for example campaigning or community development, be affected by a contract to supply services?

❑ does the organisation have the financial and staff resources for any consultancy or legal advice needed to take on the contract and prepare a bid?

❑ is the organisation ready to take on a new role and does it have the capacity to manage the growth this may involve?

❑ will the organisation be obliged to take on the authority's staff if the contract is for services previously provided by the authority?

You will need to take legal advice on this last point. The **Transfer of Undertakings (Protection of Employment) Regulations, 1981** as amended, mean that if an organisation takes over activities from another employer, for example a local authority, the staff who were employed by that employer may be automatically transferred on the same terms and conditions so that the organisation becomes their employer for one year only. The law is uncertain in this area and Government advice on contracting out of services is generally considered to be incorrect. The advice provided up to April 94 has probably also been superseded by a court decision on the effect of the Transfer of Undertaking Regulations to the contracting out of cleaning at a hospital.

## Costing the service

Consider the following possible costs in addition to that of providing the service:

❑ local authority rates of pay for staff if applicable;

❑ project management costs and overheads;

- organisational and restructuring costs;

- pensions and maternity cover;

- training and consultancy costs;

- legal advice;

- contingency for redundancy payments if the contract is terminated or not renewed;

- costs of monitoring and evaluation;

- annual increments for staff;

- inflation;

- possible VAT and tax liability;

- additional insurance;

- any additional equipment or adaptations to premises required to meet the contract requirements.

## Is the contract acceptable?

Organisations should ensure that they are satisfied with the contract and in particular the following points:

- length of the contract;

- arrangements for renewal;

- insurance obligations and in particular any indemnity clauses where the organisation agrees to cover any claims;

- whether payments are in arrears or in advance and their frequency, and whether interest can be charged on late payments;

- the extent to which payments are guaranteed and the circumstances in which they can be withheld;

- increases in payments to cover inflation and annual increments;

- provisions for changes to payments if the service required alters, and arrangements for dealing with disputes in such cases;

- the mechanism for dealing with complaints and disputes, including arbitration where other measures fail;

- rules on confidentiality;

- provision for VAT if applicable;

- reviews of the contract and the services provided;

- monitoring of the services provided (organisations themselves should monitor services using both qualitative and quantitative measures);

- penalty and termination clauses if either party defaults, and protection against termination by the authority in unwarranted circumstances;

- clauses guaranteeing equal opportunities in recruitment and services delivered under the contract, including a complaints procedure for users;

- the right for the organisation to have the final say on who uses the service;

- the rights of service users in relation to both the group and the authority: this is often not included in contracts.

Where possible try to draw up a contract in partnership with the authority requiring the service and in consultation with service users.

For further details see *Getting reading for contracts: a guide for voluntary organisations.*

# Equipment contracts

Many organisations enter into leasing contracts for equipment, including computers, photocopiers and cars.

Leases are often for a fixed term and then continue automatically unless the required notice to terminate them is given. A lessee who wants to dispose of equipment before the term has finished must either pay off all the charges to the end of the contract or acquire other equipment from the owner.

Before signing up for any equipment lease make sure that the full terms and conditions of the lease are understood, and in particular note:

- any routine charges made;

- whether the service provided for those charges is limited in any way, for example it may exclude maintenance or servicing;

- when servicing or maintenance is provided, whether this is for the full period of the lease (this is often not the case and it can cost a substantial amount to take out a maintenance contract when the service period has finished in order to encourage the purchase or hire of a new machine);

❑ whether the owner can increase the charges and if there is a maximum limit on any increases;

❑ whether the maintenance contract is limited, for example if it excludes breakdown if the lessee is at fault or whether certain expensive parts of the machine are excluded;

❑ whether the owner guarantees to continue servicing and maintenance throughout the contract or if he or she can decide to discontinue the service. Also note the position if the owner goes out of business: will anyone who acquires the ownership still have an obligation to maintain the machine?

❑ whether VAT is charged on top of the basic charges.

# Booklist

**The arts funding guide**, *Anne-Marie Doulton (editor)*, Directory of Social Change (1994), £15.95

**Basic fundraising leaflets**, Directory of Social Change, £7.50

**Beginner's guide to contracts**, *Jo Woolf*, London Voluntary Service Council (1992), £7.95

**The central government grants guide**, *Anne-Marie Doulton (editor)*, Directory of Social Change (1993), £12.95

**Changes to the law on smaller lotteries: some guidance notes for local authorities and societies**, Home Office (1994), free

**Charities, trading and the law**, *Stephen Lloyd*, Directory of Social Change (1994), price not fixed

**Community business and council estates**, *Trevor Watling*, London Voluntary Service Council (1989), £4.50

**Contracts in practice**, *Ken Edwards*, National Council for Voluntary Organisations and Directory of Social Change (1992), £8.95

**Costing for contracts**, *John Callaghan*, National Council for Voluntary Organisations and Directory of Social Change (1992), £8.95

**Data protection: putting the record straight**, *Roger Cornwell and Marie Staunton*, Liberty (1985), £3.95

**Directory of grant making trusts 1993/94**, Charities Aid Foundation (1993), £50.00

**Equal opportunities in voluntary organisations — reading list no 2**, National Council for Voluntary Organisations (1993), £2.50

**From grants to contracts**, *Keith Hawley*, National Council for Voluntary Organisations and Directory of Social Change (1992), £8.95

**Getting ready for contracts: a guide for voluntary organisations**, *Sandy Adirondack and Richard Macfarlane*, Directory of Social Change (1993), £8.95

**The London grants guide**, *Lucy Stubbs (editor)*, Directory of Social Change (1992), £12.50

**Lotteries and the law**, The Gaming Board (1994), free

**The major companies guide**, Directory of Social Change (1994), £14.95

**Publish and still not be damned**, *Richard Gutch, David Miliband and Richard Percival*, National Council for Voluntary Organisations (1988), £3.00

**The Data Protection Act, 1984 guidelines**, Data Protection Registrar, free

**The lottery gamble: a guide to the National Lottery**, *Margaret Bolton*, National Council for Voluntary Organisations (1993), £6.00

**The right side of the law: a guide to the Government's rules on publicity produced by local authorities and voluntary organisations**, Local Government Information Unit (1993), £5.00

**Trading by charities**, Charities' Tax Reform Group (1994), £4.35

# Chapter 10: Facing closure

There are many reasons why voluntary organisations might close down; for example some groups may wish to stop operating after achieving a specific purpose, others may have no choice and be forced into closure through lack of funds.

Whatever the reason, closing down is not straightforward. This is especially true if an organisation employs staff, rents or owns property, or leases equipment. Facing closure becomes even more complicated, and indeed serious, if a group cannot meet its financial obligations.

This chapter starts by discussing the steps an organisation can take if it is in financial difficulty and faces possible closure. It then looks at the procedures for winding up the organisation if closure cannot be avoided because of insolvency. It also looks at the processes for closing down the organisation if it is still solvent, for example because it has fulfilled its objectives. The legal and technical terms introduced in the text are explained in the glossary at the end of the chapter.

**A note of caution: this chapter cannot be a substitute for expert legal and financial advice. When facing closure, professional expertise is essential.**

## Is closure necessary?

An organisation should consistently monitor its financial position so that it can spot potential problems as early as possible. If the answer to any of the following questions is 'yes', then a group is running into financial difficulties and should either start thinking of closure or ensure that alternative plans are put into action immediately to put it back on an even keel financially:

❏ is there an unanticipated overdraft;

❏ is expenditure greater than income;

❏ are there any large debts that it has difficulty in paying;

❏ is future income (in most cases grants) at considerable risk?

The next step is to work out the group's exact financial position in order to discover how long it can remain solvent. Once an **incorporated** organisation becomes insolvent, and there is no reasonable

prospect of it ever being able to pay off debts, then it must cease operating immediately. In an **unincorporated** organisation, the committee will be liable for the debts, so in theory it could decide to continue operating. In practice, few committee members are likely to wish to increase their liability, so an unincorporated organisation should also cease its activities.

## Liabilities

Forecast the expenses the organisation is likely to incur over the next few months. These could include:

❏ employees' wages and employer's national insurance;

❏ rents and rates for premises;

❏ running costs, such as electricity, telephone and building repairs;

❏ administrative costs, such as phone, post and travel;

❏ bank charges;

❏ VAT payments;

❏ Inland Revenue payments.

Also consider the actual costs of closure. These include:

❏ the legal fees for disposing of a lease and for winding up a limited company or an industrial and provident society (see 'Winding up', below);

❏ redundancy, and outstanding holiday and maternity payments;

❏ legal and financial advice on the closure;

❏ outstanding costs, such as rent for the remaining period of a lease on equipment or premises.

## Assets

Examine the organisation's assets and likely income. These could include:

❏ money in the bank and cash in hand;

❏ further grant instalments;

❏ money owed to the organisation;

❏ stock, for example unsold publications;

❏ fixed assets such as land, buildings, equipment and vehicles.

CHAIRPERSON – GRANTS COMMITTEE

When assessing fixed assets, make sure it is possible to sell the goods. As a condition of grant aid many funders do not allow organisations to sell their premises or equipment. Also check the constitution to see whether there are any restrictions on selling assets.

## Solvency and insolvency

The statement of assets and liabilities will show whether or not the group is insolvent.

An organisation is insolvent if its total assets are worth less than its total liabilities or it is unable to pay its debts as they become due, ie within the normal credit limits.

Sometimes the expression 'technical insolvency' is used. An organisation can be described as technically insolvent if its liabilities exceed its assets but it is still able to pay immediate debts. Provided that there is a reasonable prospect of the assets becoming worth more than the liabilities in the future, the organisation will not have to be wound up as being insolvent. Similarly, an organisation is 'technically insolvent' if its assets are worth more than its liabilities but it has no ready cash to pay debts that are due immediately. Provided that creditors are prepared to wait until there is cash to pay debts, the organisation need not be wound up as being insolvent.

Any organisation that becomes insolvent will have to stop its activities and be wound up. This is true for all types of legal structure. In unincorporated organisations (unincorporated associations, trusts and friendly societies) the committee members are personally responsible for the debts of the organisation. If an incorporated organisation (company limited by guarantee or industrial and provident society) is insolvent and there is no reasonable prospect of it being able to pay its debts, it should stop trading at once. If activities continue, the limited liability which normally protects committee members against personal liability can be overridden

and they could be held personally responsible for the organisation's debts.

It is essential to recognise any financial difficulties as soon as possible as there may be an opportunity to prevent insolvency and protect committee members from financial responsibility. If there is any concern about the organisation's financial position, immediately seek advice from an accountant.

An organisation heading for insolvency has two choices. It can either implement a rescue plan to ensure that it remains solvent, or it has to be wound up. The next section examines ways in which it may be possible to rescue an organisation that is in financial difficulties.

# Planning for survival

There are a number of measures which may enable an organisation to survive.

## Reducing costs and increasing income

In most organisations, cutting down costs will involve changes to the services provided. This section looks at the various methods of reducing costs, increasing income and raising capital, and goes on to describe how to prioritise in order to make decisions.

### Reducing staff costs

Reducing costs will involve some difficult choices. In many organisations staff costs form the largest proportion of expenditure and therefore the greatest savings would be made through redundancies or by changing terms and conditions. Although the committee is responsible for these decisions, it is essential to consult with staff throughout the planning process. Consultation with staff is important even if redundancy or redeployment is not necessary, since restrictions on expenditure will affect working conditions and require their cooperation.

Although redundancies are the obvious way of reducing costs, there may be other options. These include:

❑ restricting recruitment;

❑ redeploying staff (but providing for the cost of retraining if necessary);

❑ offering early retirement (making sure that there is no loss of pension rights);

❑ introducing short-time working (reducing hours of work);

❏ laying off workers for a temporary period in the hope of obtaining new funding;

❏ agreeing with workers that they should become self-employed (but see below).

Staff who are laid off or required to work short time have certain rights. If the lay off or short-time working lasts more than four consecutive weeks, or more than six weeks in any 13, then the worker may (not more than four weeks after the lay off or short-time working has finished) give written notice of his or her intention to claim redundancy payment. The worker must then give the requisite notice to terminate his or her contract, and will be entitled to be considered redundant.

An agreement with a member of staff to become self-employed should be used only where both the organisation and employee can benefit. It should never be used as a way of simply reducing costs whilst those concerned carry out their original jobs but with a different legal status and reduced rights. This method of reducing costs is most appropriate for people who enjoy the liberty of working for more than one organisation, and can therefore be genuinely self-employed. By agreeing to the arrangement, they are gaining an element of freedom in their work whilst the organisation can reduce its costs but still benefit from their expertise. Before introducing this option, make sure that those concerned are aware that by becoming self-employed, workers give up their pension rights and rights to unemployment benefit, and have to pay their own national insurance. Also consider the financial implications for the organisation. Self-employed workers will invariably be more expensive, on a daily rate at least, than those on an organisation's payroll.

Chapter 3 describes the rules concerning self-employed status. Chapter 4 looks at the legal rights of staff where reorganisation is necessary and results in redeployment. A later section of this chapter looks at the law and good practice governing redundancy procedures.

## Reducing premises costs

Premises can form another large element of expenditure. The cost of premises may be reduced by moving to cheaper accommodation if this is possible. Another option is to share or sublet current premises. Chapter 6 looks at the implications of this option in more detail.

### Property owned by the organisation
The **Charities Act, 1993** sets out procedures that a registered charity must follow if it wants to dispose of premises.

A charity cannot dispose of its premises to a trustee,

an employee, any person or organisation which gave it the premises (which could include a local authority), or any relative of any of those people, without the consent of the Charity Commissioners. In all other cases, a charity can sell the premises without consent provided that it:

❏ has obtained a written report from a qualified surveyor on the proposed sale;

❏ has advertised the sale as the surveyor has advised; and

❏ is satisfied it is getting the best possible price.

If the land was given to the charity for its charitable objects, there is an additional requirement that the intention to sell is advertised in newspapers, and members of the public have time to express their views. In all cases, obtain legal advice and inform your solicitor that your organisation is a registered charity.

A second option is to rent the building or part of it to another group. The local council for voluntary service or an estate agent may have details of groups looking for premises. It is also possible to advertise in voluntary sector press, such as *Voluntary Voice* or *Third Sector*. Again, charities have to meet certain requirements under the **Charities Act, 1993** before letting out premises, and legal advice should be obtained.

In both cases, check to see whether the constitution allows these options to be pursued.

### Premises on lease
Organisations renting premises may be able to dispose of the lease and move to cheaper premises, or to sublet. Check the terms of the lease to establish whether any of the following options are possible.

### Assigning the lease
Assigning a lease means finding another tenant to take on the remaining period. Not all leases allow the premises to be assigned, and any such move would usually require the landlord's consent. If the lease is assigned, make sure that the new tenants are financially viable, otherwise you could still be liable for the rent. Unless a landlord is explicitly prepared to release the original tenant from obligations under the lease when it is assigned, that tenant remains liable for the rent for the full term if the new tenant fails to pay.

### Surrendering the lease early
Some organisations may have considered the possibility of uncertain funding when negotiating the lease and it may allow notice to quit to be given at the same time each year. Alternatively the landlord may agree to accept early surrender and release the group

from the continuing rent payments. However, this is unlikely unless the landlord is a local authority, or the premises could be leased to another tenant at a higher rent.

Also check whether the organisation is under an obligation to put the premises back to their original state when the lease is ended, or is responsible for repairs on leaving the building.

### Subletting
There must be provision in the lease for this; again make sure the tenants can pay the rent.

### Sharing premises
The lease may restrict the ability to share the premises. Even if this is the case, it may be worth approaching your landlord to see if he or she objects.

### Premises on a licence
Check the terms of the licence and in particular how much notice must be given and whether there is an obligation to carry out repairs.

## Reducing other costs

### Equipment
It may be possible to sell equipment both to save on running costs and to raise capital. If this is the case the group must establish who owns each major item, and whether there are restrictions on selling, for example some local authorities attach conditions on grant aid which prevent groups from selling off equipment. If in doubt check with the funders. As an insolvent organisation has a general responsibility to try and do its best for its creditors, the equipment should be sold for the best possible price.

Another possibility is to give equipment away to other groups. A charity can give equipment away only to another charity with similar objects. Check the constitution to see whether this option is permitted. If not, ask the Charity Commission for advice on how to proceed.

If equipment is bought on credit or hire purchase, check the terms of the agreement. Under some credit agreements you are merely renting the equipment until the payments are completed; with others you own it as soon as you start paying.

If equipment is rented, check the terms of the lease (see chapter 9). It may be for a fixed term, in which case the group could be liable for the rent of the whole period. As with leases of premises, the owner may be prepared to accept an early termination of the lease or allow the equipment to be transferred to someone else. However, both options are unlikely.

### Sharing costs
It may be possible to reduce expenditure by sharing with other organisations the costs of services and equipment, for example library facilities, administrative support such as bookkeeping and typing, the ownership of and/or leasing cost of computers, photocopiers and fax machines.

### Reducing administrative costs
Ways of reducing administrative costs include cutting the use of telephones, using second class post, reducing staff travel, limiting the use of external printing facilities, reducing the quality of stationery, and minimising the fees of external consultants such as auditors, accountants and solicitors.

An organisation covering a wide geographical area could make savings by using the telephone, including conference calls, or using modems or faxes, rather than getting people together in one place for a meeting.

## Increasing income

As well as reducing the running costs, an organisation may be able to find ways of increasing its income. See the booklist for details of publications on fundraising. There are a number of **funding information services** throughout the country which are able to give advice to voluntary organisations on possible sources of funding and making applications. For details see *Finding Funds* or contact the *Funding Information Service for London*.

Make sure you consider the following:

❑ **trust funding**, particularly for specific pieces of work such as publications, conferences, research or an innovative project;

❑ **business sponsorship**, particularly for pieces of work that will give the company some publicity, for example publications or conferences;

❑ **introducing or increasing charges for services or membership**. Although increased costs may discourage those most in need of services, it may be possible to introduce a tiered charging structure for services and membership, with higher fees for those who can afford to pay;

❑ **bidding for services under contract.** Many voluntary organisations are now contracting with local authorities, government departments, health authorities and trusts to provide services. Such contracts can offer a secure income. However, contracting has major implications for an organisation: it is discussed in detail in chapter 9;

❑ **setting up a profit-making subsidiary.** Some skills within an organisation could be provided on a commercial basis. As charities cannot be profit-making, those considering selling services would probably have to set up a subsidiary company which transferred its profits to the charity. See chapter 1 for further details.

❑ **improving marketing**. Some voluntary organisations many be able to raise substantial sums by concentrating on effective marketing of their services. As well as increasing income, an expanded market means organisations are reaching many more people and improving their service delivery.

## Amalgamation

A further option is to amalgamate with another organisation. Legal advice is essential if this possibility is being considered. This option is likely to involve changes to employees' terms and conditions (which are discussed in chapter 3), and possibly redundancies.

## The rescue plan

Prioritising objectives and services should be a regular feature of the management of an organisation but it is particularly important when services may have to be reduced.

There is no single method of prioritising services to cut costs, but the following information will help to inform decision making:

❑ a breakdown of each service currently provided;

❑ the services, in order of priority, that need to be provided to meet objectives;

❑ the best estimate of the costs of each service;

❑ additional income that could be raised from, or for each service;

❑ the additional expenditure and possible income of any new service;

❑ any other possible methods of generating income, the likely amount that might be raised and the expenditure and staff time that would be involved;

❑ ways of reducing the costs of premises, equipment and administration, the savings that could be achieved and the effect that any changes would have on services;

❑ savings that could be made by freezing recruitment, redeployment, short-time working and redundancy.

Because staff are likely to be affected by any decision to cut costs, it is important to consult them throughout the process of drawing up a rescue plan.

This should include asking staff for their ideas. Individuals who may be made redundant, have changes made to their employment terms and conditions or be redeployed should be consulted in private before a final decision is made.

# Closing down

## Insolvency

If a rescue plan is not viable then closure is probably inevitable, particularly if the organisation is insolvent. If, by ceasing activities, an organisation can pay off all its debts, it could consider maintaining a legal existence. For example a company can remain an inactive shell, and an unincorporated association can retain a steering committee, ready to start again if new funding becomes available. If the group is also a registered charity, the Charity Commissioners will want to be assured that it is still fulfilling its objectives. Provided the period before restarting activities is not too long or the charity continues to carry on some services (for example a law centre management committee could organise volunteers to give advice sessions) the Commissioners would probably be satisfied.

Once a formal decision has been made to close down because an organisation is insolvent, it ceases to be recognised as a going concern and exists only for the purposes of disposing of its assets. The first task is to inform the following of the decision:

❑ the employees and unions (see 'Redundancy');

❑ the group's accountant and auditor;

❑ the group's solicitor;

❑ the group's bank manager;

❑ the Charity Commission, if appropriate;

❑ Companies House if appropriate;

❑ the Registrar of Friendly Societies, if appropriate;

❑ the group's funder(s);

❑ past and current committee members;

❑ anyone with a fixed charge or mortgage over the group's property;

❑ all creditors;

❑ service users.

The management committee should select people to take responsibility for closing down the organisation, for example the finance officer and treasurer. The group must also consider the appropriate method of winding up (see below). From now on it must not interfere with its remaining assets, including money in the bank, cash in hand, stocks, equipment and perhaps also the premises. Similarly, if it is insolvent the organisation must not pay any sums to its creditors as this would be 'fraudulent preference'.

In practice, this means an organisation cannot pay any money into an overdrawn account, allow any equipment to be moved from the premises, or even pay staff wages. The organisation should, however, continue to collect any money owing to it, but may only put it into an account which is in credit.

Each day the organisation remains in its premises or employs staff it is incurring debts that it may be unable to pay. The creditors would include the utility companies, British Telecom and the landlord. In order to cut down overheads, only those people specifically engaged in winding up the organisation should remain on the premises, and they should occupy the minimum possible space.

Records of decisions and action taken must be kept, to protect the organisation and its members against any charges of fraudulent trading or fraudulent preference.

# Who is liable?

The final responsibility for debts depends on the organisation's legal structure (see chapter 1).

## Incorporated organisations

If the organisation is registered as a company limited by guarantee or an industrial and provident society, then the organisation, rather than the members of the management committee, is responsible for the debts. In companies, individuals are liable only up to the value of their guarantee (usually between £1 and £5). In industrial and provident societies they will have to pay only the amount due on any shares (usually £1). However, committee members who carry on running an organisation when they know it is insolvent could be found guilty of wrongful trading under the **Insolvency Act, 1986.** The Act says that if a company or industrial and provident society is wound up because it is insolvent, committee members can be found personally liable for any outstanding debts of the organisation if they carry on its activities when they know, or ought to know that there is no reasonable prospect of the organisation avoiding insolvency.

Individual members of a management committee who back a loan with a personal guarantee remain responsible for its repayment, even if the organisation is a company or industrial and provident society.

Likewise, individuals who have guaranteed payment of rent or equipment under a lease will remain personally responsible for payments.

## Unincorporated associations

An unincorporated association does not have a separate legal existence, independent of the people who manage it. This means that a group cannot enter into any financial or legal commitments in its own right; the members themselves have to act on behalf of the group. So if the group cannot pay its debts, a creditor is entitled to bring a court case against those responsible for authorising transactions to recover the money owed.

A committee member or trustee cannot avoid liability by resigning before the organisation runs into debt.

## Closing down a solvent organisation

A solvent organisation may decide to close down, for example because it has fulfilled its objects. If it can pay all its debts, including redundancy payments and the cost of disposing of premises and equipment, there are no restrictions on who can be paid during the closing down process. The management committee should select people to take responsibility for closing down the organisation and ensure that relevant people are informed of the decision.

# Redundancy

This section describes the law governing redundancy procedures and gives some suggestions for good practice.

## The definition

In legal terms, redundancy occurs when:

❑ the employer has ceased, or plans to cease carrying out the business for which the employee was employed or at the place where the employee was employed; or

❑ the requirements to carry out particular work have ceased or diminished, or are expected to do so, or the requirements to carry out the work at the place where the employee was employed have ceased or diminished or are expected to do so.

Employees who are dismissed by an organisation which has run out of money to pay them and decides to close will become redundant. Possible claims for redundancy following reorganisation and redeployment are discussed in chapter 4.

## Notifying those involved

As soon as any redundancies are planned, the employer must inform the following.

### The unions

If the workers belong to a union recognised for the purposes of negotiating, the employers have a legal duty under the **Trade Union and Labour Relations (Consolidation) Act, 1992** to consult union representatives at the earliest available opportunity.

As well as the general duty to consult the union as soon as possible about the proposed redundancy of *any* employee, the Act also lays down the following minimum periods of consultation:

- ❑ if the employer proposes to make 100 or more workers redundant in one workplace within a 90 day period, the unions must be consulted at least 90 days before the first dismissal takes effect;

- ❑ if the employer proposes to make between 10 and 99 workers redundant within a 30 day period, the employer must consult the unions at least 30 days before the first dismissal takes effect.

The union representatives must be told in writing:

- ❑ the reasons for the proposed redundancies;

- ❑ the number of workers affected and their job titles;

- ❑ the total number of employees carrying out those jobs;

- ❑ the proposed method of selecting people for redundancy;

- ❑ the proposed method of carrying out the dismissals;

- ❑ the proposed method of calculating redundancy payments.

Consultation must include consideration of ways of avoiding the dismissals, reducing the number of dismissals and mitigating the consequences of the dismissals, and must be undertaken with a view to trying to reach agreement with the union.

### Employment Department (ED)

Under the **Trade Union and Labour Relations (Consolidation) Act, 1992** the employer must notify the ED of any proposal to make more than ten people redundant. The period of notice which must be given is the same as that for consultation with the unions (see above). A copy of the notice to the ED must be given to the union.

### The employees

Under the **Employment Protection (Consolidation) Act, 1978** each employee must be given a written notice of redundancy. This should be either the legal minimum time or the period of notice agreed in their terms and conditions of service, whichever is the longer. If an organisation does not give advance notice, it must pay wages for the period of notice. This is separate from any obligation to give the employee redundancy pay (see below). The legal minimum notice required is as follows:

TYPICAL ... THE DIRECTOR ALWAYS GETS TO HEAR ABOUT EVERYTHING BEFORE THE REST OF US!

❏ one week after one month's and up to two years' service;

❏ one week for each year of continuous employment after two years' service, up to a maximum of 12.

## Offers of alternative work

Under the **Employment Protection (Consolidation) Act, 1978** employers must consider offering a worker threatened with redundancy another post, if one exists. The alternative work must either be similar to the previous job or suitable for the employee.

If the terms and conditions of the new job are different, the employee is entitled to a four week trial period before accepting the arrangement. This period can be extended by agreement if retraining is necessary. The right to redundancy pay is preserved during the trial period, but once the new job is accepted redundancy rights are lost.

## Time off to look for work

Employees who have been given notice of redundancy have the legal right to reasonable time off work with pay, provided that:

❏ they are full time (16 hours or more a week) and have had two years of service; or

❏ they are part time (between 8 and 16 hours a week) and have had five years of continuous service.

*The House of Lords has decided that the law which provides part-time workers with less protection than those working full time is discriminatory and unlawful. The Government will therefore introduce changes to bring the rights of part-time and full-time workers into line. At the time of writing (August 94), the details of these changes had not been announced.*

There is no legal definition of 'reasonable', but it is good practice to allow as much time off to look for work as the person needs.

## Selection for redundancy

The employer has a legal duty to select people for redundancy in a fair and reasonable manner. It is automatically unfair dismissal if the choice is made because of trade union membership or non membership, or in breach of a previously agreed procedure. Similarly, an employer must not discriminate, either directly or indirectly, on the grounds of race or sex.

Procedures and criteria for selection for redundancy should be reviewed to ensure that they do not indirectly discriminate against any group of people,

for example arrangements which state that part-time workers should be laid off first could affect women disproportionately; 'last in — first out' arrangements could adversely affect black workers.

## Redundancy pay

The **Employment Protection (Consolidation) Act, 1978** governs statutory redundancy pay. To be eligible under the Act, an employee must be:

❏ continuously employed for more than two years if full time (working 16 hours or more a week);

❏ continuously employed for more than five years if part time (working between 8 and 16 hours a week);

❏ dismissed for reasons of redundancy;

❏ aged over 18 years;

❏ under 65 or the normal retirement age, if this is lower than 65; it must be the same for men and women.

The amount of redundancy pay given depends on the employee's age, length of service and weekly pay. The rates are:

❏ half a week's pay for every complete year of service in which the employee is aged between 18 and 21 years;

❏ one week's pay for every complete year of service in which the employee is aged between 22 and 40 years;

❏ one and a half week's pay for each complete year of service in which the employee is 41 years or over but below retirement age.

The maximum number of years to be counted is 20. The Government sets an upper limit each year on the amount of weekly pay that can be counted. In April 94 the figure was set at £205. The employer is responsible for paying this lump sum. Employees within one year of retirement age have their redundancy pay reduced.

## Good practice

The law provides a safety net for workers who are made redundant. However, the provisions outlined above are far from generous. Employers should look at ways of introducing better terms into employees' contracts.

Improvements on the legal minimum include:

❏ keeping workers as fully informed as possible and consulting them about all the options;

❏ helping staff find alternative work;

❏ arranging for counselling in redundancy;

❏ extending the period of redundancy notice given;

❏ extending the number of weeks' redundancy pay;

❏ increasing the maximum figure for 'weekly' pay;

❏ treating all the workers equally under the redundancy procedure, regardless of age or length of service.

Consider carefully the group's financial position before agreeing to better financial provisions. The decision to make staff redundant will be made when a group does not have enough assets and income to cover its costs. The contractual liability to employees is a debt. If these liabilities are increased, a group may have to close earlier, which is against everyone's interests. Also remember that if a group cannot pay its employees the amount stated in their contracts, the management committee of an unincorporated association may become personally liable.

## Redundancy Fund

If a company becomes insolvent and is unable to pay employees' salaries and redundancy pay, the workers can claim some of the money owed to them from the Government's Redundancy Fund.

Employees may claim:

❏ statutory redundancy pay;

❏ statutory maternity pay;

❏ a basic award of unfair dismissal compensation, made by an industrial tribunal (but only if redundancy payment is not made);

❏ repayment of an apprenticeship premium;

❏ a compensatory award for the employer's failure to give statutory notice of redundancy;

❏ up to eight weeks' arrears of pay, to a maximum limit;

❏ up to six weeks' holiday pay;

❏ unpaid contributions to an occupational pension scheme;

❏ pay for the statutory period of notice.

An employee who is still owed money after receiving these awards (for example for any additional arrears of wages) would have a claim for some priority debts

against the employer. The employee would therefore become a 'preferential creditor' (see below). This means the claim would rank higher than those of some creditors, but equally with national insurance, income tax deducted at source, VAT and other preferential debts.

Employees are always advised to seek help from their unions, a law centre or the local Department of Employment office when making these claims.

# Winding up

## Unincorporated associations

The mechanisms for winding up an unincorporated association will be set down in its constitution. The procedure would probably require a resolution agreeing to the dissolution to be passed at a general meeting. The group's constitution may also state how any balance or remaining assets should be distributed if the group is solvent.

If an unincorporated association becomes insolvent, legal advice is essential. Any liabilities incurred can be treated as personal liabilities for its management committee members or trustees. There is no legal procedure for winding up the assets of an unincorporated association, but such a group should try as far as possible to use the procedure that a company has to follow. If the group is in debt, it may be best to call a meeting of its creditors to see whether they will accept a share of what remains.

It is important to check whether there are any outstanding responsibilities — for example rent for premises or charges for leased equipment — before winding up. This is because the committee members will be liable for these debts if the organisation does not pay them or get them released. The options are:

❏ get agreement for these to be waived;

❏ pay outstanding charges in one lump sum; or

❏ keep the organisation in existence until the lease ends.

A group will need to consider how to transfer any assets remaining after it has paid its debts. The decision should be made at the meeting which formally winds up the group. Most constitutions allow the committee or a general meeting to select another organisation to which the assets can be transferred. If a group is a charity, assets must be transferred to another charity.

Before an organisation is wound up, final accounts will need to be prepared and submitted to the final meeting for approval. Once the organisation has been wound up, the bank account should be closed and headed notepaper destroyed. Where relevant the Charity Commissioners should be informed and sent a copy of the final accounts.

## Incorporated organisations

An incorporated organisation can be wound up in one of the following ways:

❑ going into voluntary liquidation;

❑ using the courts to appoint the Official Receiver;

❑ using a debenture to appoint a receiver.

### Voluntary liquidation

This is the most common option. It differs from compulsory liquidation in that the decision to liquidate is made by the organisation rather than the courts. There are two types: a members' voluntary liquidation and a creditors' voluntary liquidation. Both procedures are described in the following section.

#### Members' voluntary liquidation
This occurs when an organisation is solvent but decides to wind up. The process of winding up is therefore comparatively straightforward.

An accountant should be appointed and given all the financial information about the organisation so that a Declaration of Solvency may be sent to Companies House. The Declaration must state that the organisation is able to pay all its debts within one year of the start of the wind up.

Once the **Declaration of Solvency** has been registered, the organisation can appoint a liquidator, who can then distribute the assets. The liquidator must be a qualified insolvency practitioner, usually an accountant.

In this kind of liquidation assets will remain after all the debts have been paid. In practice, most constitutions will require these assets to be given to another organisation with similar objects. If the organisation is a charity, they must be transferred to another charity.

#### Creditors' voluntary liquidation
This takes place when an organisation is insolvent. It should call a meeting of all its creditors and present them with a statement of affairs. This should describe the organisation's financial situation at the time of the decision to wind up.

The creditors now in effect own the organisation's assets, and must decide how they are to be distributed. To do this they appoint a liquidator, who must be a qualified insolvency practitioner, and set a

fee. Alternatively, the creditors may petition the court to appoint the Official Receiver as the liquidator.

### The Official Receiver

The organisation itself, or one or more of the creditors can petition the court to appoint the Official Receiver from the Department of Trade and Industry (DTI) who will decide whether the organisation should be wound up. A statement of affairs, which analyses the history of the organisation and details its assets, liabilities and debts, should be prepared by an accountant within 14 days of the appointment of the Official Receiver. A liquidator is then appointed. This could be the Official Receiver from the DTI, or another person chosen by the creditors. This process is commonly known as compulsory liquidation.

### Receivership by debenture

A debenture is a form of contract which states that an investor (such as a bank) has security over an organisation's assets (such as its premises and equipment) in the event of liquidation. A debenture holder has the option of appointing a receiver. The receiver would then decide whether it is in the debenture holder's interest to appoint a liquidator.

### The liquidation

As soon as a liquidator is appointed the committee members and members lose all their powers and responsibilities. It becomes the duty of the liquidator to disperse the assets in a certain order of preference laid down by company law. This is as follows:

1. Secured creditors (debenture holders) with a fixed charge (over specific property).

2. The liquidator's costs.

3. Preferential creditors who are:
   - the local council, for all local rates;
   - the Inland Revenue, for land tax, income tax and national insurance contributions;
   - employees, for outstanding wages, salaries and accrued holiday pay.

4. Secured creditors with a floating charge (over some or all of the group's assets).

5. Unsecured creditors - the ones who are left.

## Dissolution

Once the assets have been distributed, the liquidator will call a general meeting of the creditors and members to report on the liquidation. After three months the Registrar of Companies will strike the company off the register. It will then be dissolved.

# Glossary

**Creditors' meeting**
A meeting called by members or directors of a group in order to appoint a liquidator.

**Creditors' voluntary liquidation**
The process whereby a liquidator is appointed by a meeting of creditors.

**Declaration of solvency**
A report by an accountant to the Registrar of Companies in a members' voluntary liquidation declaring that a group is solvent.

**Debenture**
A form of securing charges over a loan or investment.

**Fraud**
Intent to deceive for one's own benefit.

**Fraudulent preference**
Preferring one creditor to another whilst knowingly insolvent.

**Fraudulent trading**
Trading with intent to defraud creditors or for any other fraudulent purpose.

**Wrongful trading**
Carrying on the business of the organisation knowing that it is going to wind up as insolvent or where it should be known that it will.

**Insolvency**
The situation where liabilities are more than assets or an inability to pay debts as they fall due.

**Liquidator**
Person appointed by the court or by the creditors to wind up the affairs of the company. It may be the Official Receiver or an insolvency practitioner.

**Liquidation**
The process of collecting and disposing of assets in order to wind up.

**Members' voluntary liquidation**
The process whereby a group's members decide to wind up a solvent organisation.

**Official Receiver**
An employee of the Department of Trade and Industry appointed upon petition to the court to look into the affairs of the group and/or to act as a liquidator.

**Preferential creditors**
Those paid in preference to others when the assets of the group have been gathered, according to the ranking of debts in the Companies Act.

**Provisional liquidator**
The Official Receiver, (who sets up the meeting whereby the liquidator is appointed).

**Receiver**
The person who is appointed by a creditor, for example a bank, to look into the running of a group in an attempt to salvage it or appoint a liquidator.

**Solvency**
The ability to pay debts as they fall due and the situation where assets are more than liabilities.

**Statement of affairs**
The members' or directors' statement of a group's current financial position, usually presented by a liquidator at a creditors' meeting.

**Technically insolvent**
The situation when assets are less than liabilities on the balance sheet but there is other cash to pay debts and the situation can be retrieved, or where assets are worth more than liabilities and, even though debts cannot be paid, all the creditors have agreed to wait.

**Winding up**
A legal process whereby a group is dissolved, its property is administered for the benefit of its creditors, and any surplus is administered according to the Companies Act and charity law.

# Booklist

**Finding funds: general information of funding for voluntary groups**, National Council for Voluntary Organisations, £7.50

**Managing your solvency: a guide to insolvency and how to ensure that you continue as a going concern**, *Michael Norton (editor)*, Directory of Social Change (1994), £9.95

Free leaflets regarding redundancy are available from the Employment Department

# Publishers and addresses

**ACAS**
Clifton House, 83-117 Euston Road, London NW1 2RB: 071 396 0022

**ACAS — publications**
PO Box 404, Leicester LE4 9ZZ

**ACTS**
Transport House, Smith Square, London SW1P 3JB: 071 828 7788

**Angal Collection Boxes and Devices Limited**
104 Felsham Road, London SW15 1DQ: 081 788 1059

**Association of Community Technical Aid Centres**
The Royal Institution, Colquitt Street, Liverpool L1 4DE: 051 708 7607

**British Insurance Brokers' Association**
Biba House, 14 Bevis Marks, London EC3A 7NT: 071 623 9043

**British Standards Institute**
Sales Department, Linford Wood, Milton Keynes MK14 6LE: 0908 221166

**CATCH**
2 West End Lane, London NW6 4NT: 071 372 7990

**Charities Advisory Trust**
Radius Works, Back Lane, London NW3 1HL: 071 794 9835

**Charities Aid Foundation**
48 Pembury Road, Tonbridge, Kent TN9 2JD: 0732 771333

**Charities' Tax Reform Group**
12 Little College Street, London SW1P 3SH: 071 222 1265

**The Charity Commission**
St Alban's House, 57/60 Haymarket, London SW1Y 4QX: 071 210 4477

**City Centre**
32-35 Featherstone Street, London EC1Y 8QX: 071 608 1338

**Commission for Racial Equality**
Elliot House, 10-12 Allington Street, London SW1E 5EH: 071 828 7022

**Commission for Racial Equality — Publications**
Lavis Marketing, 73 Lime Walk, Headington, Oxford OX3 7AD: 0865 67575

**Community Accountancy Project**
18 Ashwin Street, London E8 3DL: 071 249 7109

**Community Matters**
8/9 Upper Street, London N1 0PQ: 071 226 0189

**Community Trading Services Limited**
8/9 Upper Street, London N1 0PQ: 071 354 9569

**Companies House**
Crown Way, Maindy, Cardiff CF4 3UZ: 0222 388588

**Contributions Agency**
Leaflets available from social security benefits offices (listed in phone book under 'Benefits Agency' or 'Social Security')
Local offices listed in the phone book

**Croner Publications Ltd**
Croner House, London Road, Kingston, Surrey KT2 6SR: 081 547 3333

**Data Protection Registrar**
Springfield House, Water Lane, Wilmslow, Cheshire SK9 5AX: 0625 535777

**Department of Transport**
2 Marsham Street, London SW1P 3EB: 071 276 0800

**Directory of Social Change**
Radius Works, Back Lane, London NW3 1HL: 071 284 4364

**Disabled Living Foundation**
380-384 Harrow Road, London W9 2HU: 071 289 6111

**Employment Department**
Leaflets available from local offices and jobcentres

**Employment Department Overseas Labour Section**
West 5, Moorfoot, Sheffield S1 4PQ: 0742 594074

**Employment Service**
Leaflets available from jobcentres

**Equal Opportunities Commission**
Overseas House, Quay Street, Manchester M3 3HN: 061 833 9244

**Federation of Independent Advice Centres**
13 Stockwell Road, London SW9 9AU: 071 274 1839

**Funding Information Service for London**
LVSC, 356 Holloway Road, London N7 6PA: 071 700 8115

**The Gaming Board for Great Britain**
Berkshire House, 168-173 High Holborn, London WC1V 7AA: 071 306 6269

**Give As You Earn**
Foundation House, Coach and Horses Passage,
The Pantiles, Tunbridge Wells, Kent TN2 5TZ:
0892 512244

**Health Education Authority**
Hamilton House, Mabledon Place, London WC1H
9TX: 071 383 3833

**Health and Safety Commission**
Rose Court, 2 Southwark Bridge, London SE1 9HS:
071 717 6000

**Health and Safety Executive**
Rose Court, 2 Southwark Bridge, London SE1 9HS:
071 717 6000

**Health and Safety Executive — publications**
HSE Books, PO Box 1999, Sudbury, Suffolk CO10 6FS:
0787 881165

**HMSO**
49 High Holborn, London WC1V 6HB (visitors)
or write to PO Box 276, London SW8 5DT
071 873 0011 (enquiries); 071 873 9090 (orders)

**Home Office**
50 Queen Anne's Gate, London SW1 9AT:
071 273 3108 (lotteries publication)

**Home Office Charity Law Section**
Room 1370, 50 Queen Anne's Gate, London SW1 9AT:
071 273 2989

**The Industrial Society**
48 Bryanston Square, London W1H 7LN: 071 262 2401

**Inland Revenue**
Publications available from Tax Enquiry Centres and
Tax Offices (listed under 'Inland Revenue')

**Joint Council for the Welfare of Immigrants**
115 Old Street, London EC1V 9JR: 071 251 8706

**Lambeth ACCORD**
336 Brixton Road, London SW9 7AA: 071 274 2299

**Legal Action Group**
242-244 Pentonville Road, London N1 9UN:
071 833 2931

**Lesbian and Gay Employment Rights**
St Margaret's House, 21 Old Ford Road, London E2
9PL: 081 983 0694

**Liberty**
21 Tabard Street, London SE1 4LA: 071 403 3888

**Local Government Information Unit**
1-5 Bath Street, London EC1V 9QQ: 071 608 1051

**London Hazards Centre**
Headland House, 308 Gray's Inn Road, London
WC1X 8DS: 071 837 5606

**London Voluntary Service Council**
356 Holloway Road, London N7 6PA: 071 700 8107

**The Lotteries Council**
Peter Broderick, Honorary Secretary, Community
Publishing (Avon) Ltd, PO Box 215, Pamwell House,
Pennywell Road, Bristol, Avon BS 99 7QX:
0271 541111

**Migrant Support Unit**
6-20 John Mews Road, London WC1 2XN:
071 916 1646

**MSF**
Park House, 64-66 Wandsworth Common North Side,
London SW18 2SH: 081 871 2100

**National Council for Voluntary Organisations**
Regent's Wharf, 8 All Saints Street, London N1 9RL:
071 713 6161

**New Ways to Work**
309 Upper Street, London N1 2TY: 071 226 4026

**The Pensions Trust**
15 Rathbone Street, London W1P 2AJ: 071 636 1841

**Planning Aid for London**
Calvert House, 5 Calvert Avenue, London E2 7JP:
071 613 4435

**RADAR**
12 City Forum, 250 City Road, London EC1V 8AF:
071 250 3222

**Tolley's Publishing Co Ltd**
Tolley House, 2 Addiscombe Road, Croydon, Surrey
CR9 5AF: 081 686 9141

**Unison**
1 Mabledon Place, London WC1H 9AJ: 071 388 2366

**Voluntary Action Camden**
1st floor, Instrument House, 207-215 Kings Cross
Road, London WC1X 9DB: 071 837 5544

**Volunteer Centre UK**
Carriage Row, 183 Eversholt Street, London NW1
1BU: 071 388 9888

**Women's Design Service**
Johnson's Yard, 4 Pinchin Street, London E1 1SA:
071 709 7910

Goldsmiths
UNIVERSITY
OF LONDON

Centre
for Public and
Voluntary Sector
Development